I0122057

FM 3-21.12

The Infantry Weapons Company

July 2008

Distribution Restriction: Approved for public release; distribution is unlimited.

Headquarters, Department of the Army

Published by Books Express Publishing
Books Express Publishing, 2011
ISBN 978-1-78039-935-5

Books Express publications are available from all good retail and online booksellers. For
publishing proposals and direct ordering please contact us at: info@books-express.com

Field Manual
No. 3-21.12

Headquarters
Department of the Army
Washington, DC, 1 July 2008

The Infantry Weapons Company

Contents

Distribution Restriction: Approved for public release; distr bution is unlimited.

Figures

Tables

Preface

This field manual provides a doctrinal framework for the Infantry weapons company assigned to Infantry battalions in an Infantry brigade combat team (IBCT). It is a companion to FM 3-21.10, *The Infantry Rifle Company*, much of which applies to the Infantry weapons company and as such will not be repeated herein. This manual will discuss on the unique characteristics of the Infantry weapons company, including principles, tactics, techniques, procedures, and terms and symbols. It will also cover what the Infantry weapons company brings to the Infantry battalion and the battlefield. Among topics covered in FM 3-21.10 but omitted here are the characteristics and fundamentals of urban operations, risk management and fratricide avoidance, heavy and Stryker unit employment, sniper employment, improvised explosive devices, operations in a chemical, biological, radiological, and nuclear (CBRN) environment, media considerations, pattern analysis, and situational understanding.

It focuses on the employment of the Infantry weapons company while fighting as a pure company or combined arms team under the command of an Infantry weapons company commander. This framework will help Infantry weapons company leaders effectively--

- Exploit weapons company-unique capabilities.
- Employ the company using unit weapon fundamentals.
- Reduce the vulnerability of the unit.
- Plan and conduct full-spectrum operations.
- Accomplish missions in various tactical situations, from stability and civil support to high-intensity combat.
- Win on the battlefield.

Although organization for combat may require the detachment of individual weapons company platoons to other units, this manual does not cover detailed operations of detached platoons. It only provides a general discussion of coordination and operational issues pertaining to detachments.

The main target audience for this manual includes Infantry weapons company commanders, executive officers, first sergeants, platoon sergeants, and platoon leaders. Others who may find it useful include military instructors, evaluators, training and doctrine developers, and other Infantry company commanders, including those at headquarters and headquarters company and rifle companies; Infantry battalion staff officers; service school instructors; and commissioning source instructors.

This manual applies to the Active Army, the Army National Guard (ARNG)/Army National Guard of the United States (ARNGUS), and the United States Army Reserve (USAR) unless otherwise stated.

The proponent is the US Army Training and Doctrine Command. The preparing agency is the US Army Infantry School. You may send comments and recommendations by any means—US mail, e-mail, fax, or telephone—as long as you use or follow the format of DA Form 2028 (*Recommended Changes to Publications and Blank Forms*). You may also phone for more information.

E-mail	BENN.CATD.Doctrine@conus.army.mil
Office/Fax	COM 706-545-7114/7500 (DSN 835)
US Mail	Commandant, USAIS
	ATTN: ATSH-ATD
	6751 Constitution Loop
	Fort Benning, GA 31905-5593

Unless this publication states otherwise, masculine nouns and pronouns may refer to either men or women.

This page intentionally left blank.

Chapter 1

Introduction

"Battles are won by fire and movement. The purpose of movement is to set the fire in a more advantageous place." -- GEN G.S. Patton Jr.

As the operational environment (OE) in which the Infantry must operate continues to evolve, so does the Infantry. Infantry units must continually adapt in order to meet the threat. The Infantry weapons company is a response to meet these changing conditions. This chapter discusses the mission, organizational structure, characteristics, and weapon systems of the Infantry weapons company found in the Infantry battalions of the Infantry brigade combat team (IBCT).

Section I. OVERVIEW

Infantry weapons companies are uniquely equipped to provide the Infantry battalion with additional capabilities. Their organization structure and equipment provide the battalion with additional heavy weapons firepower, maneuverability, and long-range communications.

ORGANIZATION

1-1.   The Infantry weapons company is organic to an Infantry battalion assigned to an IBCT. In each IBCT Infantry battalion, there is a headquarters company, three Infantry rifle companies, and one Infantry weapons company as shown in Figure 1-1. The weapons company has approximately 80 personnel. It is a fully mobile unit consisting of weapons carrier vehicles and a variety of heavy weapons systems.

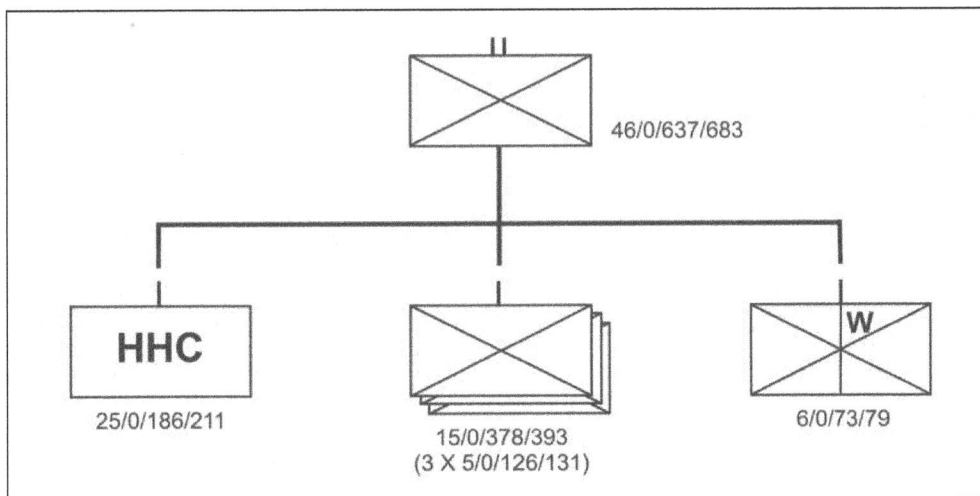

Figure 1-1. The Infantry Battalion, IBCT.

BATTLEFIELD FUNCTIONS

1-2.   The mission of the Infantry weapons company is to provide mobile heavy weapons and long range close combat missile fires to the Infantry battalion. The inherent versatility of the weapons company as part of the Infantry battalion also makes it well suited in employment against asymmetrical threats in full spectrum operations. Mass and depth are key components to employing heavy weapons assets. During tactical operations, heavy weapons units can suppress, fix, or destroy enemy at long ranges, allowing other Infantry units or combined arms teams to maneuver. The weapons company provides the Infantry battalion with a highly mobile, multi-functional element that can:

- Deliver precision long-range, large-caliber direct fires to destroy enemy armored vehicles and fortifications.
- Deliver massed heavy machinegun and grenade launcher fires to engage enemy personnel, destroy light vehicles, and provide area suppression.
- Move rapidly on the battlefield to shift combat power where it is needed.
- Communicate over longer distances than units using man-packed radios.
- Employ long-range thermal weapons sights to detect and engage enemy forces during hours of darkness.
- Conduct moving or stationary observation, reconnaissance, screen, and guard missions.
- Provide security and control for armed convoy escorts.
- Coordinate, mass, and shift long-range direct fires.
- Control and execute mounted combat and reconnaissance patrols.
- Support the assaults of other units with massed supporting fires.
- Provide responsive and flexible over-watch of moving elements.
- Provide effective and wide-ranging outer cordon forces.
- Integrate indirect and aerial fires with the unit's direct fire plan.
- Task organize with one or more rifle platoons, or attached armored forces, into a powerful and flexible combined arms team.
- Detach one or more Assault platoons to augment rifle companies within the battalion.
- Conduct unit self-sustainment and maintenance within its capability.

CHARACTERISTICS

1-3.   The Infantry weapons company is uniquely equipped with heavy weapons to support the maneuver of the rifle companies within the Infantry battalion. The heavy weapons contained in the weapons company include a mix that can be tailored to a particular mission based on mission, enemy, terrain, troops, time, civilians (METT-TC). The company maneuvers in all types of terrain, climates and visibility conditions.

ARMS ROOM CONCEPT

1-4.   Infantry weapons companies are currently equipped with four types of heavy weapons. The selection and employment of weapon system or systems to use for a particular mission is termed the "Arms Room Concept." The heavy weapons systems currently available in the weapons company are the tube-launched, optically-tracked, wire-guided (TOW) Improved Target Acquisition System (ITAS), the MK-19 40mm Grenade Machine Gun, the M2 .50 caliber Machine Gun, and the Javelin Close Combat Missile System. Each vehicle-mounted system is also equipped with a tripod for ground mount operations. Only one of these systems can be mounted on each individual vehicle at a time. Javelins may be carried in the vehicle along with a vehicle-mounted system. During movements, other weapon systems not mounted, along with any additional equipment, may be carried in trailers. When trailers are not feasible, non-mission essential equipment may be left in a stay behind position. During mission planning, leaders must determine which weapons systems are best suited for that particular mission and configure the vehicles appropriately. While all of the heavy weapons vehicles can mount the MK-19 and the M2, only two per platoon are equipped to mount the ITAS. There are two ITAS, two M2 .50 caliber machine guns, two MK-19 40mm Grenade Machine Guns, and two Javelin Close Combat Missile Systems per platoon for a total of 24 mountable heavy weapons systems per company. For any given mission, only four of the six vehicular mountable systems may be mounted in each platoon. The remaining systems may be left in the stay behind position.

CAPABILITIES

1-5.   The heavy weapon systems available to the weapons company provide direct fire against personnel, vehicles, armored or other hard targets to support maneuver of Infantry. Vehicular mounted communications systems may be used to enhance long range communications for the battalion offering communications relay if necessary. Optic systems supplied with the heavy weapons may also aid in security and information gathering.

OFFENSIVE CAPABILITIES

1-6.   A weapons company may initially provide the base of fire in a battalion attack in order to suppress, fix, or destroy the enemy in position. It may also engage enemy in planned engagement areas, isolate objectives by destroying enemy counterattacks, or destroy withdrawing enemy forces. It is also well suited to protect the battalion's flanks. Within the confines of the rules of engagement, the company's heavy weapons may also be useful in urban operations with tasks such as creating entry points into buildings, engagement of snipers, and destruction of reinforced structures.

DEFENSIVE CAPABILITIES

1-7.   Weapons companies can be positioned forward of the defensive area to participate in security operations or to overwatch reconnaissance units or obstacles. As the enemy closes, they can displace to positions that provide direct fires into an engagement area. They may also be positioned throughout the depth of the decisive area of operation to cover likely armor avenues of approach, perform reconnaissance or assist in route security. During counterattacks, the weapons company can provide overwatching support-by-fire (SBF) positions for the maneuvering element.

STABILITY AND CIVIL SUPPORT CAPABILITIES

1-8.   Whether conducting stability operations in a foreign nation or domestic civil support operations, the weapons company brings with it a host of capabilities including transportation, mobility, enhanced optics, and communications assets. These capabilities can be creatively employed to assist both of these operations. For further discussion, see Chapter 6 and Chapter 7 of this manual.

LIMITATIONS

1-9.   Although the weapons company's vehicles provide protection against small arms and fragmentation, these vehicles lack protection against large caliber direct and indirect fires and are still vulnerable to enemy antiarmor weapons.

1-10.   The weapons carrier vehicle provides increased mobility and can maneuver the weapons quickly to advantage locations on the battlefield. However, certain types of terrain such as steep slopes, thick vegetation, mud and other restrictive areas, may restrict vehicular travel. Weather may also prevent vehicles from operating at full capacity.

1-11.   The inherent maintenance requirement for the vehicles and heavy weapons are greatly increased for the weapons company over those of the rifle company. This requirement creates a large increase in responsibilities for the logistical personnel for the company.

1-12.   The ITAS fires TOW missiles. TOW missiles are accurate, but missile flight time is long and obstacles may interfere with the flight path. The slow rate of fire and the visible launch signature of the TOW missile increase the weapons squad's vulnerability especially if a vehicle mounted ITAS engages within an enemy's effective direct-fire range (no standoff). Units can reduce this vulnerability by displacing often and by integrating their fires with those of automatic weapon systems and with other antiarmor weapons in the platoon. Vulnerability is further decreased through the use of obstacles and indirect fires.

ORGANIZATION

1-13.   Figure 1-2 shows the organization of the weapons company. The company consists of a company headquarters and four assault platoons. Each assault platoon has two sections consisting of two squads each and a leader's vehicle. Each squad contains four Soldiers and a vehicle mounting the heavy weapons.

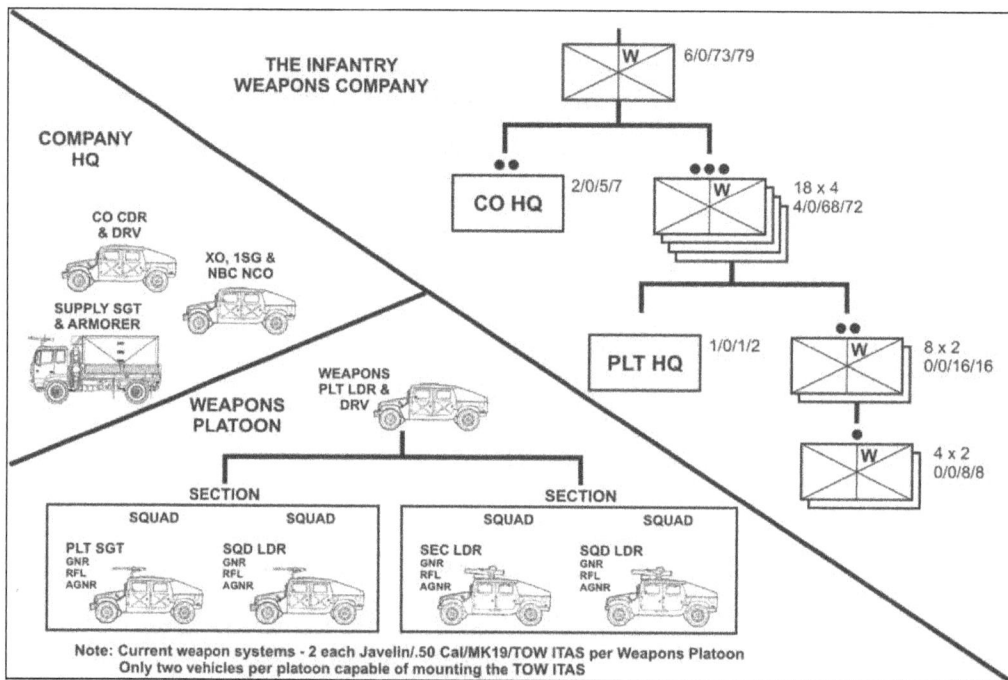

Figure 1-2. The Infantry Weapons Company. IBCT.

Section II. DUTIES AND RESPONSIBILITIES OF KEY PERSONNEL

This section describes the duties and responsibilities of key personnel in the Infantry weapons company.

COMPANY COMMANDER

1-14.   The company commander leads by personal example and is responsible for everything the company does or fails to do. His principle duties include the key areas of tactical employment, training, administration, personnel management, maintenance, force protection, and sustainment of his company. He must integrate and synchronize a mix of forces for full spectrum operations including other combined arms and maneuver elements, civil affairs, psychological operations (PSYOP), interpreters, media, unmanned aircraft systems (UAS), and robotics teams. The commander:

- Commands and controls through his subordinate leaders.
- Employs his company to accomplish its mission within the battalion commander's intent and concept.
- Selects the best location to maneuver the platoons and other elements.
- Conducts mission analysis, troop-leading procedures (TLP), and issues operation orders for company tactical operations.
- Maintains and expresses situation awareness and understanding.
- Resources the platoons and other elements and requests battalion support when needed.
- Ensures that the company command post (CP) effectively tracks the battle situation and status.
- Provides a timely and accurate tactical picture to the battalion commander and subordinate units.
- Implements effective measures for force protection, security, and accountability of forces and systems.
- Develops the leadership and tactical skill of his platoon leaders.
- Conducts direct fire coordination, principal advisor to the battalion commander on direct fire coordination and may perform as the battalion direct fire coordinator.

EXECUTIVE OFFICER

1-15.   The executive officer (XO) is second in command. His primary role is to assist the commander in mission planning and accomplishment. He assumes command of the company as required and ensures that tactical reports from the platoons are forwarded to the battalion tactical operations center. The XO locates where he can maintain communications with the company commander and the battalion. His responsibilities include:

- Planning and supervising, before the battle along with the first sergeant, the company's sustainment operations and is responsible for the company command post. He ensures that precombat inspections are complete. He plans and coordinates logistical support with agencies outside the company while the first sergeant does the same internally. He prepares or aids in preparing paragraph 4 of the company operation order (OPORD). He may also help the company commander plan the mission.

- Performing duties as the unit maintenance officer.

- Coordinating with higher, adjacent, and supporting units. He may aid in control of critical events of the battle such as a passage of lines, bridging a gap, or breaching an obstacle; or, he may assume control of a platoon attached to the company during movement.

- Performing as landing zone or pickup zone control officer. This may include straggler control, casualty evacuation, resupply operations, or air-ground liaison.

- Leading a quartering party. The quartering party is an element consisting of representatives of various company elements. Their purpose is to precede the company and reconnoiter, secure, and mark an assembly area.

- Leading a detachment. A detachment consists of a group of personnel assigned other tactical tasks such as shaping or sustaining force leader in a company raid or attack or control of the company machine guns.

- Leading the reserve, leading the detachment left in contact during a withdrawal, controlling attachments to the company, or serving as movement control officer.

FIRST SERGEANT

1-16.   The first sergeant is the senior noncommissioned officer (NCO) and normally the most experienced Soldier in the company. He is the expert on individual and NCO skills. He helps the commander prepare, coordinate, and supervise all activities that support the unit mission. He operates where the commander directs or where he can best influence a critical point or what is viewed as the unit's decisive point. The first sergeant's duties include:

- Supervising routine operations. This can include enforcing the tactical standing operating procedures (TSOP); planning and coordinating both training and full spectrum operations; and administering replacement operations, logistics, maintenance, communications, field hygiene, and casualty evacuation operations.
- Supervising, inspecting, and influencing matters designated by the commander as well as areas that depend on his expertise such as Soldier care, force protection, security, and accountability.
- Assisting the XO and keeping himself prepared to assume the XO's duties, if needed.
- Leading task-organized elements or subunits for the company's shaping effort or other designated missions.
- Leading the company casualty evacuation (CASEVAC) efforts and running the company casualty collection point (CCP) for company missions.

FIRE SUPPORT OFFICER

1-17.   The fire support officer (FSO) is attached to the company from the battalion fire support platoon and helps plan, coordinate, and execute the company's fire support. During planning, he develops a fire support plan based on the company commander's concept and guidance. He coordinates the fire support plan with the battalion fire support officer. During planning, the fire support officer:

- Advises the commander of the capabilities and statuses of all available fire support assets.
- Helps the commander develop the OPORD to ensure full integration of fires into the concept. Refines field artillery and mortar targets to support the maneuver plan.
- Designates targets and fire control measures and determines method of engagement and firing responsibility.
- Determines the specific tasks and instructions required to conduct and control the fire plan.
- Briefs the fire support plan as part of the company OPORD, and coordinates with platoon leaders to ensure they understand their fire support responsibilities.
- Integrates platoon targets into the company target overlay and target worksheet, and sends the resulting products to the battalion fires cell.
- During the battle, normally locates near the commander. This allows greater flexibility in conducting or adjusting the fire support plan. At times, locates away from the commander to better control supporting fires. Informs the commander of key information on the radio net.
- Understands Infantry tactics in order to integrate fires effectively, and if the company commander becomes a casualty, may assume temporary control of the company until the XO can do so.
- Coordinates the employment of the joint air attack team (JAAT), close air support (CAS), attack helicopter, and UASs.
- Ensures the indirect fire plan is part of each company rehearsal.

RADIO OPERATOR

1-18.   The radio operator supervises operation, maintenance, and installation of organic wire, and frequency modulation (FM) communications. This includes sending and receiving routine traffic and making required communication checks. The radio operators duties include:

- Monitoring the communications nets, relaying information, and keeping the commander informed of significant events if necessary.

- Rendering clear, accurate, and timely situation reports (SITREP).
- Performing limited troubleshooting of organic communications equipment. Serves as the link between the company and the battalion for communications equipment maintenance.
- Supervising all aspects of communications security (COMSEC) equipment, to include requesting, receipting, maintaining, securing, employing, and training for COMSEC equipment and related materials.
- Advising the company commander in planning and employing the communications systems. Based on the commander's guidance, assists in preparing paragraph 5 of the OPORD.

SUPPLY SERGEANT

1-19.   The supply sergeant requests, receives, issues, stores, maintains, and turns in supplies and equipment for the company. He coordinates requirements with the first sergeant, the XO and the battalion S-4. If located in the Infantry battalion trains, the headquarters and headquarters company commander may provide guidance and assistance to supply sergeants. His responsibilities include

- Controlling the supply trucks that are organic to the company.
- Monitoring tactical situation.
- Anticipating logistical requirements (Chapter 11).
- Communications using the battalion administrative/logistical radio and digital network.

CHEMICAL, BIOLOGICAL, RADIOLOGICAL, AND NUCLEAR NCO

1-20.   The chemical, biological, radiological, or nuclear (CBRN) NCO helps the company commander plan CBRN operations. He conducts and supervises CBRN training within the company (decontamination, monitoring, survey, and equipment maintenance operations) and inspects detection and protective equipment for serviceability. His duties include:

- Operating forward with the company CP and helping the senior radio operator with CP operations and security.
- Recommending mission-oriented protective posture (MOPP) levels to the commander (based on guidance from the battalion CBRN NCO and the current situation).
- Conducting continuous CBRN vulnerability analysis.
- Ensuring connectivity with the joint warning and reporting network.
- Acting as liaison with supporting chemical units if necessary.
- Reporting, analyzing, and disseminating CBRN attack data manually or digitally using the CBRN Warning and Reporting System, and nuclear, biological and chemical (NBC)1, NBC4, and spot reports from digital systems.
- Planning and supervising decontamination and monitoring and survey operations.
- Requesting CBRN equipment and supplies.
- Maintaining and calibrating equipment.

ARMORER

1-21.   The armorer is a supply specialist whose duties focus on organizational maintenance and repair of the company's small arms weapons. He assures accountability and security of weapons and ammunition under his control and evacuates weapons for repair or replacement, if required. Normally, he helps the supply sergeant in the brigade support area (BSA), but he may operate forward with the company CP to support continuous CP operations and to fix equipment forward.

COMBAT MEDIC

1-22.   The combat medic is the first individual in the medical chain who makes medically substantiated decisions based on medical military occupational specialty (MOS)-specific training. A combat medic may be attached to the weapons company to provide emergency medical treatment for sick, injured, or wounded company personnel. Emergency medical treatment (immediate far forward care) consists of those lifesaving steps that do not require the knowledge and skills of a physician. Emergency medical treatment procedures performed by the combat medic may include opening airways, starting intravenous fluids, controlling hemorrhages, preventing or treating shock, splinting suspected or confirmed fractures, and relieving pain. The emergency medicine performed by the combat medic is supervised by the battalion surgeon or physician's assistant. The combat medic is responsible for:

- Providing guidance to the company commander pertaining to Army Health System (AHS) support issues.
- Triaging disease non-battle injured (DNBI), wounded, or ill friendly and enemy personnel for priority of evacuation as they arrive at the company CCP.
- Overseeing sick-call screening for the company.
- Requesting and coordinating the evacuation of DNBI or wounded personnel under the directions of the company first sergeant.
- Assisting in the training of the company personnel on first aid (self-aid and buddy-aid) and combat lifesavers in enhanced first-aid procedures.
- Requisitioning Class VIII supplies from the battalion aid station (BAS) for the company according to the TSOP.
- Assisting the commander with medical planning, advises on higher headquarters' AHS plan, and recommending locations for company CCPs.
- Monitoring the tactical situation, and anticipate and coordinate Health Service Support (HSS)/Force Health Protection (FHP) requirements and Class VIII resupply as necessary.
- Advising the company commander and first sergeant on mass casualty operations.
- Keeping the first sergeant informed on the status of casualties, and coordinate with him for additional HSS requirements.

ASSAULT PLATOON LEADER

1-23.   The assault platoon leader (PL) leads his Soldiers by personal example. He is responsible for all the platoon does or fails to do and has complete authority over his subordinates. This centralized authority enables the PL to maintain unit discipline and unity and to act decisively. The demands of modern combat or full spectrum operations require the PL to exercise initiative without continuous guidance from higher commands. He must know his Soldiers as well as how to employ the platoon, its weapons, and its systems. He relies on the expertise of the Platoon Sergeant and regularly consults with him on all platoon matters. As part of his key tactical responsibilities, the platoon leader:

- Leads the platoon in accomplishing its mission according to the company and battalion commanders' intent and concept.
- Performs TLPs for missions assigned to the platoon.
- Locates where he can best maneuver the squads and the fighting elements, and then synchronizes their efforts.
- Anticipates the platoon's next tactical move.
- Requests and controls assets.
- Ensures force-protection measures are implemented.
- Maintains all-round, three-dimensional security.
- Controls emplacement of key weapon systems.

- Ensures security measures are implemented at the limit of advance.
- Provides a timely and accurate tactical picture to the commander.

ASSAULT PLATOON SERGEANT

1-24.   The assault platoon sergeant is the platoon's most experienced NCO and second in command. He is accountable to the platoon leader for the leadership, discipline, training, and welfare of the platoon's Soldiers. He sets the example in everything. His expertise includes tactical maneuver, employment of weapons and systems, logistics, administration, security, accountability, force protection, and Soldier care. As part of his traditional tactical responsibilities, the platoon sergeant:

- Locates and acts where best to help control the fight or other platoon operations.
- Assures that the platoon is prepared to accomplish its mission by supervising precombat checks and inspections.
- Helps develop the squad leaders' tactical and leadership skills.
- Supervises platoon sustainment operations.
- Receives the squad leaders' administrative, logistical, and maintenance reports and requests for rations, water, fuel, and ammunition.
- Coordinates with the company first sergeant or XO for resupply.
- Runs the platoon CCP; directs the medic and aid and litter teams; forwards casualty reports; manages personnel strength levels, receives and orients replacements.

Section III. PREPARATION FOR WAR

Infantry units are organized and equipped to close with and kill the enemy, to destroy his equipment, and to shatter his will to resist. This close personal fight requires combat-ready units with skilled Soldiers and leaders. These units are developed into agile combat forces by tough, thorough, and demanding training. This takes leaders who understand the effective employment of all Infantry forces in a complex OE. As leaders train their units, they too should strive to enhance their leadership abilities and seek to polish their decision-making and leadership skills with each training exercise.

LEADERS

1-25.   Leadership is a skill that can be practiced and improved upon. A competent leader is one that not only ensures his unit is prepared, but one that prepares himself as well. A leader must be able to exercise effective command in combat by gaining a clear understanding of the fight before him, and then use his skills as a tactician and competent decision maker to lead his unit. A distillation of World War experiences was prepared in 1939 for the Infantry Journal under the, supervision of Colonel George C. Marshall. The handbook contained a caution that should be heeded by all those who expect from history detailed instructions for conduct in specific situations. An excerpt of Col Marshall's thoughts published in the journal follows:

"The art of war has no traffic with rules, for the infinitely varied circumstances and conditions of combat never produce exactly the same situation twice....

"It follows, then, that the leader who would become a competent tactician must first close his mind to the alluring formula that well-meaning people offer in the name of victory. To master his difficult art he must learn to cut to the heart of a situation, recognize its decisive elements and base his course of action on these. The ability to do this is not God-given, nor can it be acquired overnight; it is a process of years. He must realize that training in solving problems of all types, long practice in making clear, unequivocal decisions, the habit of concentrating on the question at hand, and an elasticity of mind, are indispensable requisites for the successful practice of the art of war.

"The leader who frantically strives to remember what someone else did in some slightly similar situation has already set his feet on a well-traveled road to ruin.

"Every situation encountered in war is likely to be exceptional. The schematic solution will seldom fit. Leaders who think that familiarity with blind rules of thumb will win battles are doomed to disappointment. Those who seek to fight by rote, who memorize an assortment of standard solutions with the idea of applying the most appropriate when confronted by actual combat, walk with disaster, rather, it is essential that all leaders---from subaltern to commanding general---familiarize themselves with the art of clear, logical thinking. It is more valuable to be able to analyze one battle situation correctly, recognize its decisive elements and devise a simple, workable solution for it, than to memorize all the erudition ever written of war.

"The American Army's call for the use of imagination, backed up by a knowledge of history, may well be what accounts for its repeated successes."

WARRIOR ETHOS

1-26.   At the core of the American Soldier are the values that drive his spirit, commitment and ethical behavior. These values, the Army Values, shape the behavior of the Soldier and reflect the common foundation of character for all Soldiers known as the Warrior Ethos. Put into practice, the Warrior Ethos reflect a Soldiers' unrelenting determination to do what is right with pride, both in uniform and out, and a total commitment and to victory at peace and war. On the battlefield every Soldier must remain focused on mission accomplishment and be ingrained with the principles of--

- I will always place the mission first.
- I will never accept defeat.
- I will never quit.
- I will never leave a fallen comrade.

1-27.   The Army has developed a three-pronged strategy for the Warrior Ethos Implementation. This strategy addresses Warrior skills, Warrior culture, and mental and physical toughness. The implementation itself must be infused throughout the Army both from the bottom up and from the top down. For a further discussion of the Warrior Ethos, see FM 6-22, Army Leadership, OCT 2006 and FM 3-21.75 (Warrior Ethos and Soldier Combat Skills).

EVERY SOLDIER AS A SENSOR

1-28.   The successful resolution of ground combat depends on the Infantry. Individual Soldiers, molded into a disciplined and well-led team, create a combat-ready force. To ensure maximum combat effectiveness, Soldiers must master a diverse set of skills. An important skill all personnel must actively employ is labeled *Every Soldier as a Sensor* or ES2. ES2 means that Soldiers are trained to observe details related to critical command information requirements while in an area of operations (AO). Their reporting must be competent, concise, and accurate in their reporting. Their leaders understand how to optimize the collection, processing, and dissemination of information in their unit to enable generation of timely intelligence. The individual Soldier is the Infantry's most precious resource.

Following the fundamentals of heavy weapons employment increases the probability of destroying targets and enhances survivability.

PROVIDE MUTUAL SUPPORT

1-29.   Mutual support is a condition that exists when elements are able to support each other by direct fire in order to prevent the enemy from attacking one position without being subject to direct fire from one or more adjacent positions. To establish mutual support, unit sections and platoons may be employed with overlapping primary and secondary sectors of fire Figure1-3. If one squad, section or platoon is attacked or forced to displace, the other units continue covering the assigned area. In order to achieve this effect, the heavy weapons squads are positioned so that fires directed at one squad or section can suppress only those units.

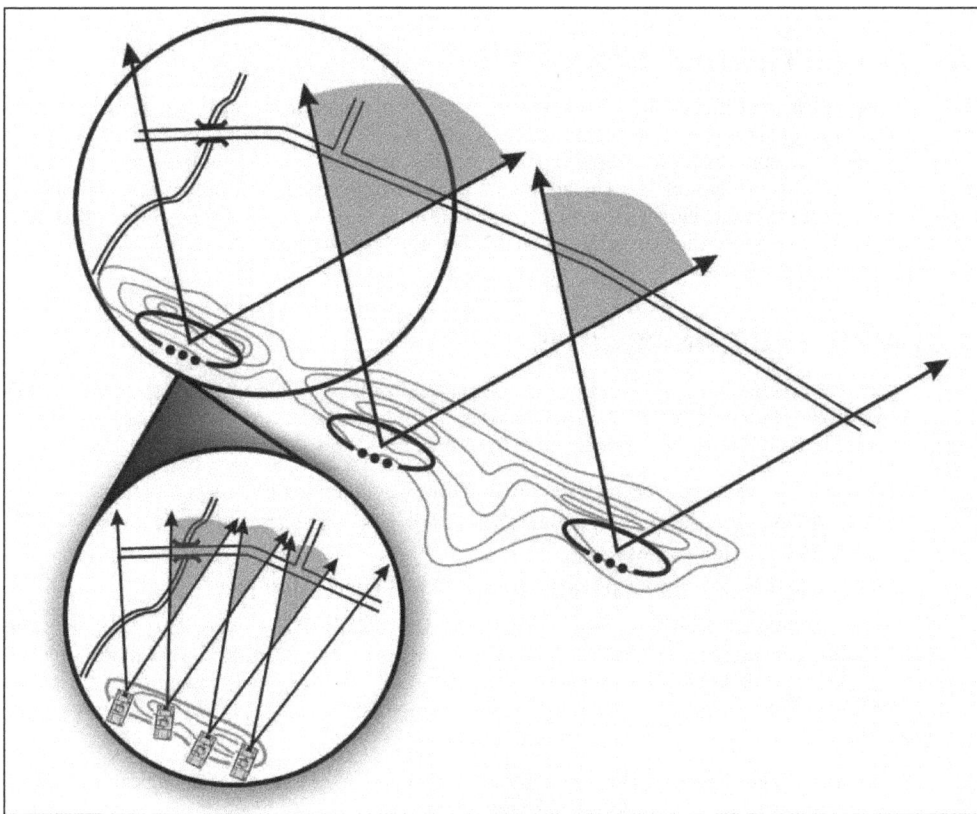

Figure 1-3. Overlapping fires.

ESTABLISH SECURITY

1-30.   Because most weapons company personnel are needed to man the weapons and operate the vehicles, local security against a dismounted threat may be a challenge for them in some circumstances. When the weapons company is positioned near other friendly Infantry units, those units may assist in protecting against possible attack by dismounted enemy Infantry. Though the weapons company is not always collocated with other units, Infantry units positioned near them should be able to cover dismounted avenues of approach to weapons unit's positions. However, the weapons company is always responsible for insuring its own local security whether friendly units are positioned near them or not. Weapons units moving with Infantry provide their own local security. During halts, the driver or assistant gunner may dismount to assist in securing the flank and rear sectors.

SEEK FLANK SHOT ENGAGEMENTS

1-31.   Heavy weapons squads, sections and platoons should be positioned to engage tanks or armored vehicles from the flank. Frontal engagements at enemy armor are less desirable for the following reasons:

- An armored vehicle's protection is greatest to the front.
- An armored vehicle's firepower and crew are normally oriented to the front.
- A frontal engagement increases the chance of detection and suppression by enemy armored vehicles.
- An armored vehicle provides a smaller target from the front.

TAKE ADVANTAGE OF STANDOFF

1-32.   Standoff is the difference between a friendly weapon's maximum range and an enemy weapon's maximum effective range. The ITAS maximum range provides it with a standoff advantage over many other weapon systems. Despite this advantage, engaging enemy armored vehicles at greater standoff ranges may not always be tactically feasible. The additional tracking time required to fire an ITAS missile beyond 2,000 meters gives a frontal target more time to maneuver against the friendly position and provides a flanking target more time to reach cover. Additionally, the terrain may not provide the fields of fire to support standoff distance engagements.

USE COVER AND CONCEALMENT

1-33.   Cover and concealment are critical to the survival of heavy weapons units and must be analyzed along with the other factors of METT-TC. An analysis of all of these factors is necessary for the heavy weapons units to be effective, to survive, and to overcome the following inherent weaknesses:

- The gunner is vulnerable because he is exposed while employing the weapon systems.
- The ITAS missile has a long flight time and must be continually tracked by the gunner.
- The ITAS has a slow rate of fire.
- Indirect fire systems may suppress the gunner decreasing his effectiveness...

1-34.   When employing heavy weapon systems, leaders should avoid conspicuous terrain, disperse weapons laterally and in depth so that no single enemy weapon can suppress two weapons squads, and disperse weapons squads to reduce casualties and equipment damage that could result from enemy mortar and artillery fires. The considerations for weapon system employment also apply during route selection and movement.

- Offensive Considerations. Determine the routes where cover and concealment are good, identify areas along the approaches to the objective where cover and concealment are poor, and consider using smoke or conducting missions during limited visibility to provide concealment.

• Defensive Considerations. Focus on locations with good fields of fire. Determine how the enemy can use the available cover and concealment and look at it from his point of view, both in daylight and at night.

EMPLOY IN DEPTH

1-35.   Heavy weapons squads are often employed in depth. In the offense, routes and firing positions should be selected to support the forward movement of attacking units. In the defense, weapons squads can be positioned forward then moved to positions in depth as the enemy closes, or the squads may be positioned in depth initially.

EMPLOY AS PART OF A COMBINED ARMS TEAM

1-36.   Skillful integration of Infantry, armor, engineer, and indirect fire assets improves the survivability and lethality of heavy weapons units.

• Infantry rifle units and platoons can assist in providing local security for the heavy weapons elements. Heavy weapons units also support the maneuver of Infantry forces.

• Heavy weapons units support the maneuver of armor forces. Heavy weapons may focus on destroying lightly armored enemy vehicles and dismounted Soldiers at long ranges, allowing the tanks to focus on destroying enemy tanks.

• Combat engineers focus on support of close combat and help shape the battlefield by enhancing mobility, countermobility, and survivability. General and geospatial engineers augment that support and provide other specialized capabilities. Mobility is enhanced as engineers provide expertise and assistance in breaching, clearing, gap crossing and other aspects of mobility support. Countermobility support is focused on the emplacement of tactical obstacles that reduce the enemy's ability to maneuver, mass, or reinforce, and increase his vulnerability to direct and indirect fires. To accomplish this, obstacles must disrupt, fix, turn, or block the enemy. To be effective, the obstacles must be covered by both direct and indirect fire. Survivability includes supporting the construction of fighting positions, other types of survivability positions, and those aspects of protection related to hardening as well as camouflage, concealment, and deception.

• Weapons unit leaders must be part of the indirect fire planning process at higher levels. They must coordinate frequencies, call signs, and priorities of fire. The Fire Support Officer habitually attached to the company from the battalion Fires Support Platoon can assist in this coordination. To do this, the weapons unit leaders should contact the attached fire support team (FIST) and the battalion mortar platoon. They should also contact the battalion fires cell or the fires battalion if there is no FSO or FIST Team. Indirect fires (artillery and mortars) are used to--

-- Destroy or neutralize the enemy. Slow the enemy rate of advance.

-- Destroy or disrupt enemy formations. Cause enemy vehicles to button up.

-- Suppress accompanying enemy artillery and antitank guided missile (ATGM) support by fire.

-- Fire white phosphorous/hexachloroethane (WP/HC) smoke to conceal weapon system firing signatures and to cover the movement of weapons squads between positions. When using obscurants, weapons company commanders (or platoon leaders) must consider the degrading effects these obscurants have on friendly units. For example, covering smoke may alert the enemy to friendly movement and may reduce a leader's ability to visually control fires.

This page intentionally left blank.

Chapter 2

Planning and Preparation

The information in this chapter is provided to the commander and leaders for consideration during planning and preparing for missions. It is to be used as a guide to assist the commander during application of the troop leading procedures (TLP) for mission related decisions based on the situation, his experience, the experience of his subordinate leaders, and key planning concepts.

Section I. PLANNING

During the mission planning process, leaders will take into consideration the personnel and equipment available to him to conduct his mission. Leaders will not only consider organic assets, but also those of personnel with associated weapons and equipment that may be attached routinely or for a specific mission or time period. Leaders must understand the characteristics and capabilities of all organic and attached assets in order to best employ them for maximum effectiveness and mission accomplishment. During the mission planning process, a leader will decide how to employ the personnel, weapons and systems he selects for the mission. Selection and employment of available assets is based on the factors of mission, enemy, terrain, troops, time, civilians (METT-TC).

BATTLE COMMAND

2-1.   Battle command is the art and science of understanding, visualizing, describing, directing, leading, and assessing forces in operations against a hostile, thinking, and adaptive enemy. Battle command applies leadership to translate decisions into actions by synchronizing forces and warfighting functions in time, space, and purpose to accomplish missions. These command skills are developed over time through study, practice, and judgment. The commander visualizes the operation, describing it in his intent and concept of the operation, and directs the actions of subordinates *within* his intent. He directly influences operations by his personal presence and his command and control (C2) system. He uses the war fighting functions (WFF) to organize, prepare, coordinate, integrate, synchronize, and execute his plan. That is, he considers everything he has or knows about an operation for each WFF.

2-2.   Visualizing, describing, and directing are aspects of battle command and leadership common to every commander. Technology, the fluid nature of operations, the increased volume of information that commanders must process, and today's battlefield underline the importance of the commander's ability to visualize, describe, and direct operations. Assessment is also an integral part battle command. Commanders must continually assess the threat, friendly forces, and effects throughout all three aspects of battle command.

TROOP-LEADING PROCEDURES

2-3.   TLPs begin when the leader receives the first indication of an upcoming mission and continue throughout the operational process of planning, preparing, executing, and assessing. The TLP comprise a sequence of actions that help leaders use available time effectively and efficiently to issue orders and execute tactical operations. TLPs are not a hard and fast set of rules. Some actions may be performed simultaneously. They are a guide that must be applied consistent with the situation and experience of the commander and his subordinate leaders. The standard Army planning process embedded within the TLPs consist of a series of interrelated subprocesses. For a detailed explanation of each process refer to FM 3-21.10.

PLANNING CONSIDERATIONS

2-4.   The unique characteristics of a weapons company requires leaders to take some additional factors into consideration during mission planning. Along with their tactical organization for combat, weapons company leaders must also include in mission planning their selection of weapons systems, communications, and vehicle load and modification considerations. As mentioned earlier, leaders will not only consider organic assets, but also those of attached personnel and their associated weapons and equipment. Selection and employment of the available assets is based on the factors of METT-TC.

WEAPON SELECTION CONSIDERATIONS

2-5.   The mix of weapons in a weapons company includes systems that can effectively engage troops, field fortifications, lightly armored and armored vehicles. The arms room concept allows for flexibility in weapons configuration for specific missions given to the weapons company. Considerations during selection of weapons systems must include an analysis of the terrain and threat in conjunction with the characteristics and capabilities of each weapon system. Table 2-1 shows weapons characteristics to assist in weapons planning.

Improved Target Acquisition System

2-6.   The Improved Target Acquisition System (ITAS) is a multipurpose weapon used for long-range engagement of targets. It can be employed in all weather conditions. It fires a tube-launched, optically-tracked, wire-guided (TOW) missile that provides a long-range capability against armored vehicles, heavily fortified bunkers, buildings, and dug-in or fortified enemy positions. The ITAS optics system, the Target Acquisition System (TAS), can also be used to increase visibility for reconnaissance, surveillance, and security operations. For planning purposes, TOW missiles have a maximum range of 3,750 meters and a minimum range of 200 meters for the TOW 2B. TOW missiles have the ability to defeat all known armor units they may encounter during combat operations. For detailed information on all ITAS characteristics and TOW munitions, refer to FM 3-22.32 and FM 3-22.34.

M2, .50 caliber, Machine Gun

2-7.   The M2 can be used against personnel and light armored vehicles with accurate fires past 2,000 meters. It is effective in restrictive terrain such as wooded areas. For detailed information on M2 characteristics and munitions, refer to FM 3-22.65.

MK-19, 40mm, Grenade Machine Gun

2-8.   The MK-19 is capable of laying down a heavy volume of close, accurate, and continuous fire. As a point weapon, it can penetrate up to 2 inches of steel armor at ranges out to 1,500 meters. As an area weapon, it can inflict personnel casualties out to 15 meters from impact at ranges out to 2,000 meters. Like the M2, the MK-19 can be employed in restrictive terrain conditions. It may also be used to cover dead space. For detailed information on all MK-19 characteristics and munitions, refer to FM 3-22.27.

Javelin Close Combat Missile System

2-9.   The Javelin is a dual-mode, man-portable AT missile with the capability to engage and defeat all known armor including tanks and other armored vehicles. When there is no armored vehicle threat, the Javelin can be employed in a secondary role of providing fire support against point targets such as bunkers and crew-served weapons positions. The Javelin command launch unit (CLU) can be used as an aid to reconnaissance, security operations and surveillance. The Javelin supports the fires of ITAS and can cover secondary armor avenues of approach and provide observation posts with an antiarmor capability. The Javelin has a maximum effective range of 2000 meters. For detailed information on all Javelin characteristics and munitions, refer to FM 3-22.37.

Optics

2-10.   All heavy weapons within the weapons company have optics systems. These systems provide the company with the ability to acquire targets at long range during daylight or limited visibility. All of the systems have magnification and thermal imaging capability (see Table 2-1) allowing thermal acquisition of targets at night or in dense forest or brush areas during light. Besides target acquisition, these can be used for both day and night observation. Some environmental conditions that affect all optics include limited visibility, night, infrared clutter, and infrared crossover.

Table 2-1. Weapons characteristics.

	Close Combat Missiles		Machine Guns	
	TOW [1]	Javelin [2]	MK19 [3]	M2 [4]
Maximum Range (M)	3,750	2,000	2,212	6,764 ball and AP 1,800-2,450 tracer burnout
Maximum Effective Range (M)	3,750	2,000	1,500 point target 2,212 area target	1,500 point target (single shot) 1,830 area target
Minimum Range/Arming Distance (M)	200 (TOW 2B)	150 top attack 65 direct attack	18 to 30 M430 18 to 36 M383	NA
Flight Time	21 seconds to max range	14 sec @ 2,000 M	NA	NA
Rates of Fire (Rds/min) Sustained Rapid Cyclic	NA NA NA	NA NA NA	40 60 325 to 375	Slow fire < 40 Rapid fire > 40 450 to 550
Casualty Radius (M)	UK	UK	15	NA
Weight (lbs)	260	14 (CLU)	Gun: 72.5 MK93 Mount: 30	Gun: 84 MK93 Mount: 30
Ammunition Type	Explosive form penetrator	HEAT	HEDP HE	Ball, tracer, AP, API, and more
Ammunition Weight	54 to 66 lbs	35 lbs	About 65 lbs (50 rounds)	About 45 lbs (100 rds)
Sight Type	Integrated day and night	Integrated Day and Night	Mounts a AN-PAS 13(V)3	Mounts a AN-PAS 13(V)3
Sight Magnification	Day and night vision sight normal/zoom	Day 4X Night	Night 4X 9X	3.3X WFOV 10X NFOV	3.3X WFOV 10X NFOV
Wide View	4/8X	**M98A2 CLU**		
Narrow View	12/24X	4X	12X 2X zoom	

[1] FM 3-22.34: TOW Weapon System
[2] FM 3-22.37: Javelin—Close Combat Missile System-Medium
[3] FM 3-22.27: MK19 40-mm Grenade Machine Gun, Mod 3
[4] FM 3-22.65: Browning machine gun, caliber .50 HB, M2

TASK ORGANIZATION

2-11.   The battalion operations order will contain the task organization for combat depicting attachments and detachments to or from the weapons company for a particular mission. Attachments and/or detachments may be habitual or temporary for a specific operation. If the weapons company receives any attachments, the commander may further task organize within the company itself to best accomplish his mission. To provide for optimal command and control and optimize heavy weapons unit's capabilities, heavy weapons platoons are not normally task organized below platoon level.

Attachments

2-12.   Weapons companies may have habitual attachments such as a FSO and a combat medic. Other sustainment support may or may not consist of a medical evacuation or field maintenance team (Chapter 1, Chapter 10, and Chapter 11).

2-13.   Weapons companies may also receive various other attachments with one of the more common being an Infantry platoon. A typical mission for an Infantry platoon attached to a weapons company would be to provide security for the company while the company performs its primary mission such as support by fire for another maneuvering element.

Detachments

2-14.   Elements of the weapons company may also be detached out to other units. Detachments often include a weapons platoon attached to an Infantry rifle company. Specific missions given to detached units are the responsibility of the gaining unit commander and are not covered in detail in this manual. Typical missions may include, but are not limited to, establishing support by fire (SBF) in an attack engaging the enemy in a planned engagement area, or security of flanks. Special consideration needs to be given to the maintenance requirements of the detached unit due to the gaining unit not having a habitual requirement for maintenance of their specific weapons or vehicles.

Planning Checklist

2-15.   The following example checklist shows several items for consideration for units attached to the weapons company or for elements of the weapons company detached to other units.

- Radio communications between units
- Command and support relationship
- Communications requirements
- Unit tactical standing operating procedure (TSOP)
- Unit situation report (SITREP), tactical situation, nature of mission
- Current operation orders (OPORD) with graphics
- Signal operating instructions (SOI) (current frequencies, call signs, challenge, and password)
- Digital communications
- Special instructions
- Special equipment
- Location of units
- Reporting times
- Duration of mission
- Link up information and location
- Coordination and contact points
- Pre-combat checks and pre-combat inspections
- Support and sustainment requirements

Upon receipt of an OPORD, weapons company units must ensure they are prepared for the mission. This includes personnel, equipment and vehicle preparation. Once the decision is made on heavy weapons configurations for the vehicles they must be mounted for the mission.

VEHICLE LOAD CONSIDERATIONS

2-16.   Load configurations for vehicles and trailers will vary between units. During mission planning and preparation leaders will need to plan for what equipment will be taken and where it will be carried. See FM 3-21.10 and TM 9-2320-280-10 for additional information on vehicle load considerations. At a minimum leaders should consider;

- How much of what type of ammunition will be carried where?
- Will trailers be taken or left in a separate location?
- Where will non-mounted weapon systems be carried or stored?
- Where will any special equipment taken be stored?
- How will the nature and duration of the mission alter the standard load configuration?
- Will any vehicle modifications alter the load plan?

2-17.   Vehicle commanders must ensure that any externally stowed items are secured from theft and do not constitute a fire hazard if the vehicle is attacked by an improvised explosive device (IED), rocket-propelled grenade (RPG), or other flammable device. External stowage should be minimized or modified to lessen the threat of vehicle fire and not restrict the view or movement of gunners or passengers providing security. All loose items stored inside the vehicle must be secured to prevent theft or becoming secondary missiles in the event of a mine or IED strike or a roll over. Commanders should consider stowing flammable items that are mission essential inside the vehicle behind armored portions of the vehicle, and securing non-mission-essential and nonflammable items outside the vehicle. Other considerations follow:

- Use on-board ammunition storage containers such as 60-mm mortar ammunition cans. These hold several types of ammunition. This saves the crew a lot of time when they have to switch between ammunition for crew-served weapons.
- Carry complete spare wheel and tire assemblies rather than just spare tires. This reduces the time needed to change a flat, and will often allow a crew to repair a vehicle after a mine strike.
- Consider equipping every vehicle or every other vehicle with wheeled vehicle tow bars, so that vehicles can recover or tow each other. Tow bars are better than cables, since no driver is needed in the towed vehicle.
- Consider emplacing civilian or military fire extinguishers in fixed positions inside the vehicle. Normally, locate them to protect the crew rather than the vehicle. This helps ensure crew survivability. Carry additional loose fire extinguishers to fight vehicle fires.

2-18.   Commanders should establish load plan standing operating procedures (SOP) for sensitive items. They should account for ammunition and additional special equipment such as breach kits, demolitions, and first aid equipment. They should also account for any additional weapons.

UP-ARMORED HMMWVS

2-19.   The Army started adding armor to its high mobility multipurpose wheeled vehicles (HMMWV) years before Operation Iraqi Freedom, but attacks from small arms, rocket-propelled grenades, and IEDs prompted the Army to place an urgent priority on shortening production schedules and beefing up protection for vehicles already in the field. However, both RPGs and IEDs can defeat many armored vehicles, and will likely defeat any wheeled vehicle at the point of detonation, with or without an armor package.

2-20.   Factory produced up-armored HMMWVs provide level-one armor protection. They provide all-around protection, both glass and on the armament on the side, front, rear, sides, top, and bottom. "Add-on" up-armor kits, or level-two armor protection, are also factory-produced in the United States, and is installed on existing 'soft-skinned HMMWVs. However, "add-on" up-armor kits only provide front, rear, and side glass protection, while leaving the top and the bottom of the vehicles vulnerable. Level-three armor refers to the stop-gap measure use of steel plates that have been approved, and which are cut for vehicles, and then either welded or bolted on a vehicle.

2-21.   In addition to increased armor protection, up-armored HMMWVs feature more rugged suspension systems able to handle the added weight and ballistic- resistant glass. They also include air conditioners that enable crews to operate with the windows up, even in stifling temperatures.

UNIT-INSTALLED PROTECTION

2-22.   Improvised armor and other protection have been added to vehicles by American Soldiers at least since World War II. Units may be permitted to add additional improvised armor and other protective devices to supplement the existing protection on their vehicles. Examples of these include wire cutters and reinforced bumpers. Besides the strain on engines and suspensions, there are some other factors to consider when adding armor:

* What is the primary enemy threat? For example, if the threat is 7.62-mm guns, RPGs, IEDs, or mines, how well can the vehicle's armor protect the crew from each threat? What threats must be protected by increased offensive capabilities?
* If the enemy is employing mines, consider whether the armor and weight associated with mine strike protection is practical versus armor, which protects against other threats.
* Consider armoring critical pieces of the vehicle itself such as the fuel system, communication system, and cooling system. Ensure added armor does not reduce cooling airflow around electronic equipment.
* Use of Kevlar blankets from disabled HMMWVs or the M2 Bradley spall liner to 'armor' HMMWV seats and to add lightweight armor to other areas of the vehicle.
* Does the gunner have enough protection? Consider his legs and lower body, which will be exposed through the middle of the vehicle as well, and which are not covered by body armor.
* Does the protection interfere with the firing of the primary weapon? For example, a wire cutter on a vehicle may interfere with firing the missile.

2-23.   Inherent with light-wheeled vehicle operations in combat are the risk associated with the reduced protection compared to more heavily armored systems. While the up-armored HMMWVs found in the weapons company do increase their protection, the vehicles and personnel are still at risk from heavy weapons and high explosives. Other risks such as low-lying power lines and wires may also impose a hazard to occupants of the vehicle. Modifications to the HMMWVs such as the unit-installed wire cutters and wire guards should be considered to reduce the risk of injury due to these hazards. See FM 3-21.10 for additional information on vehicle modifications.

VEHICLE WEIGHT, OBSERVATION, AND SURVIVABILITY

2-24.   Force protection is directly linked to mission success and must always be an important consideration in the planning and execution of missions that employ soft-skinned vehicles. The balance between the protection of vehicles and crews, observation, and the employment of weapons is critical. The additional weight of additional armor also places a strain on other vehicle components, such as the engine and the suspension. Normally, heavily armored vehicles, especially wheeled vehicles with extra armor such as the up-armored HMMWV, severely limit crew and passenger observation in restrictive and urban terrain. They can also limit weapons employment at close ranges. At times, insurgent and terrorist enemy forces target vehicles with poor security, because they seem easier to destroy and less likely to respond effectively. Commanders must analyze enemy trends and events in their area of operations (AO) before deciding on the appropriate levels of armor versus offensive capabilities, mission demands, and crew survivability. Other considerations might include--

- Can the vehicle suspension support additional armor and still carry the payload?
- Can the vehicle crew and passengers provide all-round security for themselves?
- Will additional armor affect vehicle mobility over rough terrain or in restrictive urban areas?
- Does the vehicle have sufficient power, acceleration, and speed?
- Can the vehicle crew and passengers quickly and safely mount or dismount? Can they do so under fire?

PRECOMBAT CHECKS AND INSPECTIONS

2-25.   Precombat checks (PCC) and precombat inspections (PCI) are critical to the success of any combat mission. These checks and inspections are leader tasks and cannot be delegated below squad leader level. They ensure that the Soldier is prepared to execute the required individual and collective tasks that support the mission. Checks and inspections are part of the TLPs that protect against shortfalls that could endanger Soldiers' lives and jeopardize the successful execution of a mission. PCCs and PCIs must be tailored to the specific unit and the mission requirements. Each mission and each patrol may require a separate set of checklists. One of the best ways to ensure PCCs and PCIs are complete and thorough is with full-dress rehearsals. These rehearsals, run at combat speed with communication and full mission-equipment, allow the leader to envision minute details, as they will occur on the battlefield. If the operation is to be conducted at night, Soldiers should conduct full-dress rehearsals at night as well. PCCs and PCIs should include back briefs on the mission, the task and purpose of the mission, and how the Soldiers' role fits into the scheme of maneuver. The Soldiers should know the latest intelligence updates and the rules of engagement (ROE), and be versed in medical evacuation (MEDEVAC) procedures and sustainment requirements. Table 2-2 lists sensitive items, high-dollar value items, issued pieces of equipment, and supplies. This table should spur thought--it is not a final list.

Table 2-2. Example precombat check and inspection list.

ID card	T&E mechanisms	Grappling hook
ID tags	Spare barrels	Sling sets
Ammunition	Spare barrel bags	PZ marking kit
Weapons	Extraction tools	ANCD
Protective mask	Asbestos gloves	Plugger or GPS
Knives	Barrel changing handles	Handheld microphones
Flashlights	Headspace and timing gauges	NVDs
Radios and backup communication	SAW tools	Batteries and spare batteries
Communication cards	Basic issue items	Picket pounder
Nine-line MEDEVAC procedures	Oil and transmission fluids	Engineer stakes
OPORD	Antifreeze coolant	Pickets
FRAGOs	Water	Concertina wire
Maps	MREs	TCP signs
Graphics, routes, objectives, LZs, and PZs	Load plans	IR lights
Protractors	Fuel cans	Glint tape
Alcohol pens	Fuel spout	Chemical lights
Alcohol erasers	Tow bars	Spare handsets
Pen and paper	Slave cables	Pencil with eraser
Tripods	Concertina wire gloves	Weapon tie downs
Pintles		

Chapter 3

Movement

In combat, units are positioned on the battlefield in order to gain the maximum advantage possible over the enemy. This is accomplished through tactical movement and maneuver. This chapter discusses mounted movement techniques and formations available to the company commander for moving his unit. Some are secure and slow, while others are faster, but less secure. Some work well in certain terrain or tactical situations, but not so well in others. Some offer security, but take longer; others offer speed, but less security. The commander must consider the overall movement plan including the unique advantages and disadvantages of each movement technique and formation.

Section I. MOVEMENT FORMATIONS AND TECHNIQUES

Tactical movement is used to position units on the battlefield and prepare them for contact. Maneuver is movement while in contact combined with supporting fire. At company level, movement and maneuver overlap considerably. The process by which units transition from tactical movement to maneuver is called "actions on contact" and are covered in Chapter 4. The formation and technique used are determined by the commander based on mission, enemy, terrain, troops, time, civilians (METT-TC) conditions and the likelihood of enemy contact. Platoons will also employ movement formations and techniques within a company movement.

FORMATIONS

3-1.   Mounted movement formations describe the specific locations of the company's elements in relation to each other. They are guides on how to arrange the unit for movements. Each formation aids control, security, and firepower to varying degrees. The following factors should be considered in determining the best formation to use.

- Mission.
- Enemy situation.
- Terrain.
- Weather and visibility conditions.
- Speed of movement desired.
- Degree of flexibility desired.
- Ability to command and control.

3-2.   The company moves using seven basic mounted movement formations including the company column, wedge, line, vee, diamond, box and echelon right or left. They also employ two stationary formations during temporary halts, the coil and the herringbone. Below is a brief description and diagram of each type formation.

COLUMN FORMATION

3-3.   Figure 3-1.The company uses the column when moving fast, when moving through restricted terrain on a specific route, or when it does not expect enemy contact. Each platoon normally follows directly behind the platoon in front of it. If the situation dictates, platoons can disperse laterally to enhance security.

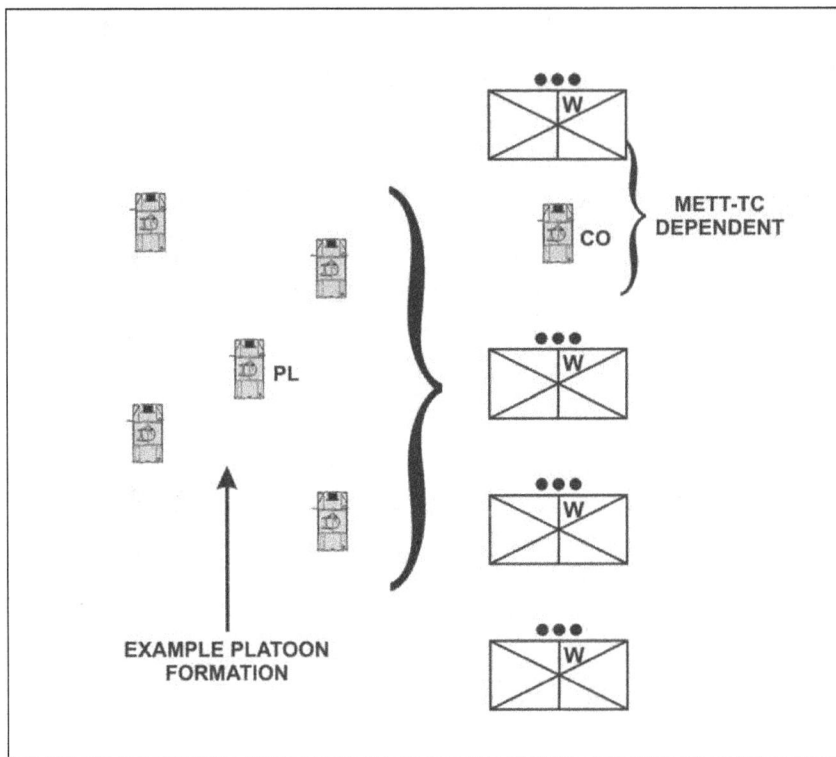

Figure 3-1. Column formation.

WEDGE FORMATION

3-4.   Figure 3-2. When the enemy situation seems unclear or when contact might occur, leaders often use the wedge formation.

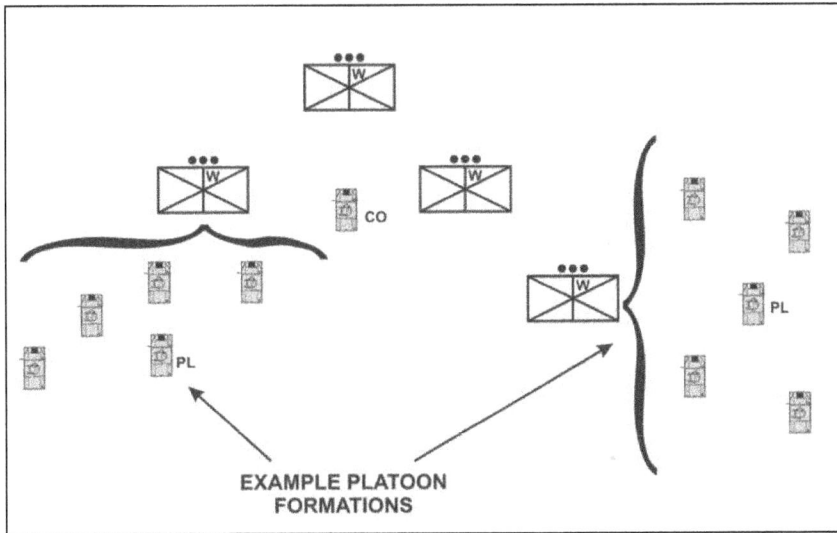

Figure 3-2. Wedge formation.

LINE FORMATION

3-5.   Figure 3-3. When crossing open areas or occupying a support-by-fire position, the company may use the line formation. The line formation is normally used when no terrain remains between it and the enemy, when the enemy's antitank weapons have been suppressed, or when the company is vulnerable to artillery fire and must move fast.

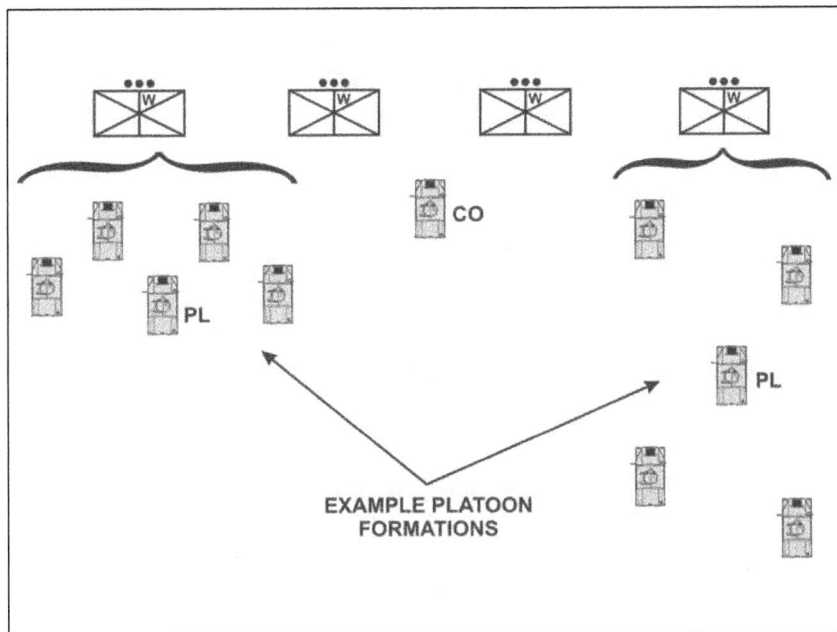

Figure 3-3. Line formation.

VEE FORMATION

3-6.   Figure 3-4. The Vee formation is used when enemy contact is possible. In the company Vee, the center platoons are located in the rear of the formation, while the flank platoons are to the front of and outside the center platoon.

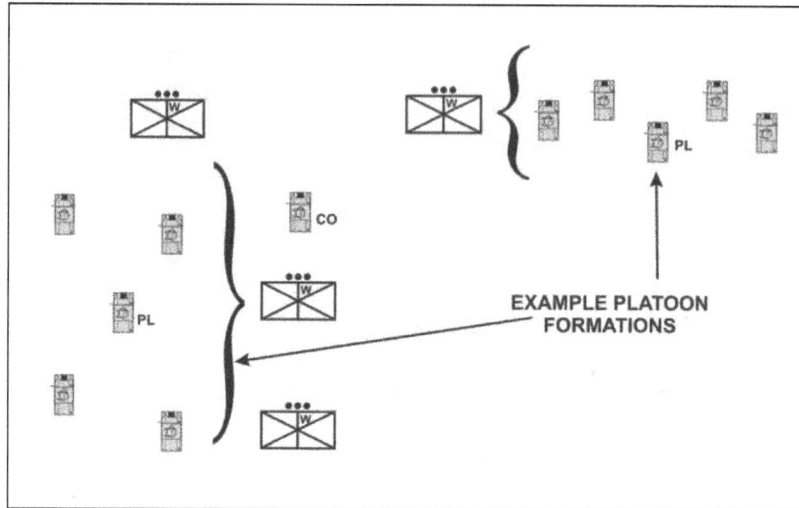

Figure 3-4. Vee formation.

DIAMOND FORMATION

3-7.   Figure 3-5. The company uses the diamond formation when they want to maintain all around security, and enemy contact is not expected. The company leads with a platoon with two platoons to the flanks and the fourth platoon in the rear.

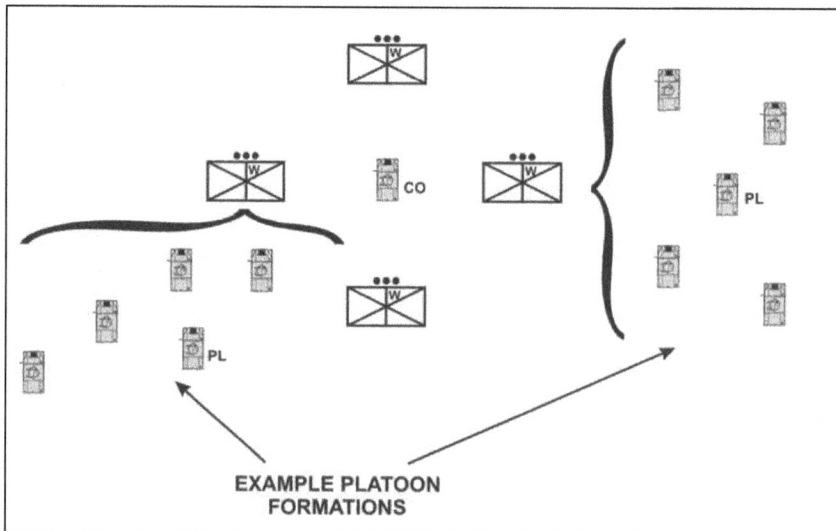

Figure 3-5. Diamond formation.

BOX FORMATION

3-8.   Figure 3-6. The box formation arranges the unit with two forward and two trail platoons. A weapons company with only three platoons would have to adopt a Vee or another formation. It is often used when executing an approach march, an exploitation, or a pursuit when the commander has only general knowledge about the enemy.

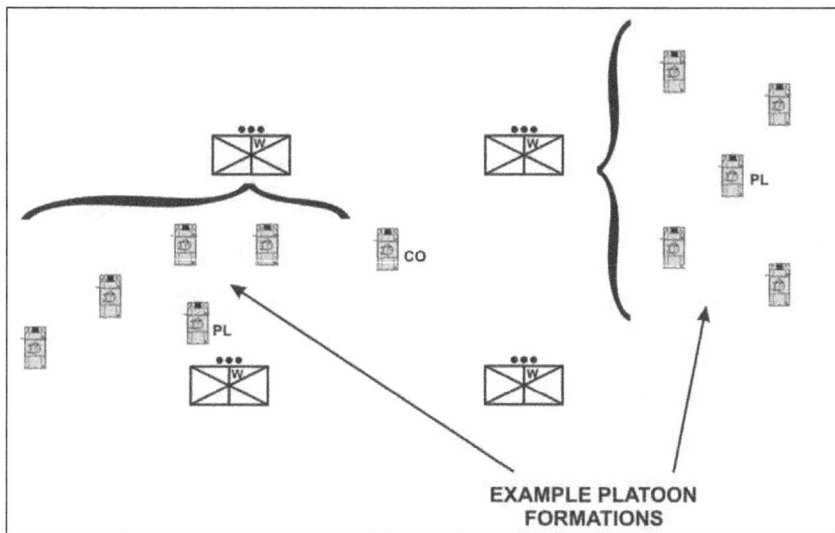

Figure 3-6. Box formation.

ECHELON FORMATION

3-9.   Figure 3-7. The echelon formation is used when the company wants to maintain security and/or observation of one flank and enemy contact is not likely. The company echelon formation (either echelon left or echelon right) has the lead platoon positioned farthest from the echeloned flank, with each subsequent platoon located to the rear of and outside the platoon in front of it.

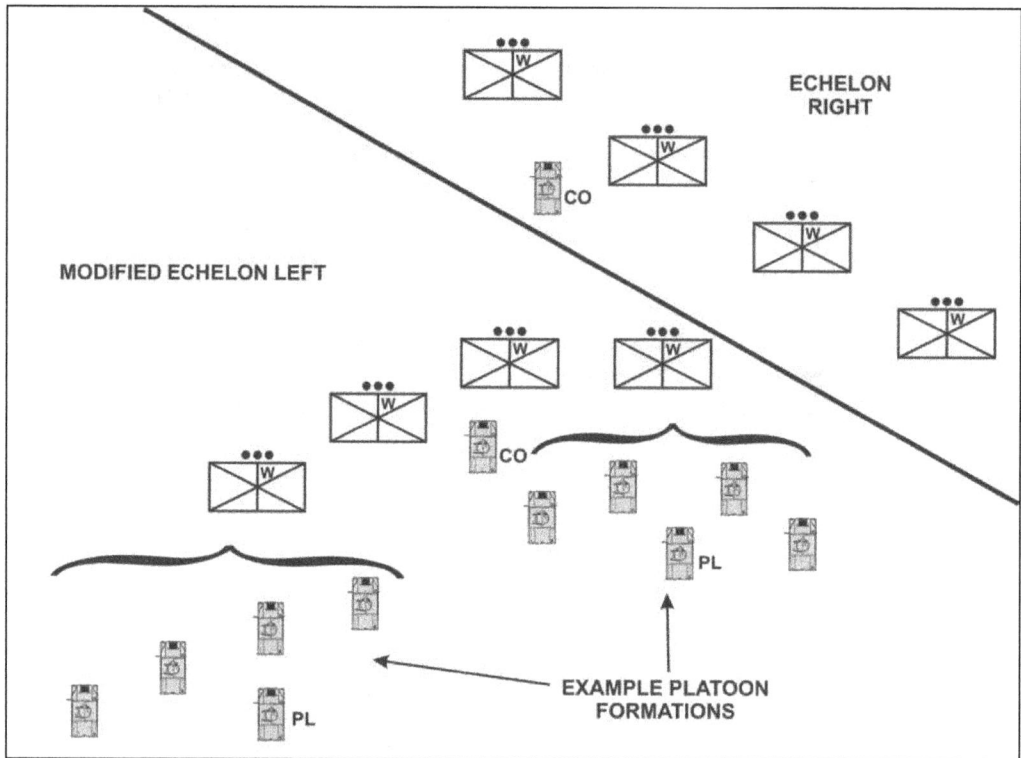

Figure 3-7. Echelon left/right formation.

COIL AND HERRINGBONE FORMATIONS

3-10.   The coil and herringbone are formations employed when elements of the company are stationary and must maintain 360-degree security.

Coil

3-11.   Figure 3-8. The coil is used to provide all-round security and observation when the company is stationary. It is also useful for tactical refueling, resupply, and issuing orders. Security is posted to include air guards and dismounted rifleman.

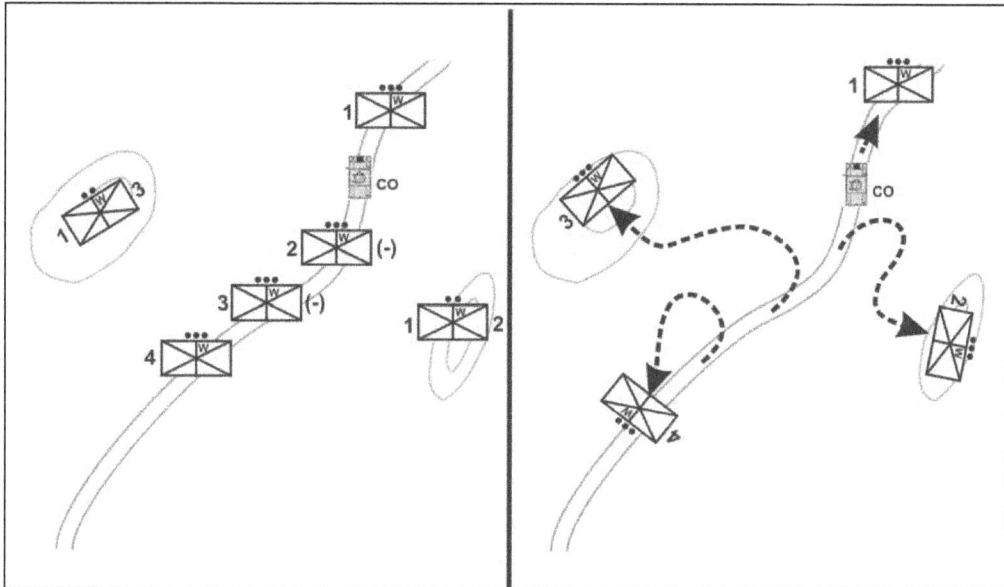

Figure 3-8. Coil formation before (left) and after (right).

Herringbone

3-12.   Figure 3-9. The company uses the herringbone to disperse when traveling in column formation. They can use it during air attacks or when they must stop during movement. It lets them move to covered and concealed positions off a road or from an open area and set up all-round security without detailed instructions. They reposition the vehicles as needed to take advantage of the best cover, concealment, and fields of fire.

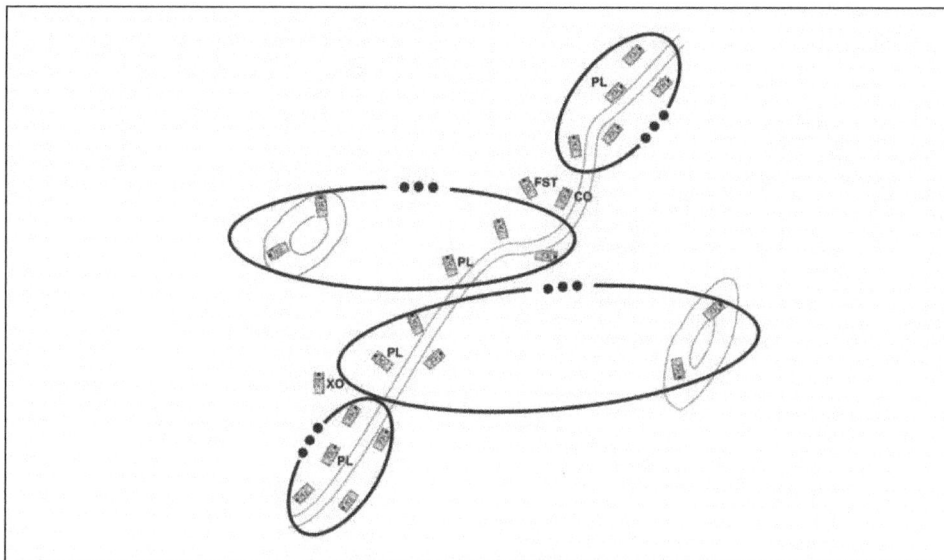

Figure 3-9. Herringbone formation.

FORMATION SELECTION

3-13.   Commanders select the formation that provides the proper control, security, and speed. Table 3-1 compares the six movement formations.

Table 3-1. Comparison of movement formations.

Formation	Security	Fires	Control	Speed
Column	Good dispersion. Limited all-round security.	Limited to front and rear. Excellent to the flanks.	Easy to control. Flexible formation.	Fast.
Line	Excellent to the front. Poor to the flank and rear.	Excellent to the front. Poor to the flank and rear.	Difficult to control. Inflexible formation.	Slow.
Wedge	Good all-round security.	Excellent to the front and good to flanks.	Easy to control but more difficult than the column. Flexible formation.	Slower than the column.
Echelon	Good to the echeloned flank and front.	Excellent to the echeloned flank and front.	Difficult to control.	Slow.
Coil	Excellent all around security.	Excellent to front rear and flanks.	Easy to control.	Used while stationary.
Herringbone	Great dispersion. Good all-round security	Good to front rear and flanks	Easy to implement. Control more difficult after dispersion.	Used to disperse to cover and concealment while traveling.

TECHNIQUES

3-14.   The company commander selects from the three-mounted movement techniques (traveling, traveling overwatch, and bounding overwatch) largely based on the likelihood of enemy contact and other METT-TC factors. As the probability of enemy contact increases, leaders adjust the movement technique to provide greater security. For example, if an enemy update received from higher headquarters states that the enemy has moved much closer to the platoon than the platoon leader anticipated, he immediately switches the technique from traveling overwatch to bounding overwatch. Figure 3-10 shows the link between the possibility of contact and movement technique. Other factors that may influence a leaders decision include--

- The type of contact expected.
- The availability of an overwatch element.
- The terrain over which the moving element will pass.
- The balance of speed and security required during movement.

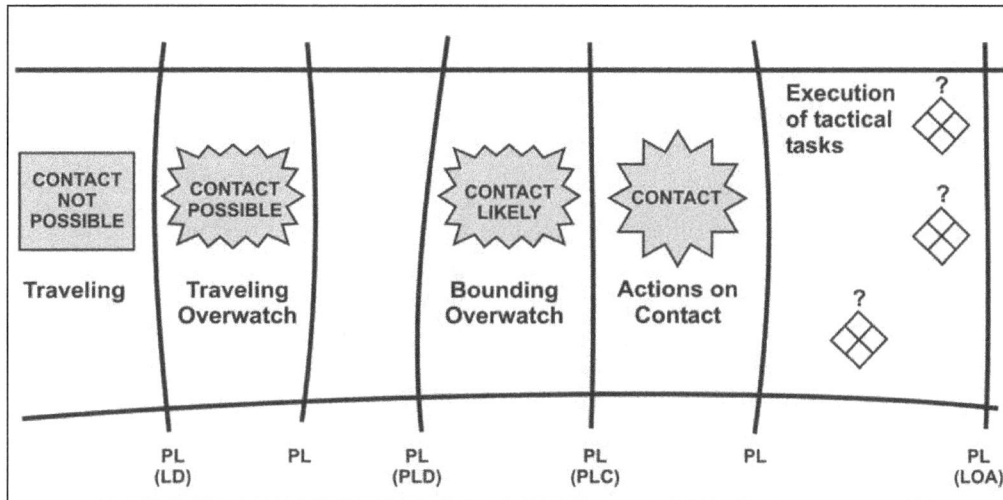

Figure 3-10. Transition from movement techniques to maneuver.

TRAVELING

3-15.   Continuous movement characterizes the traveling technique by all company elements. It is best suited for situations in which enemy contact is unlikely and speed is important. When leaders analyze the latest information on the enemy and determine that contact with the enemy is unlikely, often the traveling techniques will be used for movement. Figure 3-11 shows a traveling technique for an Infantry weapons company.

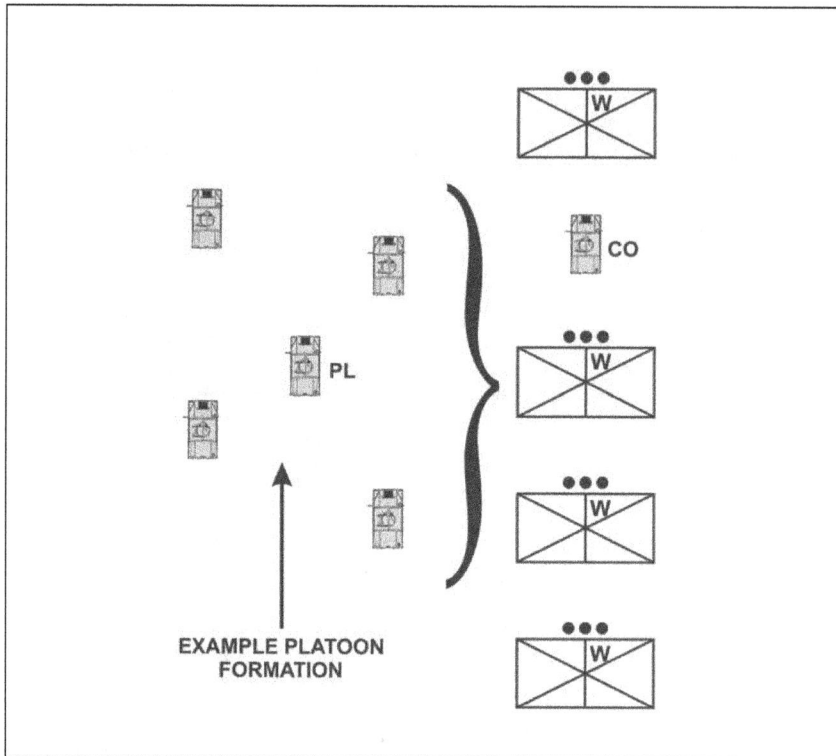

Figure 3-11. Traveling technique.

TRAVELING OVERWATCH

3-16.   Traveling overwatch is an extended form of traveling that provides additional security when speed is desirable but contact is possible. The lead element moves continuously and provides security forward of the main body. Leaders track the movement of forward security elements. The trail platoon moves at various speeds and may halt periodically to overwatch movement of the lead platoon. Dispersion between the two platoons must be based on the trail platoon's ability to see the lead platoon and to provide immediate suppressive fires in case the lead platoon is engaged. The intent is to maintain depth, provide flexibility, and maintain the ability to maneuver even if contact occurs. However, if contact is made, ideally a unit should be moving in bounding overwatch rather than traveling overwatch. Figure 3-12_ shows a traveling overwatch technique for an Infantry weapons company.

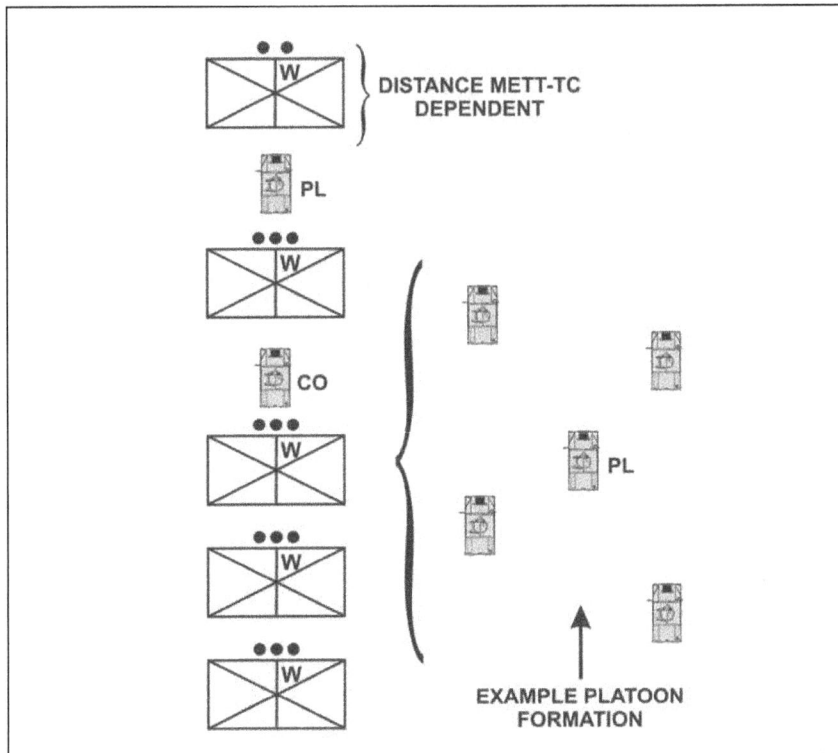

Figure 3-12. Traveling overwatch technique.

BOUNDING OVERWATCH

3-17.   Bounding overwatch is used when contact is expected. It is the most secure, but slowest, movement technique. The purpose of bounding overwatch is to deploy prior to contact, giving the unit the ability to protect a bounding element by immediately suppressing an enemy force. In all types of bounding, the overwatch element is assigned sectors to scan while the bounding element uses terrain to achieve cover and concealment. The bounding element avoids masking the fires of the overwatch element; it never bounds beyond the range at which the overwatch element can effectively suppress likely or suspected enemy positions. Ideally, the overwatch element keeps the bounding element in sight. Before bounding, the leader shows the bounding element the location of the next overwatch position. Once the bounding element reaches its overwatch position, it signals "READY" by voice or visual means to the element that overwatched it's bound. The company can employ either of two bounding methods: alternate or successive. Figure 3-13 shows a bounding overwatch technique for an Infantry weapons company.

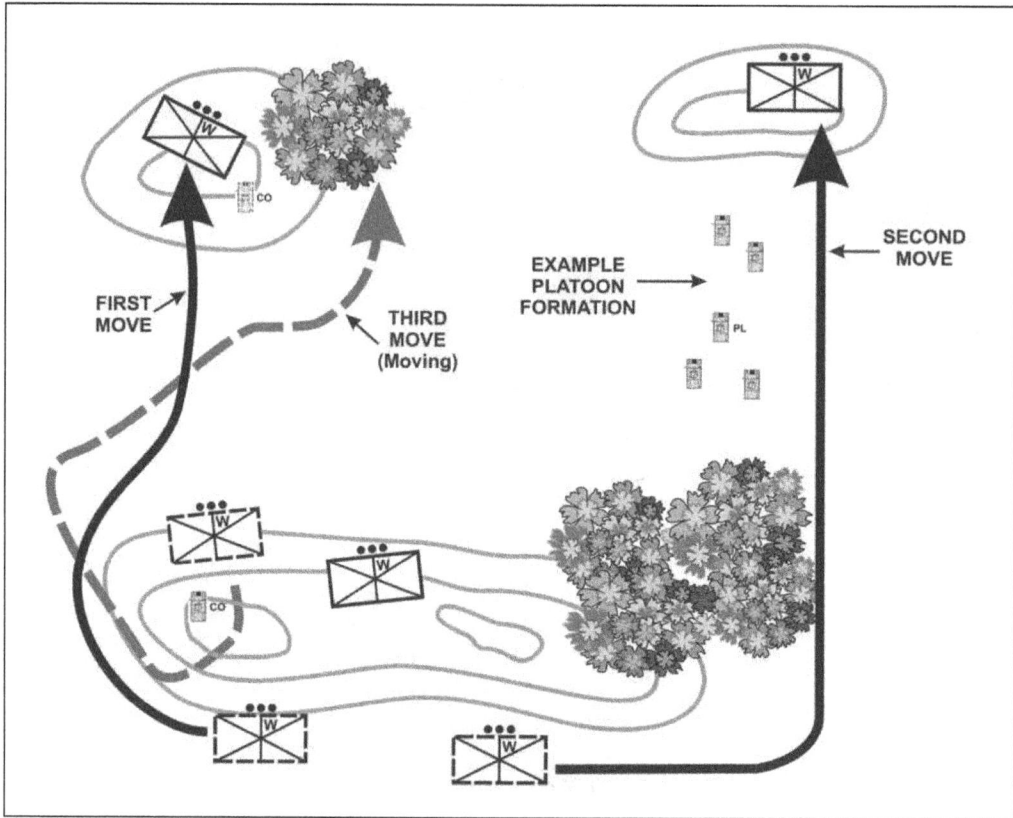

Figure 3-13. Bounding overwatch technique.

Alternate Bounds

3-18.   Covered by the rear element, the lead element moves forward, halts, and assumes overwatch positions. The rear element advances past the lead element and takes up overwatch positions. This sequence continues as necessary with only one element moving at a time. This method is usually more rapid than successive bounds.

Successive Bounds

3-19.   In the successive bounding method the lead element, covered by the rear element, advances and takes up overwatch positions. The rear element then advances to an overwatch position roughly abreast of the lead element and halts. The lead element then moves to the next position, and so on. Only one element moves at a time, and the rear element avoids advancing beyond the lead element. This method is easier to control and more secure than the alternate bounding method, but it is slower.

Section II. OPERATIONAL CONSIDERATIONS

The company commander assists in protecting his company during movement by ensuring the company is using proper movement formations and techniques. Movement should be as rapid as the terrain, mobility of the force, and enemy situation permit. The ability to gain and maintain the initiative often depends on movement being undetected by the enemy. The Infantry weapons company depends heavily upon terrain, mobility and standoff for protection from enemy fire.

MOVEMENT FUNDAMENTALS

3-20.   The Infantry weapons company commander's mission analysis helps him decide how to move most effectively and securely. When planning company movements, the commander ensures the unit is moving in a way that supports a rapid transition to maneuver. Once contact with the enemy is made, squads and platoons execute the appropriate actions on contact, and leaders begin to maneuver their units. The following fundamentals provide guidance for planning effective company movements.

Reconnoiter

3-21.   All echelons reconnoiter. The enemy situation and the available planning time may limit the unit's reconnaissance, but leaders at every level seek information about the terrain and enemy. If sufficient information is still lacking, an effective technique is to send a reconnaissance element forward of the lead platoon. Even if this unit is only 15 minutes ahead of the company, it can still provide valuable information and reaction time for the company commander.

Use Terrain and Weather Effectively

3-22.   Unlike the Infantry rifle company with the ability to move across almost any terrain, the Infantry weapons company is restricted to areas trafficable by the vehicles. This restriction is largely counteracted by the speed at which the unit can move. To the greatest extent possible, the company moves on covered and concealed routes. Moving in limited visibility may provide better concealment, and the enemy might be less alert during these periods. Leaders should plan to avoid identified danger areas or kill zones such as large open areas surrounded by covered or concealed areas.

Move as Sections or Platoons

3-23.   The advantages to moving the company by sections or platoons include--

- Faster movement.
- Better security. A small unit is less likely to be detected because it requires less cover and concealment.
- More dispersion. The dispersion gained by moving the company by sections and platoons makes it more difficult for the enemy to concentrate his fires against the company, especially indirect fires, close air support (CAS), and chemical agents. Subordinate units also gain room to maneuver.
- Better operations security (OPSEC). It is harder for the enemy to determine what the friendly force is doing with only isolated platoon, section or individual vehicle spot reports.

3-24.   When planning decentralized movements the commander should also consider the following disadvantages.

- Numerous linkups are required to regroup the company.
- May take longer to mass combat power to support a hasty attack or disengage in the event of enemy contact.

Maintain Security During Movement

3-25.   Security is critical during movement since the company is vulnerable to enemy aerial, direct and indirect fires. Since weapons companies do not often move with rifle companies during tactical movements, they are responsible for their own security. Leaders must be alert to maintain security of the unit during movements and halts. In addition to the fundamentals listed earlier, the company commander achieves security for the company by applying the following.

- Use the appropriate movement formation and technique for the conditions
- Move as fast as the situation allows. This may degrade the enemy's ability to detect the unit and the effectiveness of his fires once he detects it.
- When possible, orient weapons to cover the front, flanks, and rear during movements.
- In addition to his assigned sector, the gunner is responsible for aerial security. The leader and assistant gunner should have their weapons ready to fire out of their respective windows while scanning the terrain for the enemy.
- During halts, dismount as many Soldiers as possible for security. The gunner maintains his position behind the main weapon while the leader, assistant gunner, and driver dismount if possible. The driver should stay within arms reach of the vehicle.
- Enforce noise and light discipline.
- Enforce camouflage discipline (Soldiers and their equipment).

Employ Countermeasures

3-26.   Commanders should also consider the use of countermeasures during movements such as suppressive fires, direct and indirect, to degrade his ability to observe fire upon the unit by use of terrain or obscurant (smoke).

Employ Additional Control Techniques

3-27.   Additional movement control techniques often aid commanders in controlling company movements.

MOVEMENT CONTROL TECHNIQUES

3-28.   Using the proper formation and movement techniques helps the Infantry weapons company commander control the company, but additional control techniques are often required. The following techniques may help in controlling company movements.

GRAPHICS

3-29.   Normally the battalion assigns graphic control measures to synchronize a company movement into the battalion's movement or scheme of maneuver. The company commander may need to establish additional control measures to control his units. These may include boundaries, routes, command posts (CP), release points (RP), target reference points (TRP), and objectives on known (likely) enemy positions to control direct fires. The company commander ensures each graphic control measure is updated as needed and is easy to locate on the terrain.

RECONNAISSANCE

3-30.   Prior reconnaissance aids control during movement. It provides the commander with a better idea of where movement is more difficult and where graphic control measures are needed. Elements from the company may perform this reconnaissance, however the battalion reconnaissance platoon is more likely to conduct the reconnaissance and provide the information to other organizations. The use of unmanned aircraft systems (UAS) can also be a valuable reconnaissance asset. The Improved Target Acquisition

System (ITAS) target acquisition system (TAS) and Javelin's command launch unit (CLU) are also a valuable systems that can aid in reconnaissance.

GUIDES

3-31.   Guides who have already seen the terrain are the best way to provide control. When guides are not available for the entire movement, they should reconnoiter the difficult areas and guide the company through those. Examples: complex road interchanges, obstacle lanes, and another unit's area of operations (AO).

NAVIGATIONAL AIDS

3-32.   Even with the availability of a global positioning system (GPS), every leader should maintain positioning on his map and verify his position with terrain features. If possible, select routes that allow leaders to use prominent terrain to stay oriented.

LIMITED VISIBILITY MOVEMENTS

3-33.   The measures listed above are equally useful in limited visibility conditions. However, to aid movement in during limited visibility, the use of night vision devices (NVD) is a great asset. Leaders may also consider closing up the vehicle interval in formations while still maintaining the most dispersion possible at all times and reducing the speed of movement. Well-trained units can operate at night as they do during the day.

This page intentionally left blank.

Chapter 4

Offensive Operations

The offense is the decisive form of war. Offensive operations destroy or defeat the enemy. The weapons company can be deployed to support the Infantry companies or given a separate mission. The weapons company possesses the greatest combination of firepower and mobility available to the Infantry battalion. In the offense, the company provides tank-killing, bunker-destroying, and suppression capabilities that can influence the outcome of operations. It can also move quickly on the battlefield to support engaged units or to react to enemy movements. This chapter describes the tactics and techniques used by the weapons company during offensive operations. Many of the subjects covered in this chapter are also included in FM 3-21.10: The Infantry Rifle Company.

Section I. OVERVIEW

The outcome of decisive combat derives from offensive actions. All operations are designed to transition to and support the offense. A sound doctrinal foundation during offensive planning assists the weapons company commander in capitalizing on the tactical flexibility of his unit. For more detail on offensive planning considerations, refer to FM 3-21.10: The Infantry Rifle Company.

PURPOSE

4-1.   Offensive operations seek to seize, retain, and exploit the initiative to decisively defeat the enemy. Additionally, offensive operations accomplish the following:

- Disrupt enemy coherence.
- Secure terrain.
- Deny the enemy of resources.
- Fix the enemy.
- Gain information.
- Deceive the enemy.

CHARACTERISTICS

4-2.   The common characteristics of all offensive operations are surprise, concentration, tempo, and audacity. Based on mission, enemy, terrain, troops, time, civilians (METT-TC), the commander's plan and actions should balance these characteristics to accomplish the mission with minimal casualties.

SURPRISE

4-3.   Units achieve surprise by striking the enemy at a time, at a place, or in a manner for which he is unprepared. Surprise delays and disrupts the enemy's ability to react. The speed and lethality of the weapons company makes the use of surprise an important advantage. Surprise also reduces the vulnerability of the company. Some methods that the weapons company can use to achieve surprise are:

- Following operations security (OPSEC) procedures.
- Massed and simultaneous engagements of fires from multiple weapons units.
- Making the best possible use of vehicle speed.
- Operating during limited visibility.
- Using covered or concealed routes during tactical movements.
- Attacking in an unexpected direction such as a flank or rear.

CONCENTRATION

4-4.   Units achieve concentration by massing the effects of their weapons systems without necessarily massing their vehicles at a single location. Proper control and modern position location devices enable the leader to disperse his vehicles while retaining the ability to quickly mass the effects of the platoon's weapons systems whenever necessary. The challenge for the company commander is to concentrate combat power while reducing the enemy's ability to do the same against his unit... Examples of concentrating the firepower of the weapons company and other weapon systems include coordinating obstacle with direct and indirect fires, multiple platoons firing into an engagement area, and the use of supplementary positions to mass fires.

TEMPO

4-5.   Tempo is the ability to adjust the rate of operations relative to battle circumstances and relative to the enemy's capability to sense and react. It is the controlled rate of military action. While a rapid tempo is often preferred, tempo should be adjusted to ensure synchronization. The weapons company can utilize tempo by using its mobility advantage to position its units, and using mission-type orders and tactical standing operating procedures (TSOP) to increase its ability to more quickly maneuver against the enemy.

AUDACITY

4-6.   Audacity is characterized by violent execution of the mission and a willingness to seize the initiative. Knowledge of the commander's intent enables leaders to take advantage of battlefield opportunities whenever they present themselves. This enhances the effectiveness of the company's support for the entire offensive operation. The mobility and firepower of the weapons company enables it to attack quickly with great firepower.

TYPES

4-7.   The four types of offensive operations are movement to contact, attack, exploitation, and pursuit. The weapons company often provides support for each using support by fire or attack-by-fire positions. Its mobility advantage relative to the Infantry companies enables it to maneuver rapidly on the battlefield and may increase its tactical value during exploitations and pursuits.

MOVEMENT TO CONTACT

4-8.   Movement to contact is a type of offensive operation designed to develop the situation and establish or regain contact. The commander conducts a movement to contact (MTC) when the enemy situation is vague or not specific enough to conduct an attack. Because the enemy situation is vague, the weapons company may have one or more of its platoons attached to other units within the battalion. The weapons company may also be used in support of or in concert with the scouts to find the enemy. The weapons company also has the ability to fix the enemy once contact has been made and can guide Infantry units into an engagement.

ATTACK

4-9.   An attack is an offensive operation that destroys or defeats enemy forces, seizes and secures terrain, or both. Movement, supported by fires, characterizes the conduct of an attack. However, the commander may decide to conduct an attack using only fires. An attack differs from a MTC because enemy main body dispositions are at least partially known, which allows the commander to achieve greater synchronization. This enables him to mass the effects of the attacking force's combat power more effectively in an attack than in a MTC. Special-purpose attacks are ambush, spoiling attack, counterattack, raid, feint, and demonstration. In planning attacks, the weapons company may be used to--

- Suppress the enemy on an objective.
- Isolate the objective.
- Exploit the point of penetration and continue the attack deeper.
- Conduct a feint or demonstration (deception).
- Secure lines of communication.
- Conduct a raid using its direct fire weapons.
- Establish blocking positions by ground maneuver or air lift to destroy or canalize the enemy.

EXPLOITATION

4-10.   Exploitation is a type of offensive operation that rapidly follows a successful attack and is designed to disorganize the enemy in depth. The objective of exploitation is to complete the enemy's disintegration. The weapons company uses speed and firepower to actively seek to gain terrain or destroy enemy forces. The weapons company paired with close combat attack from army aviation can be very effective in maintaining the initiative and tempo.

PURSUIT

4-11.   A pursuit is an offensive operation designed to catch or cut off a hostile force attempting to escape, with the aim of destroying it. A pursuit normally follows a successful exploitation. The weapons company may take part in a pursuit as part of a larger force or, because of its organic transportation, may be task-organized as a pursuit force to close with and destroy the remnants of the enemy force.

SEQUENCE

4-12.   As the company commander plans an offensive mission, he generally considers a sequence of operations, which apply to many, but not all, offensive operations. Offensive operations generally follow a sequence of several events. These are assembly area operations, reconnaissance, movement to the line of departure, maneuver, deployment, assault, consolidation, and reorganization.

ASSEMBLY AREA

4-13.   The commander directs and supervises mission preparations in the assembly area to prepare the unit for the upcoming battle. This includes the mounting of the best weapon for the mission. Preparation time also allows the unit to conduct pre-combat inspections and checks, rehearsals, TLPs, and sustainment activities. For more information on action in the assembly area, see Troop Leading Procedures in FM 3-21.10; Chapter 11 in this manual, and precombat checks (PCC) and precombat inspections (PCI) checklist in Chapter 2 of this manual.

RECONNAISSANCE

4-14.   Reconnaissance should be conducted at all echelons. The enemy situation and available planning time may limit the unit's reconnaissance, but leaders at every level must aggressively seek information about the terrain and enemy. A ground reconnaissance is preferred but often not possible. Unmanned aircraft systems (UAS), Force XXI Battle Command, Brigade and Below (FBCB2), and, at a minimum, map reconnaissance may have to be used in lieu of a ground reconnaissance. If the digital map is installed, the FBCB2 allows leaders to determine the line of sight, dead space from locations, and permits the selection of tentative firing positions. However, it does not take into account man-made features and vegetation. The weapons company may be assigned recon responsibilities and can use the weapons sights for increased visibility in visual recon, perform area recon or route recon in support of the main body movement.

MOVEMENT TO THE LINE OF DEPARTURE

4-15.   When attacking from positions not in contact, the weapons company often stages in rear assembly areas, road marches to attack positions behind friendly units in contact with the enemy, and conducts a forward passage of lines. When necessary, the unit employs indirect fires, close air support (when available), and direct fire to facilitate movement.

MANEUVER

4-16.   The weapons company commander plans the approach to the objective to ensure security, speed, and flexibility. He selects the routes, techniques, and formations that protects his force and supports the actions on the objective. The unit may need to overcome enemy resistance en route to the objective and should plan accordingly. The commander will often use movement techniques such as the bounding overwatch to maneuver to support by fire positions.

DEPLOYMENT

4-17.   The weapons company deploys and moves toward the final attack-by-fire or support by fire positions. Units cover their assigned sectors of fire and may place their vehicles in hull defilade positions by using existing terrain to their advantage. They need to be prepared to seize their position and may either have scouts reconnoiter their positions or have Infantry clear the positions if necessary.

ASSAULT

4-18.   The unit's objective may be terrain- or force oriented. Terrain-oriented objectives require the unit to secure and retain a designated area and often require fighting through enemy forces. If the objective is force-oriented, an objective area may be assigned for orientation, but the unit's effort is focused on the enemy's actual disposition. The weapons company can either direct their fires onto the objective, be used to isolate it from other enemy positions, cover enemy avenues of approach, or other missions as assigned.

CONSOLIDATION AND REORGANIZATION

4-19.   The company executes follow-on missions as directed by the higher commander. Whether a raid, hasty attack, or deliberate attack, the unit organizes itself and prepares for continued operations, which may include continued offensive actions, transition to stability operations, or defensive operations. Regardless of the follow-on mission, the unit will perform site security, process any detainees, and conduct tactical site exploitation (TSE). During TSE all collected items and personnel are properly documented, photographed, and handled according to TSOP to ensure accountability and chain of custody.

During planning for the offense, the commander visualizes, describes, and directs his concept of the operation. The weapons company commander begins with a designated area of operations (AO), identified mission (s), and assigned forces. The commander then develops and issues verbally planning guidance based on his visualization in terms of the physical means to accomplish the mission.

WARFIGHTING FUNCTIONS

4-20.   The weapons company commander uses the warfighting functions to develop, review and prepare his plan and preparations for the attack. A warfighting function is a group of tasks and systems united by a common purpose that commanders use to accomplish missions and training objectives. Decisive, shaping, and sustaining operations combine all the warfighting functions to generate combat power.

INTELLIGENCE

4-21.   Intelligence is the related tasks and systems that facilitate understanding of the enemy, terrain, weather, and civil considerations. It includes tasks associated with intelligence, surveillance, and reconnaissance. The weapons company commander must understand the enemy's strengths and weaknesses. Ideally, this knowledge will be available during troop leading procedures (TLP). The commander must analyze all combat information received via command updates and through a common operational picture gained with FBCB2 if available. Additionally, the commander should conduct personal reconnaissance or request UAS overflights of his AO as the situation permits. The weapons company may also gather information through reconnaissance to be used for intelligence.

MOVEMENT AND MANEUVER

4-22.   The movement and maneuver function move forces to achieve a position of advantage in relation to the enemy. It includes tasks associated with projecting, protecting and employing forces. Maneuver is the means by which commanders mass the effects of combat power to achieve surprise, shock, momentum, and dominance. For example, the weapons company may support maneuver by supplying heavy machine gun fire in support of a maneuvering Infantry unit. Movement is necessary to support that function and to assure the protection, dispersion and displacement of the force as a whole. The weapons company role in support of movement may be in the form of support such as convoy security for other mobile forces.

FIRES

4-23.   Fire support provides collective and coordinated use of indirect fires and close air support (CAS) through the targeting process. All fires in support of the weapons company and other units are external to the weapons company itself. The commander may employ supporting fires in the offense to achieve a variety of tactical goals:

- To suppress enemy weapons systems that inhibits movement.
- To fix or neutralize bypassed enemy elements.
- To prepare enemy positions for an assault.
- To obscure enemy observation or screen friendly maneuver.
- Illuminate enemy positions.

PROTECTION

4-24.   The weapons company continually seeks ways increase its own protection and assist in providing protection to other units. They employ both active and passive security measures using techniques such as cover and concealment and site security. Protection preserves the force so the commander can apply maximum combat power. Preserving the force includes protecting personnel, physical assets, and information. Protection facilitates the ability of the commander to maintain the integrity and combat power of the deploying force. For a discussion of active and passive defensive measures (Chapter 5, Section II). Protection focuses on several tasks:

- Area security.
- Defend against air and missile attack and aerial surveillance.
- Counter rockets, artillery, and mortars.
- Survivability operations.
- Casualty prevention.
- Antiterrorism.
- Protection against deliberate and accidental CBNR to include improvised explosive devices.
- Battlefield obscuration.
- Information protection.
- Fratricide avoidance.
- Personnel recovery operations.
- Safety.

Employment of Air Defense Systems

4-25.   In offensive situations, air defense elements accompany the main attack. They may maneuver with the lead company, orienting on low-altitude air avenues of approach. When the unit is moving or in a situation that entails short halts, the short range air defense (SHORAD) element positions its vehicles and man portable air defense system to assure mutual support between systems and coverage to the company. The Stinger gunners can dismount to provide air defense when the unit reaches the objective or pauses during the attack.

SUSTAINMENT

4-26.   Sustainment provides support and services to ensure freedom of action, extend operational reach, and prolong endurance. Unit endurance is primarily a function of its sustainment ability. Key sustainment planning considerations for the weapons company during offensive operations include--

- Increased consumption of Class III supplies.
- Vehicle maintenance requirements.
- Class V projection planned throughout the depth of the operation.

COMMAND AND CONTROL

4-27.   Command and control support the commander in exercising authority and direction. It includes those tasks associated with acquiring friendly information, managing relevant information, and directing and leading subordinates. The commander determines where to position himself on the battlefield in order to most effectively influence the operation. The weapons company may assist communications for other units such as using their more powerful radios in providing a long-range communications relay for rifle companies. In the offense to effectively command and control:

- The communications standing operating procedures (SOP) for the company must be clear, simple and redundant.
- Daylight and limited visibility markings must be understood by all.
- Radio transmissions must be clear and concise to enhance offensive command and control (C2).
- Units establish SOPs that dictate message recipients to insure critical information reaches the commander, without burdening him with routine digital traffic.

WEAPONS SELECTION

4-28.   The selection of weapons is based on a careful analysis of METT-TC, especially enemy and terrain. If the enemy is capable of employing tanks and mechanized elements, then the weapons company commander should consider having a mix of heavy weapons. Table 4-1 shows some very general selection guidelines for the current weapons in the weapons company based on the enemy and terrain. Ultimately, thorough planning and analysis should result in a weapons ready posture, to include engagement criteria and engagement priorities for each weapon system (Chapter 9).

Table 4-1. General weapons employment guidelines.

Weapon	Enemy		Terrain	
	Tank & Mechanized	Infantry	Open	Close
ITAS	✓		✓	
MK19	✓	✓	✓	✓
M2		✓	✓	✓
Javelin	✓		✓	

SELECTION OF SUPPORT AND ATTACK-BY-FIRE POSITIONS

4-29.   The weapons company commander carefully studies the battalion's scheme of maneuver and selects tentative support and attack-by-fire positions throughout the battalion's AO. He selects the best locations for those fire positions directed by battalion and selects others throughout the AO. He is especially careful in the selection of positions that support the capture of any intermediate and final objective. He also identifies positions that can cover any enemy avenues of approach into the battalions AO and fire positions to support the Infantry's consolidation on the objective and positions to stop any counterattacks. The weapons company commander therefore selects positions to--

- Comply with those directed in the battalion operation order OPORD or FRAGO.
- Support the battalion's movement through the AO.
- Support the capture of intermediate and final objectives.
- Cover any potential enemy avenues of approach into the battalion's AO.
- Support the Infantry's consolidation on the objective(s).
- Maximize standoff capabilities of the weapon system.
- Stop any counterattacks.
- Continue the attack.

Section III. MOVEMENT TO CONTACT

The purpose of a movement to contact is to gain or reestablish contact with the enemy. A movement to contact is most often executed through one of two techniques, the approach march and the search and attack. When operating as part of a higher unit's movement to contact, the weapons company normally employs the same technique as that unit. The company commander must consider the mounted capabilities of his company during both techniques. Considerations that may assist the commander in developing his concept include the time available, the speed of movement, the enemy situation, and security. For additional information on these techniques, see FM 3-21.10.

OVERVIEW

4-30.   The weapons company normally conducts a movement to contact as part of the battalion. An Infantry battalion may be given a movement to contact mission as the lead element of an attack or as a counterattack element of a brigade combat team (BCT) or higher-level unit. Reconnaissance, surveillance and flexibility are essential in gaining and maintaining the initiative. The movement to contact terminates with the occupation of an assigned objective or when enemy resistance requires the battalion to deploy and conduct an attack in order to continue forward movement. The battalion normally moves with a security force, a main body and a rear guard. Often the security force consists of a company size element formed into a reconnaissance force and an advance guard. The weapons company may be part of the battalion's main body or may have one or more of its platoons attached to the advanced guard. It should be prepared to deploy and attack the enemy with concentrated heavy weapons firepower at the decisive point on the battlefield.

APPROACH MARCH TECHNIQUE

4-31.   An approach march is the advance of a combat unit when direct contact with the enemy is intended. During offensive operations, the commander can choose to have all or part of his force conduct an approach march as part of the movement to contact. A battalion conducts movement to contact in a manner that allows it to maneuver to develop the situation fully, to maintain freedom of action, and if required, to defeat the enemy once contact is made. The approach March technique can facilitate the commander's decisions by allowing freedom of action and movement of the main body.

SEARCH AND ATTACK TECHNIQUE

4-32.   The search and attack may be used in a noncontiguous AO and against an enemy operating in dispersed elements. It is organized into finding, fixing, and finishing forces. The search and attack techniques purpose is to find the enemy with a small element (squad, section, or platoon) and, if possible, fix and destroy him. If the finding force is not strong enough to fix and finish the enemy, then the fixing force (normally a company for a battalion level operation) is committed to fixing and, if possible, finishing off the enemy. If the fixing force is not strong enough, then it fixes the enemy and the finishing force completes the destruction of the enemy. This cascading effect allows the battalion to commit the smallest force to destroy the enemy while retaining the ability to "pile on" other units if required. The weapons company may have a platoon attached to the fixing force and the rest of the company as part of the finishing force. It can be used to support the attack-by-fire or use attack-by-fire positions to cordon the objective area.

Section IV. ACTIONS ON CONTACT

In both offensive and defensive operations, contact occurs when a member of a weapons company encounters any situation that requires an active or passive response to a threat or potential threat. Contact may occur in different forms through a variety of circumstances. These may happen through:

- Visual (friendly elements may or may not be observed by the enemy).
- Physical or direct fire with an enemy force.
- Indirect fire.
- With obstacles of enemy or unknown origin.
- With enemy or unknown aircraft.
- Involving chemical, biological, radiological or nuclear (CBRN) conditions.
- Involving electronic warfare tactics.
- With nonhostile elements such as civilians.

COMMANDER'S ANALYSIS

4-33.   Company commanders analyze the enemy throughout the troop-leading procedures to identify all likely contact situations that may occur during a mission. Through the planning and rehearsals conducted during troop-leading procedures, leaders develop and refine course of actions (COA) to deal with probable enemy actions. The COAs eventually become the foundation for the unit's scheme of maneuver. During the troop-leading process, the leader must evaluate a number of factors to determine impacts on the unit's actions on contact.

TIME REQUIREMENTS

4-34.   Company commanders must understand that properly executed actions on contact require time at section, platoon, and company levels. To develop the situation fully, a subordinate unit may need to execute extensive lateral movement, conduct reconnaissance-by-fire, and call for and adjust indirect fires. Each of these activities requires time. The commander must balance the time required for subordinate elements to conduct actions on contact with the need of his organization or the higher headquarters to maintain tempo and momentum. In terms of slowing the tempo of an operation, however, the loss of a platoon or team is normally much more costly than the additional time required to allow the subordinate element to properly develop the situation.

STEPS

4-35.   The weapons company should execute actions on contact using a logical, well-organized, four-step, decision-making process:

    1. Deploy and report.
    2. Evaluate and develop the situation.
    3. Choose a COA.
    4. Execute the selected COA.

4-36.   The four-step process is not intended to generate a rigid, lockstep response to the enemy. Rather, the goal is to provide an orderly framework that enables the unit and its subordinate elements to survive the initial contact and then to apply sound decision-making and timely actions to complete the operation. Ideally, the unit will acquire the enemy before being sighted by the enemy. It then can initiate physical contact on its own terms by executing the designated COA. For more detail, see FM 3-21.10: The Infantry Rifle Company.

Section V. ATTACKS

An attack is a type of offensive operation characterized by movement supported by fire. The purpose of an attack is to destroy an enemy force or to seize terrain. The attack should always try to strike the enemy where he is weakest. The company can attack independently or as part of a battalion or larger element. This section discusses the types of attacks including the hasty attack, the deliberate attack, and special-purpose attacks. It also quickly discusses follow on actions of the exploitation and pursuit. For a more detailed explanation of attacks, exploitation and pursuit see FM 3-21.10.

TYPES

4-37.   The two basic types of attack are the hasty attack and the deliberate attack. The primary difference between them is the extent of planning and preparation conducted by the attacking force, but no clear distinction exists between deliberate and hasty attacks. Attacks range along a continuum. At one end of this continuum, the company commander issues a FRAGO that directs a hasty attack with rapid execution of battle drills by forces immediately available. These attacks rely on an implicit understanding and frequency modulation (FM) radio (or digital) communication with detailed orders and appropriate branches or sequels that make understanding explicit. Information on the general enemy situation may come from a movement to contact, and the unit launches a hasty attack as a continuation of the meeting engagement. The weapons company normally supports the attack from support by fire positions or has an independent mission, often to isolate the objective, for attack-by-fire positions. It can also conduct reconnaissance by fire primarily with its machine guns. In the attack, the company maneuvers along the lines of least resistance using the terrain for cover and concealment. This indirect approach affords the best chance to achieve surprise on the enemy force. All attacks, whether hasty or deliberate, depend on synchronization for success. They require planning, coordination, and time to prepare.

HASTY ATTACK

4-38.   A hasty attack is used to--

- Maintain momentum.
- Exploit a tactical opportunity.
- Regain the initiative.
- Prevent the enemy from regaining organization or balance.
- Gain a favorable position that may be lost with time.

4-39.   Because its primary purpose is to maintain momentum or take advantage of the enemy situation, the hasty attack is normally conducted with only the resources that are immediately available. Maintaining unrelenting pressure through hasty attacks keeps the enemy off balance and makes it difficult for him to react effectively. Rapidly attacking before the enemy can act often results in success even when the combat power ratio is not as favorable as desired. With its emphasis on agility and surprise, however, this type of attack may cause the attacking force to lose a degree of synchronization. To minimize this risk, the commander should maximize use of standard formations and well-rehearsed and thoroughly understood battle drills and SOPs. By maintaining situational understanding and assigning on-order and be-prepared missions to subordinate units as the situation warrants, the weapons company is better able to transition into hasty attacks. The hasty attack is often the preferred option during continuous operations. It allows the commander to maintain the momentum of friendly operations while denying the enemy the time needed to prepare his defenses and to recover from losses suffered during previous action. Hasty attacks normally result from a movement to contact, successful defense, or continuation of a previous attack. The weapons company, with its inherent speed and firepower, can move quickly into firing positions to support the Infantry attack. It can also isolate the objective from attack-by-fire positions.

DELIBERATE ATTACK

4-40.   The weapons company typically will conduct a deliberate attack as part of a larger force. It often conducts a deliberate attack by itself when it has an attack-by-fire mission or has been task organized with Infantry units. Deliberate attacks follow a distinct period of preparation, which is used for extensive intelligence, surveillance, and reconnaissance (ISR) operations, detailed planning, task organization of forces, fires planning, preparation of troops and equipment, coordination, rehearsals, and plan refinement. The deliberate attack is a fully synchronized operation that employs every available asset against the defending enemy. It is characterized by a high volume of planned fires (direct and indirect), use of major supporting attacks, forward positioning of resources needed to maintain momentum, and operations throughout the depth of enemy positions. Thorough preparation allows the attacking force to stage a combined-arms and fully integrated attack. Likewise, however, the enemy will have more time to prepare his defensive positions and integrate fires and obstacles. The factors of METT-TC dictate how thoroughly these activities are accomplished.

4-41.   The weapons company commander plans for the commitment of his company in compliance with battalion orders. He conducts a METT-TC analysis, gives his order, and prepares for the attack. The following are some of the tasks that are done by the commander and his primary subordinates, the executive officer and the first sergeant, prior to a successful deliberate attack:

- Develops his scheme of maneuver and fire plan.
- Briefs his platoon leaders.
- Conducts rock drills and briefbacks to ensure subordinates understand their missions.
- Coordinates indirect fires with the fire support officer.
- Coordinates with the Infantry company commanders to ensure his maneuver and fire plan supports their plans.
- Assigns targets.
- Conducts rehearsals.
- Vehicles are mounted with the best weapon's mix for the mission and additional ammunition is brought forward.
- Routes to support by fire and attack-by-fire positions are reconnoitered by leaders and marked.
- Check equipment for serviceability.

SPECIAL-PURPOSE ATTACKS

4-42.   The weapons company could possibly receive a mission to conduct a raid, ambush, spoiling attack, counterattack, feint, or a demonstration. The weapons company can use both support by fire and attack-by-fire positions during these types of attacks. Its mobility is an advantage. Any attachments however, such as Infantry, should be equally mobile. The commander selects weapons based on a detailed analysis of the factors of METT-TC.

Raid

4-43.   This is a limited-objective form of attack entailing swift penetration of hostile terrain. A raid operation always ends with a planned withdrawal to a friendly location upon the completion of the assigned mission. A raid is not intended to hold territory. The weapons company can conduct an independent raid, a raid in conjunction with other ground forces, or it can participate in a higher unit offensive operation that encompasses several related raids or other related operations. For more information on the weapons company and their involvement in raids, see Chapter 8, Section VI of this manual.

Ambush

4-44.   An ambush is a surprise attack, from concealed positions, on a moving or temporarily halted enemy. It may take the form of an assault to close with and destroy the enemy, or it may be an attack-by-fire only, executed from concealed positions. An ambush does not require that ground be seized or held. Although the execution of an ambush is offensive in nature, the unit may be directed to conduct an ambush in a wide variety of situations. The weapons company can ambush enemy units from support by fire positions. Ideally, the weapons units strike from a flank and, in the case of an enemy convoy, destroy the lead and rear vehicles, and then destroy the rest in detail. Priority targets include enemy systems that can return effective fire or control such as tanks, heavy automatic weapons, and command and control systems.

Spoiling Attack

4-45.   This is a limited-objective attack to delay, disrupt, or destroy the enemy's capability to attack. Units mount spoiling attacks from defensive postures to disrupt expected enemy attacks. A spoiling attack attempts to strike the enemy while he is most vulnerable--during his preparations for attack in assembly areas and attack positions or while he is on the move prior to crossing his line of departure. In most respects, units conduct spoiling attacks like any other attack. They may be hasty (when planning time is short) or deliberate (when the unit has obtained adequate forewarning). The weapons company can effectively support a spoiling attack or conduct one by establishing attack-by-fire positions.

Counterattack

4-46.   This is an attack by defensive forces to regain the initiative or to deny the enemy success with his attack. Commanders conduct counterattacks either with a reserve or with lightly committed forward elements. They counterattack after the enemy launches his attack, reveals his main effort, or creates an assailable flank. The weapons company commander conducts a counterattack much like other attacks, but synchronizing them within the overall defensive effort requires careful timing. Counterattacks made by the weapons company however, may be limited to movement to better terrain in order to bring fires on the enemy.

Feint

4-47.   The feint is in many ways identical to other forms of the attack. Its purpose is to cause the enemy to react in a particular way, such as by repositioning forces, committing its reserve, or shifting fires. The key difference between the feint and other attack forms is that it is much more limited in scope, with an extremely specific objective. The scale of the operation, however, usually is apparent only to the controlling headquarters. For the element actually conducting the feint, such as a weapons company, platoon, or section, execution is just as rapid and as violent as in a full-scale attack. The grenade machine guns may be very effective during a feint by delivering a high volume of high explosive into the target area.

Demonstration

4-48.   The demonstration is an attack whose purpose is to deceive the enemy about the location of the decisive operation. The purpose of a demonstration is similar to that of a feint, but the friendly force does not make contact with the enemy. The mobility of the weapons company allows it to demonstrate then reposition quickly to another predetermined location on the battlefield.

EXPLOITATION

4-49.   A company normally takes part in exploitations as part of a larger force; however, all company commanders should prepare to exploit tactical success at the local level. Any action must be within the higher commanders' intent and concept of the operation.

PURSUIT

4-50.   The objective of the pursuit is the total destruction of the enemy force. The weapons company may take part in a pursuit as part of a larger force or, because of its organic transportation, may task-organize a pursuit force that can close with and destroy the remnants of the enemy force. It can also fix the enemy in place to allow the Infantry units' time to maneuver and destroy the enemy. In the pursuit the weapons company commander should be aware of the locations of friendly units and not maneuver beyond the mutual support of the rest of the battalion.

Section VI. OFFENSIVE MANEUVER

Two common ways a weapons company can support a battalion or company in the offense by conducting a support by fire mission or an attack-by-fire mission. Both type missions are shown in Figure 4-1.

SUPPORT-BY-FIRE FORCE

4-51.   The combination of fire and movement first needs a unit to remain stationary and provide protection through fires for the assaulting forces by destroying, suppressing, or fixing enemy forces. This is a mission well suited for the weapons company due to their mix of heavy weapons. The decision on weapon selection is based on a detailed METT-TC analysis. Ideally, their positions would be selected prior to movement. The support by fire force avoids fratricide by using FBCB2, direct fire control measures (DFCM), and visual confirmation. The integration of these direct fires into the scheme of maneuver, known as direct fire control, is essential to battlefield success. For more information on direct fire control, see Chapter 9 of this manual.

4-52.   As the support by fire force, the weapons company occupies support by fire positions that afford effective cover and concealment, unobstructed observation, and clear fields of fire. Once it is in position, it has the responsibility both for placing the effects of direct fires on known enemy forces and for aggressively scanning assigned sectors of observation. In doing so, it identifies previously unknown enemy elements and then fires upon them. The protection provided by the support by fire force allows the assaulting force to continue its movement and to retain the initiative even when it is under enemy observation or within range of enemy weapons.

4-53.   The assaulting force can either be other units, such as Infantry companies or scouts, or elements from the weapons company itself. Movement in a maneuver situation is inherently dangerous. It is complicated not only by the obvious potential for harm posed by enemy weapons but also by the uncertainty caused by unknown terrain and other operational factors. The assaulting force must therefore take full advantage of whatever cover and concealment are provided by the terrain.

ATTACK-BY-FIRE

4-54.   An attack-by-fire mission may be conducted as a stand-alone mission. It may also be used to engage enemy elements by firing on a position other than an assault conducted by another unit on a separate objective. The purpose of an attack-by-fire is to mass the effects of direct and indirect fire systems from one or multiple locations on an enemy to destroy, suppress, fix, or deceive him without closing with him. This mission may be used to help allow freedom of operations of other forces on a separate objective. A commander assigning this task to a subordinate must also state the desired effect on the enemy, such as destroy, suppress, fix, or deceive. A commander normally employs this task when the mission does not dictate or support close combat and occupation of a geographical objective by another friendly force. The commander may assign the force conducting an attack-by-fire mission with either a sector of fire, an engagement area, or an objective. He may also assign it an axis of advance and a force-oriented objective. The attack-by-fire unit can also cover an enemy avenue of approach. An attack-by-fire closely resembles the task of support by fire but ground forces do not close with the enemy.

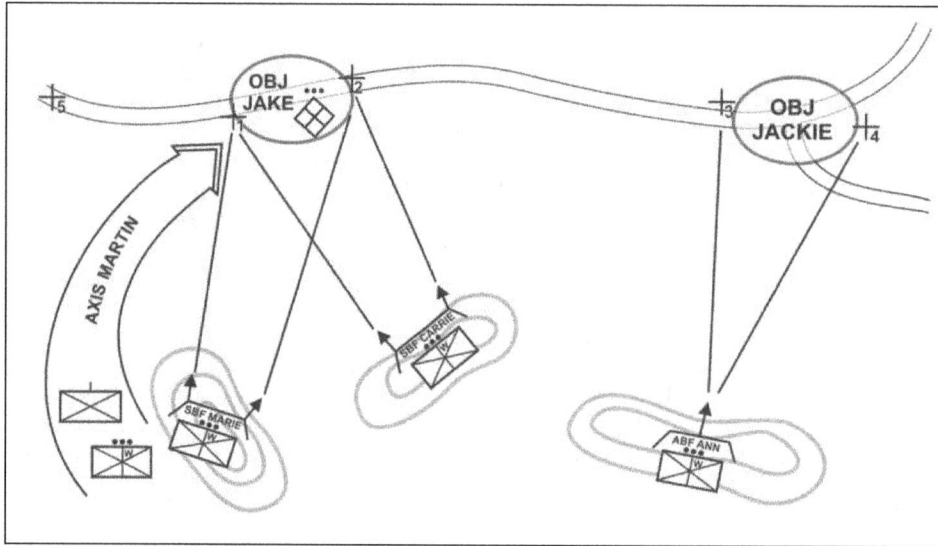

Figure 4-1. Support-by-fire on Objective Jake and attack-by-fire on Objective Jackie.

USE OF TERRAIN FOR COVER AND CONCEALMENT

4-55.   While maneuvering, the all units should use terrain to provide cover and concealment. Some techniques include:

- Not moving forward from a firing position. Back away from your position and go around on the low ground.
- Staying on low ground as much as possible. Moving on top of ridgelines and over hilltops silhouettes (skylines) vehicles.
- Scanning the ground for indicators of an obstacle or minefield such as disturbed earth, out-of-place features, and surface-laid mines.
- Selecting the formation and movement technique that maximizes the unit's battle space while minimizing gaps and dead space.
- Bounding fore, covering dead space and gaps. The overwatch element cannot cover all of the assaulting unit's gaps and dead space. Vehicle crews keep the distance of each move (or bound) within the direct fire range of the overwatch element.
- Planning actions at danger areas. If necessary, the vehicle crew dismounts and either observes around blind spots or checks the trafficability of a route or defile before the vehicle moves over or through these locations.
- Reducing the vehicle signature, such as creating dust clouds, as much as possible.
- Prior to conducting an operation, leaders can use FBCB2 to analyze line of sight (LOS) to identify tentative overwatch positions.

HASTY OCCUPATION OF A POSITION

4-56.   The weapons company and platoons may use this method if it is fixed or suppressed by enemy fire and no longer has the ability to move forward or bypass. It may also set up a hasty defense when the enemy executes a hasty attack. The company or platoons maintain contact or fixes the enemy in place until additional combat elements arrive or until it is ordered to move. When the unit must conduct a hasty defense, the commander has responsibility for continuing to develop the situation. The actions are the same as those for actions on contact.

Chapter 5

Defensive Operations

The weapons company contributes to success in the defense by employing long-range direct fires to destroy enemy forces with fire from its heavy weapons. The weapons unit's mobility, heavy weaponry, and thermal observation devices make it an important part of the battalion's defense. The weapons unit can perform several missions in the defense including defending from a battle position(s), establishing firing positions in the main battle area (MBA), participating in security operations, and serving as a reserve.

Section I. OVERVIEW

Though the outcome of decisive combat derives from offensive actions, commanders may find that it is necessary to defend. Once they make this choice, they must set the conditions for the defense that allows friendly forces to withstand and hold the enemy while they prepare to seize the initiative and return to the offense. A thorough understanding of the commander's intent is critical in defensive operations, which demands precise integration of combat, support, and sustainment elements.

PURPOSE

5-1.   The Army conducts defensive operations to defeat an enemy attack, buy time, economize forces, or develop conditions favorable for an attack. Defensive actions alone are not normally decisive and are frequently followed by an offensive action.

CHARACTERISTICS

5-2.   The characteristics of the defense are preparation, security, disruption, massing effects, and flexibility. These are the defensive fundamentals for the weapons company. These fundamentals should be considered when planning or conducting company defensive operations. (See Chapters 9 and 10, FM 3-90, for further discussion on mobile and area defenses.)

PREPARATION

5-3.   The critical element affecting preparation for the defense is the time available and proper time management. Time management begins with receipt of the warning order, operation order (OPORD), or fragmentary order (FRAGO). Effective use of available time allows the company commander and platoon leaders to conduct a thorough reconnaissance of engagement areas, battle positions (BP), displacement routes, friendly positions, axes for possible enemy attacks and axes for friendly counterattacks. Coordination with other units is also critical. The weapons company may be deployed throughout the battalion area of operations (AO) which makes it even more imperative that the commander send orders to his subordinates as soon as possible. Besides troop leading procedures, Weapons company leaders at all levels have a multitude of tasks to accomplish during the preparation phase to include:

- Ensure Soldiers, vehicles, and weapons are prepared for action.
- Establishing or confirming engagement areas and fire control measures.

- Verify exact firing positions.
- Reconnoiter and calculate time-distance factors for routes between firing positions.
- Move the unit and occupy primary positions.

SECURITY

5-4.   The company and platoons establish operations security (OPSEC) procedures to maintain security during planning, preparation, and execution of the defense. The weapons leaders integrate their security plan with that of the adjacent units. Leaders enhance their position by using early warning devices to identify potential mounted and dismounted avenues of approach. They then position early warning devices and observation posts (OP) to cover these avenues. Coordination with other unit commanders is necessary to make sure weapons units are fully integrated into the overall security plan. Weapon units must provide their own security if they are on BPs that have no other Infantry support. Units should also maintain security during movement and select routes that provide concealment and cover from enemy fire. Shorter engagement ranges and close terrain make weapons company units employing missile systems more vulnerable to dismounted enemy Infantry. Therefore, leaders should consider positioning units with or in close proximity to Infantry units. If the Infantry is not available, the weapons unit should protect itself by task organizing the unit with some Soldiers operating the missile systems and other Soldiers providing security with small arms, and machine guns. To protect themselves from enemy direct and indirect fires, Weapons units should consider constructing fighting positions even if the main weapon system remains on the vehicle.

DISRUPTION

5-5.   All defensive concepts are aimed at disrupting the attacker's synchronization. Counterattacks, indirect fires, obstacles, and retention of key terrain prevent the enemy from concentrating his strength against portions of the defense. The combination of direct fires coupled with obstacles and indirect fires can greatly reduce the enemy's ability to use his systems against us. Smoke and white phosphorous can also obscure the enemy's overwatch positions and isolate his units. Within the weapons company, units can separate dismounted Infantry from armored vehicles by using the machine guns. Destroying enemy command and control vehicles also disrupts enemy synchronization and flexibility. The weapons company should establish an engagement priority for specific types of enemy vehicles and formations.

MASSING EFFECTS

5-6.   If a defender is to succeed, he must concentrate his combat power at the decisive time and place. The weapons company can achieve this by massing its direct fires from multiple firing positions spread both laterally and in depth. Using trigger lines or other fire control measures, the weapons company can destroy many enemy vehicles and personnel in a short period of time. The proper use of fire control measures help allow fires to be distributed through the enemy's point(s) of attack. The defender also strives to obtain a local advantage at points of decision. Offensive action and the use of surprise and deception are often the means of gaining this advantage. To concentrate combat power, the defender normally must economize in some areas, retain a reserve, and maneuver to gain local superiority. Weapons company units can provide fire support to local counterattacks to maintain the integrity of the defense. The weapons company can also quickly move to provide support throughout the battle area. Indirect fires can be shifted to critical points to rapidly concentrate destructive effects.

FLEXIBILITY

5-7.   The key to the employment of the weapons company is flexibility. Flexibility is derived from sound preparation and effective command and control. The defender must be agile enough to counter or avoid the attacker's blow and then strike back effectively. Flexibility results from a detailed mission analysis, an understanding of the unit's purpose, aggressive reconnaissance and security, and, when applicable, organization in depth and the retention or reconstitution of a reserve. Supplementary fire positions on primary and secondary avenues of approach may provide additional flexibility to the unit. Alternate fire positions within the BP allow vehicles to move and continue to fire after the primary position is located by the enemy. Successive BPs provide depth for weapons company units to move to if the present original BP becomes untenable. After a thorough analysis of the terrain and enemy, reserves can be positioned to allow the unit to react to unanticipated events. With its mobility, communications, and firepower, the weapons company can also quickly reinforce threatened sectors and increase the depth of the defense behind engaged units.

TYPES

5-8.   On a large operational level, there are three types of defensive operations including the area defense, the mobile defense, and retrograde. At the company level, defensive operations as a part of a mobile or area defense will be largely transparent. As a part of these operations, a company-sized unit may defend, delay, withdraw or counterattack. The weapons company may participate in any of these operations however, with their organic mobility and firepower, they may be well suited to quickly maneuver and destroy enemy units that threaten or penetrate the battalion's position. For more information on these types of defensive operations and sequence of the defense, see FM 3-90.

AREA DEFENSE

5-9.   The area defense a type of defensive operation that concentrates on denying enemy forces access to designated terrain for a specific time rather than destroying the enemy outright. The focus of the area defense is on retaining terrain where the bulk of the defending force positions itself in mutually supporting, prepared positions.

MOBILE DEFENSE

5-10.   The mobile defense is a type of defensive operation that concentrates on the destruction or defeat of the enemy through a decisive attack by a striking force. The mobile defense focuses on defeating or destroying the enemy by allowing him to advance to a point where he is exposed to a decisive counterattack by the striking force. The decisive operation is an attack conducted by the striking force. The weapons company is often part of a strike force due to its mobility, speed, firepower, and command and control capability.

RETROGRADE

5-11.   The retrograde is a type of defensive operation that involves organized movement away from the enemy. The enemy may force these operations, or a commander may execute them voluntarily. The retrograde is a transitional operation; it is not conducted in isolation. It is part of a larger scheme of maneuver designed to regain the initiative and defeat the enemy. The weapons company may often be used to cover the withdrawal of Infantry units.

Section II. PLANNING CONSIDERATIONS

This section discusses warfighting functions and defensive planning as well as the selection of defensive fighting positions.

WARFIGHTING FUNCTIONS

5-12.   The weapons company commander uses the warfighting functions to develop, review and prepare his plan and preparations for defensive operations. The warfighting functions (WFF) are critical tactical considerations that provide a means of reviewing plans, preparation, and execution. Commanders visualize, describe, direct, and lead operations in terms of the warfighting functions. The synchronization and coordination of activities within each WFF and among the various WFFs are critical to the successful defensive operations.

INTELLIGENCE

5-13.   Intelligence operations for the defense are similar to that of the offense. The company commander will not have complete information about enemy intentions. Therefore, he must obtain or develop the best possible intelligence preparation of the battlefield (IPB) products and conduct continuous intelligence, surveillance, and reconnaissance (ISR) collection throughout the operation. He may also need to request information from the battalion staff to answer priority intelligence requirements. ISR assets serve to help study terrain to determine the enemy's probable routes he may use for attacks; and confirm or deny strengths, dispositions, and likely course of actions (COA), especially where and in what strength the enemy will conduct offensive operations.

MOVEMENT AND MANEUVER

5-14.   The goal of effective weapons positioning is to enable the weapons company to mass direct fires at critical points on the battlefield and to enhance its survivability. To do this, the commander must maximize the strengths of his weapons systems while minimizing the company's exposure to enemy observation and fires. The following paragraphs focus on tactical considerations for weapons positioning:

Depth and Dispersion.

5-15.   Dispersing positions laterally and in depth helps to protect the force from enemy observation and fires. If the terrain allows for the development of an engagement area, the positions are established in depth allowing sufficient maneuver space within each position to establish in-depth placement of vehicles and weapons systems. Fighting positions should be positioned to allow the massing of direct fires at critical points on the battlefield.

Flank Positions.

5-16.   Flank positions enable a defending force to bring fires to bear on an attacking force moving parallel to the defender's forces. An effective flank position provides the defender with a larger and more vulnerable target while leaving the attacker unsure of the location of the defense. Major considerations for successful employment of a flank position are the defender's ability to secure the flank and his ability to achieve surprise by remaining undetected. Effective fire control and fratricide avoidance measures are critical considerations in the employment of flank positions.

Displacement Planning.

5-17.   Disengagement and displacement allow the company to retain its operational flexibility and tactical agility. The ultimate goals of disengagement and displacement are to enable the weapons company to maintain standoff ranges and to avoid being fixed or decisively engaged by the enemy. The commander considers several important factors in displacement planning. These include, but are not limited to, the following:

- The enemy situation (for example, an attack with two battalion-size enemy units may prevent the unit from disengaging).
- Disengagement criteria and disengagement line.
- Availability of indirect fires, including final protective fires (FPF) and smoke that can support disengagement by suppressing or disrupting the enemy.
- Availability of cover, concealment, smoke or other obscurants to assist disengagement.
- Obstacle integration.

- Positioning of forces on terrain that provides an advantage to the disengaging elements (such as reverse slopes or natural obstacles).
- Identification of displacement routes and times when disengagement or displacement will take place. Movements along routes are rehearsed and the time required recorded.
- The size and composition of a friendly force that must be available to engage the enemy in support of the displacing unit.

5-18.   While disengagement and displacement are valuable tactical tools, they can be extremely difficult to execute in the face of a rapidly moving enemy force. In fact, displacement in contact poses such great problems that the weapons company commander plans for it thoroughly and rehearses displacement before the conduct of the defense. Then he must carefully evaluate the situation at the time displacement in contact becomes necessary to ensure that it is feasible and will not result in unacceptable loss of personnel or equipment.

Disengagement Criteria.

5-19.   Disengagement criteria dictate to subordinate elements the circumstances under which they will displace to an alternate, supplementary, or successive battle position. The company commander establishes disengagement criteria and develops a disengagement plan to support the company scheme of maneuver. Disengagement criteria are primarily based on a specified number and type of enemy reaching a specified location (usually called the break point) to trigger displacement. Other considerations, such as ammunition supplies and friendly combat power, also influence the decision to displace. Disengagement criteria are developed during the planning process based on the unique conditions of a specific situation; they should not be part of the unit's standing operating procedure (SOP).

Direct Fire Suppression.

5-20.   The attacking enemy force must not be allowed to bring effective direct and indirect fires to bear on a disengaging friendly force. Direct fires from the supporting element, employed to suppress or disrupt the enemy, are the most effective way to facilitate disengagement. The company may receive supporting fires from another element. In most cases, however, the weapons company establishes its own supporting element. Having an internal element requires the company commander to carefully sequence the displacement of his forces.

Cover and Concealment.

5-21.   Ideally, the company and subordinate units use covered and concealed routes when moving to alternate, supplementary, or successive BPs. Regardless of the degree of protection the route itself affords, all of the units should rehearse the movement. Rehearsals increase the speed at which the unit can conduct the move and provide an added measure of security. The commander or leader makes a concerted effort to allocate available time to rehearse movement in limited visibility and degraded conditions.

Indirect Fires and Smoke.

5-22.   Artillery or mortar fires can assist the unit during disengagement. Suppressive fires, placed on an enemy force as it is closing inside the defender's standoff range, slow the enemy. The defending force engages the enemy with long-range precision direct fires and then disengages and moves to new positions. Smoke can obscure the enemy's vision, slow his progress, or screen the movement of the weapons company out of the BP or along his displacement route.

Obstacle Integration.

5-23.   Obstacles must be integrated with direct and indirect fires. By slowing and disrupting enemy movement, obstacles provide the defender with the time necessary for displacement and allow friendly forces to employ direct and indirect fires effectively against the enemy. Artillery-delivered scatterable mines and other mine laying systems can also be employed in support of the disengagement, either to block a key displacement route once the displacing unit has passed through it or to close a lane through a tactical obstacle. The location of obstacles in support of disengagement depends in large measure on an analysis of the factors of mission, enemy, terrain, troops, time, civilians (METT-TC). A major consideration for employing an obstacle is that it should be positioned far enough away from the defender that he can effectively engage the enemy on the far side of the obstacle while remaining out of range of the enemy's direct fires.

Mobility.

5-24.   During defensive preparations, mobility operations initially focus on the ability to resupply, reposition, and conduct rearward and forward passage of forces, material, and equipment. Once defensive preparations are complete, the focus normally shifts to supporting the unit's reserve, local counterattacks, and the higher headquarters (HQ) counterattack or reserve. Priorities set by the higher HQ may specify routes for improvement in support of such operations.

FIRES

5-25.   Field artillery and mortars provide long-range, lethal, accurate, and responsive fires for the indirect fire plan. To be effective in the defense, the unit must plan and execute fires in a manner that achieves the intended task and purpose of each target. Indirect fires serve a variety of purposes in the defense, including:

- Slowing or disrupting enemy movement.
- Preventing the enemy from successfully executing breaching operations.
- Destroying or delaying enemy forces at obstacles using massed fires or pinpoint munitions.
- Disrupting enemy support-by-fire elements.
- Conducting counterbattery fire missions against enemy indirect fire units.
- Defeating attacks along Infantry avenues of approach.
- Covering dead space where direct fire weapons cannot engage such as likely areas the enemy may use to mass in preparation for an assault.
- Allowing friendly elements to disengage or conduct counterattacks.
- Using smoke to screen friendly displacement or to silhouette enemy formations, facilitating direct fire engagement.
- Delivering scatterable mines to close lanes and gaps in obstacles, to disrupt or prevent enemy breaching operations, to disrupt enemy movement at choke points, or to separate or isolate enemy echelons.
- Executing suppression of enemy air defense missions to support close air support (CAS), attack aviation, and high-payoff targets.
- Providing illumination both white light and infrared.

Fire Support Assets.

5-26.   In developing the indirect fire plan, the weapons company commander must evaluate the indirect fire systems available. Organic fire support at battalion is four 120-mm towed mortars and the brigade has a battalion of 105-mm (towed). Considerations include tactical capabilities, weapons ranges, and available munitions. With assistance from the battalion or company FSO, the company commander determines the best methods for achieving the task and purpose of each target in the fire plan. Positioning of the company FSO is crucial due the fact that he is the only fire support personnel asset attached to the weapons company. Since there are no forward observers attached to the weapons platoons, the FSO must be able to observe critical targets and triggers in support of the tactical plan.

PROTECTION

5-27.   Protection relates to the actions taken to prevent or mitigate hostile actions against the unit. These actions conserve the force's fighting potential so it can be applied at a decisive time and place. Force protection incorporates the coordinated and synchronized offensive and defensive measures to enable the effective employment of the force while degrading opportunities for the enemy.

Air Defense

5-28.   The weapons company, relative to other units in the Infantry battalion, is especially vulnerable to enemy air attack. They are vulnerable because:

- There are relatively few vehicles in the Infantry battalion operating in the vicinity of the forward edge of the battle area (FEBA).
- They may be a priority target for the enemy because of its firepower and ability to rapidly maneuver.
- Vehicles can produce a pronounced signature to enemy aircraft in the form of dust, wheel tracks, glare, and heat.
- Moving targets are easier to detect than stationary targets.
- Although highly mobile, the weapons company vehicles are still confined to unrestricted and restricted terrain.
- Air defense assets are scarce and maneuver units cannot always count on receiving dedicated air defense protection.

Passive Air Defense

5-29.   Passive air defense measures are key to protecting the weapons company units from air attack. These measures include--

- Attack avoidance
  - -- Use concealment, camouflage, deception, communications security, and any other action that can prevent threat detection.
  - -- Whenever possible, static positions must provide effective overhead concealment. When concealment is not available, crews must camouflage their vehicles to blend into the natural surroundings. Crews must obliterate wheel marks leading into the concealed position and cover all shiny objects that could reflect light and attract attention.
- Damage limiting measures
  - -- Dispersion. Dispersion is one of the most successful ways to reduce the effects of threat air attack. It is essential when a unit occupies static positions, prepares to cross a water obstacle; or passes through a breached obstacle. When a weapons unit is on the move and air guards identify threat aircraft, the unit leader must make a determination on a course of action to take based on if he feels the vehicles were acquired. If undetected by enemy aircraft, actions may include vehicles dispersing quickly, moving to covered and concealed positions if possible, and stopping. From the air, a stationary vehicle is more difficult to see than a moving vehicle. Leaders must remember the infrared (IR) signature from engine heat can be acquired regardless of whether the vehicle is moving or not. If the leader feels the unit has been detected, actions may include dispersion while continuing to move to a location offering better cover and concealment.
  - -- Cover. Use natural or man-made cover to reduce the effects of threat munitions. Folds in the earth, depressions, buildings, and sandbagged positions can also provide this protection.

Active Air Defense

5-30.   Although passive measures are the first line of defense against air attack, the weapons company must be prepared to engage threat aircraft. The leader bases his decision upon the situation and upon the capabilities of weapons systems organic to his unit. Although missile systems can be effective against hovering or slow moving helicopters, the primary active air defense weapons within the weapons platoon are heavy caliber machine guns and individual weapons. All platoon members must understand that they can defend against a direct attack, but they may not engage aircraft that are not attacking them unless the weapon control status allows it. The steps in active air defense include--

Step 1--Initiate fires. The primary intent is to force aircraft to take self-defense measures that alter their attack profile and reduce their effectiveness. Leaders may use a tracer burst to designate an aim point for machine gun antiaircraft fires. Volume is the key to effectiveness; crew-served and individual weapons throw up a "wall of steel" through which aircraft must fly.

Step 2--Create a noncontiguous target. Vehicles move as fast as possible at a 45- degree angle away from the path of flight and toward attacking aircraft. Each vehicle maintains an interval of at least 100 meters, forcing aircraft to make several passes to engage the entire platoon.

Step 3--Move quickly to covered and concealed positions and stop. Vehicles freeze their movement for at least 60 seconds after the last flight of aircraft has passed.

Step 4--Send a spot report. The company commander or executive officer (platoon leader or platoon sergeant) updates the higher commander on the situation as soon as possible.

Employment of Air Defense Systems

5-31.   In the defense, short-range air defense (SHORAD) units establish battle positions based on available information and the battalion and or brigade commander's scheme of maneuver. Squads are positioned approximately 2 kilometers apart to maximize the air defense vehicles' defensive capabilities.

Survivability

5-32.   Combat engineer companies are limited in organic earthmoving equipment. They are capable of preparing hasty fighting positions during the transition to a hasty defense, but to construct survivability positions for a deliberate defense, the engineer company of the Infantry brigade combat team (IBCT) will require augmentation. It is critical that units maximize the effects of terrain when selecting positions for key weapons and vehicles.

5-33.   Because of the limited availability of engineers, weapons company units often have to prepare their own positions. To the maximum extent possible, units use natural cover and concealment as well as the use of hull down positions. Personnel shelters may be built next to firing positions to protect the crew from indirect fire. If engineer support is available, the weapons company commander prepares the area of operation for the arrival of the earthmoving equipment by marking positions and designating guides for the engineer vehicles. If time is available, vehicle positions are constructed with both hull defilade firing positions and full-defilade positions.

5-34.   An additional consideration for survivability is the possibility of dismounting the weapons systems in circumstances where mobility is not necessarily required. While dismounting the systems and hiding the vehicles may reduce mobility, it will also help reduce the signature of the position.

SUSTAINMENT

5-35.   In addition to the sustainment functions required for all operations, the weapons company commander's planning process should include the following considerations.

Pre-Positioning and Caches.

5-36.   His mission analysis may reveal that the unit's ammunition needs during an upcoming operation exceed its basic load. This requires the unit to pre-position ammunition (caches). The caches, which may be positioned either at an alternate or successive BP or in the vehicles firing position, should be dug in, camouflaged, and (if possible) guarded.

Position of Trains.

5-37.   The location of the all or part of weapons company trains is based on the sustainment needs of the company. They may be located behind the company (normally one terrain feature or 1000 meters to the rear), at the battalion combat trains area, or bringing up supplies and ammunition from the forward support company often located in the brigade support area. If available, the attached ambulance squad is located where it can move quickly to treat and evacuate casualties. Maintenance support is usually located at the battalion combat trains and releases recovery vehicles to the company as required.

COMMAND AND CONTROL

5-38.   As in the offense, command and control supports the commander in exercising authority and direction. Similarly, it includes those tasks associated with acquiring friendly information, managing relevant information, and directing and leading subordinates. The commander determines where to position himself, the executive officer (XO), and the FSO during defensive operations to effectively influence tactical actions as they develop.

SELECTION OF POSITIONS

5-39.   In the defense, weapons company units may employ their weapons either mounted or dismounted. Leaders make the decision as to mounted or dismounted employment after an analysis of the METT-TC factors. They must also consider the loss of mobility that results when a weapon system is dismounted from its vehicle.

SELECTION CRITERIA

5-40.   The company commander and platoon leaders select positions that maximize the advantages and minimize the disadvantages of the weapon system used in the position. For example, the weapons leader may position vehicles with mounted machine guns closer to the engagement area while vehicle mounted missile systems may be positioned further to the rear. Machine guns may also be positioned to cover dismounted avenues of approach into the AO. Leaders also select positions that enable the massing of fires from several firing positions.

5-41.   Indirect fires present one of the greatest dangers to the weapons company. For this reason, covered and concealed locations are critical for a weapons unit's survival. Weapons company units avoid firing positions that could be easily identified by an enemy map reconnaissance. The weapons unit leader also avoids positions that can be easily located due to their proximity to prominent terrain or man-made features. The enemy normally fires artillery and mortar fires to support an attack based on an analysis of the terrain and the likely locations of friendly forces. Therefore, choosing firing positions carefully will assist weapons company units avoid much of the enemy's planned fires.

5-42.   Firing position selection begins when each element is assigned a mission, a sector of fire or a portion of an engagement area, and a general location. Leaders select firing positions that are the optimal balance between protection and the ability to effectively engage targets. Leaders select positions that are:

- Below ridgelines and crests, preferably on the sides of hills.
- Masked by terrain or man-made features from the enemy's avenue of approach.
- As dry and as level as possible. Leaders should avoid choosing positions such as swampy areas, or steep hillsides.

5-43.   Leaders select firing positions during daylight and, if possible, position their units at night to reduce the chance of enemy detection. Leaders must not assume that darkness provides concealment for their firing positions. Through the use of night vision devices, enemy forces see almost as well in darkness as in daylight. Thermal imagery devices sense the heat emitted by vehicles and personnel. These devices provide the enemy with a capability to see through smoke, light foliage, and camouflage. Weapons squads continuously improve their positions throughout mission preparation.

5-44.   Each firing position should provide the following advantages:

- Cover to the front, flank, and, time permitting, overhead.
- Concealment from ground and aerial observation.
- Good observation and fields of fire into the assigned portion of an engagement area.
- Covered and concealed routes to, and between, positions.
- Mutual support between squad positions and with other elements.

5-45.   If engineer assets do not have the blade time to dig positions, give careful consideration to existing cover. Supplementary positions may not be an allocated engineer effort, so the same guidance provided for alternate positions applies. Designate hide positions. These are positioned where they are concealed from enemy reconnaissance assets and preferably safe from the impact of artillery fires on primary positions. Dig primary fighting positions for anticipated fighting conditions (daylight or limited visibility). Supervision of engineer assets is invaluable to ensure positions are dug to standard and to maximize the precious available time

PRIMARY, ALTERNATE, SUPPLEMENTARY, AND SUBSEQUENT POSITIONS

5-46.   Each battle position has a primary firing position. Leaders may assign any number of alternate, supplementary, and subsequent positions as a result of their analysis of the factors of METT-TC.

Primary Position

5-47.   The initial firing position from which a platoon covers an assigned sector of fire or portion of an engagement area along an enemy's most likely avenue of approach is referred to as the platoon's primary position and is the best position for engaging enemy vehicles. The company commander or platoon leader usually designates the general location of this position.

Alternate Position

5-48.   An alternate position covers the same enemy avenue of approach or sector of fire as from the primary position. The company commander or platoon leader designates the locations of alternate positions to be used when primary positions become untenable or unsuitable for the assigned task. When platoons have sufficient time and resources, they construct an alternate position to the same level of preparation as a primary position.

5-49.   An alternate position should be positioned such that the fires delivered from there can achieve the desired effects. Then, as a general guideline, it should be located 300 meters or more, METT-TC dependent, from the primary position to reduce the chance that indirect fire that suppresses the primary position also will affect the alternate position. Though terrain may not allow this much space, leaders should always consider this guideline when selecting alternate positions.

5-50.   If the platoon leader selects alternate positions, he should report the locations of each alternate position to the company commander.

Supplementary Position

5-51.   The supplementary position allows the platoon to cover an enemy avenue of approach or sector of fire that is different from that covered by the primary or alternate positions. It usually is chosen to cover avenues of approach to the flank or rear of a unit. The squads reconnoiter their specific positions and prepare range cards. Leaders will typically base occupation of a supplementary position on specific enemy actions.

Subsequent Position

5-52.   The subsequent position is a position that a unit expects to move to during the course of battle. A defending antiarmor unit may have numerous subsequent positions. These positions may also have primary, alternate, and supplementary positions associated with them as shown in Figure 5-1.

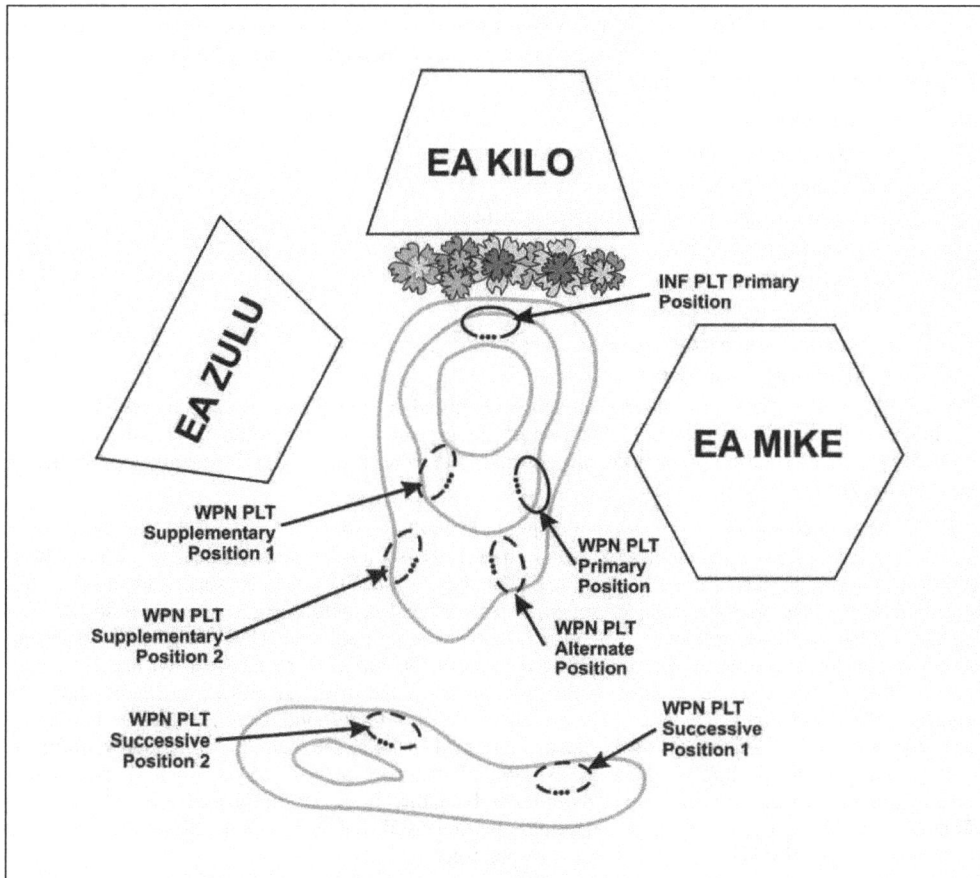

Figure 5-1. Defensive firing positions.

FIRING POSITION PREPARATION.

5-53.   The company commander or platoon leader will designate the level of preparation for each firing position based on the factors of METT-TC, with emphasis on the time available. There are three levels of preparation: reconnaissance, preparation, and occupation.

Reconnaissance

5-54.   Leaders reconnoiter the engagement area or AO and firing positions. They must get on the ground to physically inspect the terrain and determine its effects on antiarmor weapons employment and on enemy weapons employment.

Preparation

5-55.   The weapons element begins preparing a firing position as soon as the leaders complete their reconnaissance. The leaders call the vehicles forward and guide them into position. They may consider having drivers back the vehicles into position so they can leave quickly without moving toward the enemy or using time to turn around. The unit removes or camouflages all signs that the enemy could detect (such as wheel tracks, windshield reflections). Squads continue to improve the position until it is vacated. Preparation includes, but is not limited to--

- Marking the position.
- Emplacing fire control measures (as required).
- Digging the position.
- Identifying and digging ammunition caches.
- Preparing a range card.
- Emplacing protective obstacles.
- Camouflaging the position.
- Platoon and company sector sketches.
- Rehearsing occupation and disengagement.

5-56.   The unit occupies the general position identified by the platoon leader or section leader and establishes security. Each weapons squad must be prepared to fight while it prepares the position. Maintaining security during preparation allows the squad to react quickly if the enemy appears before the position has been completed.

5-57.   After selecting a firing position, a common technique leaders use to mark the position is by using stakes and then preparing a range card. This enables the squad or another squad to occupy the firing position and use the data from the range card for the position. Often three stakes are used to mark a mounted firing position. One stake is placed in front of and centered on the vehicle. It should be long enough so that the driver can see it as he moves the vehicle into position. The other two stakes are placed parallel to the left side of the vehicle and lined up with the hub on the front and rear wheels. The stakes are placed close to the vehicle with enough clearance to allow the driver to move into the position without knocking the stakes down. The stakes are driven solidly into the ground. Engineer tape or luminous tape can be placed on the friendly side of the stakes to make it easier to see them during limited visibility. Once the squad has dug the position, it camouflages it. Squad members use sod, leaves, brush, grass, or any other natural material to do so. The items should not be taken from the immediate area of the position. Camouflage nets or other man-made materials also are used, but these work best if used with natural materials. The position should look as natural as possible.

Occupation

5-58.   The company commander establishes criteria and SOPs for occupation of the position. For example:

- Vehicles approach the firing position from the rear using terrain-driving techniques on a rehearsed route.
- To reoccupy a marked position, the driver aligns his vehicle on the front stake and moves forward slowly until the two stakes on the left of his vehicle are centered on the front and rear wheels.
- The SOP includes the sequence of action and the priority of work.
- A trigger for occupation may be established based on METT-TC, specifically keying on the sequence of the enemy attack.
- Rehearsals

TYPES OF FIRING POSITIONS

5-59.   Based on a thorough analysis of the factors of METT-TC, leaders select the appropriate type of weapons firing position for the situation.

Mounted Position.

5-60.   The mounted firing position is characterized by a hull-down firing position. The vehicle is positioned behind either a natural or constructed cover with only the weapon system exposed. Leaders should seek a natural hull-down position whenever it is available. When a natural hull-down position is not available, the unit obtains, if available, engineer assistance to excavate hull-down positions. When hide positions are used, the primary firing positions should be hull-down positions. Leaders should select or construct hull-down positions so that the vehicle moves quickly into complete defilade. Routes into and out of hull-down positions should offer sufficient cover and concealment.

Dismounted Position.

5-61.   The dismounted position has cover and concealment to protect squads from direct and indirect fires. Overhead cover must be camouflaged. Overhead cover must allow room to effectively operate the selected weapon system. Individual weapons must be positioned for effective self-defense. The squad keeps the selected weapon system mounted in the vehicle while it constructs a dismounted position and the gunner prepares a range card. The tripod outlines the dismounted position. Once the position is complete, the squad emplaces the selected weapon system in the position and camouflages the position. The vehicle is place in a hide position.

Anitarmor Ambush Position

5-62.   The antiarmor ambush position can be either mounted or dismounted. The mounted position has the same criteria as above with the vehicle normally facing to the rear. If dismounted, the squad constructs a simple position that is large enough to conceal the antiarmor system and the squad until the ambush is completed. The position requires no overhead cover and the squad uses existing terrain features for this purpose. In choosing this position, the squad leader considers whether his squad can survive returned fire from the ambushed enemy element. The weight of the selected antiarmor system and the distance it must travel are important planning considerations because they prevent the squad from quickly withdrawing from the ambush site.

Urban Terrain Position.

5-63.   The squad leader considers the same crew survival question that he would for an antiarmor ambush position. Urban terrain affords the squad more cover and concealment. However, urban terrain does present certain firing limitations for close combat missile systems. For example, a ground-mounted Improved Target Acquisition System (ITAS) should be fired from a building only when the following conditions exist:

- The building is sturdy.
- The ceiling is at least 2 meters (7 feet) high.
- The room is at least 5 meters by 8 meters (17 feet by 24 feet) or larger.
- There are 2 square meters (20 square feet) of ventilation to the rear of the system (an open door 2 meters by 1 meter [7 feet by 3 feet] provides that much ventilation).
- Glass is removed from all windows and doors, the floor is swept, and any furniture and other objects that could be blown around are removed from the room.
- Squad members in the room are wearing hearing protection and ballistic eye protection and are positioned forward of the rear end of the launch tube.

Section III. TACTICAL EMPLOYMENT

This section describes the tactics and planning considerations available to the company commander as he prepares his defense. The weapons company commander's analysis determines the most effective control measures needed for each defensive mission.

CONTIGUOUS AND NONCONTIGUOUS DEFENSE

5-64.   Despite the increasing noncontiguous nature of operations, there may be situations where commanders describe decisive, shaping, and sustaining operations in spatial terms. Typically, contiguous operations involve conventional combat and concentrated maneuver forces. Ground forces share boundaries and orient against a similarly organized enemy force. Terrain or friendly forces secure flanks and protect sustainment operations. Noncontiguous operations are now more common than ever. Stability operations are normally noncontiguous. In noncontiguous operations, smaller, lighter, more mobile, and more lethal forces sustained by efficient, distribution-based sustainment systems lend themselves to simultaneous operations against multiple objectives. Situational understanding, coupled with precision fires, frees commanders to maneuver against multiple objectives. Swift maneuver against several objectives supported by precise, concentrated fires induces paralysis and shock among enemy troops and commanders.

CONTIGUOUS DEFENSE

5-65.   This tactic allows interlocking and overlapping observation and fields of fire across the battalion front. A thorough analysis of METT-TC results in the balanced positioning of forces along and in depth from the FEBA. Since he is rarely able to defend in strength along the entire length of his assigned FEBA, he must accept risk in some areas to provide strength in other, more vulnerable, areas. Actions conducted in the security area should identify the area that the enemy intends to attack in sufficient time to reinforce that area, shift reserves, and to mass fires. Indirect fires are used to slow and disrupt the attack. The weapons company is able to move rapidly to threatened areas and provide the means to mass long-range fires. Weapons platoons may be rapidly detached or released back to the weapons company as required to support the battalion commander's scheme of maneuver. The weapons company does not have to move as a unit but rather displaces from their positions and move independently, under the control of the company commander, to the threatened area and occupy pre-reconnoitered positions with the units arriving first occupying the most important positions or those furthest away. The battalion commander may also keep weapons company units in non-threatened areas while having the weapons company commander or the counterattack force commander in charge of the remainder. Indirect and direct fires are coordinated throughout the battle. Priority targets are also identified and destroyed.

5-66.   Should the enemy have an air assault capability, the weapons company can quickly move to contain the enemy forces until Infantry units can deploy. It can have platoons detached and be part of the battalion reserve. The type of terrain that is good for Infantry in the contiguous defense however, may limit the movement of the weapons company units and may have the battalion commander detach more platoons to his Infantry companies. The weapons company can also have platoons attached to units, such as the scouts, placed forward of the main battle area to provide security, intelligence, and kill the enemy with long-range fires. The weapons company's weapons systems optic systems provide a major enhancement to normal day/ night observation capabilities of the Infantry battalion.

Weapons Configuration and Targeting

5-67.   If an enemy Infantry or Infantry heavy force is attacking, the weapons company will predominantly arm itself with antipersonnel weapons such as machine guns. Against a mechanized enemy or mechanized heavy team, the weapons company will choose to predominantly arm itself with missile systems. However, the weapons company commander usually determines the weapons mix for his platoons based on his mission analysis of the battalion's OPORD\FRAGO and may not have the time to change the mix at the beginning of the attack and may decide to retain a balanced weapons mix able to engage a wide array of enemy forces.

Enemy Penetration

5-68.   A contiguous defense often has the space required to absorb an enemy penetration and then maneuver forces around the penetration to hit its flanks while a counterattack is prepared and executed. The weapons company is capable of rapid maneuver to the flanks of the penetration and delivering mass fires. If the battalion is forced to withdraw to successive positions, then the weapons company can be employed to cover this movement and not allow the Infantry forces to become decisively engaged.

NONCONTIGUOUS DEFENSE

5-69.   The noncontiguous defense is the most decentralized and dynamic defense conducted by an Infantry battalion. This type of defense orients on the enemy and not terrain. To be successful, this defense depends on surprise, offensive action, and the initiative of small-unit leaders. It is characterized by aggressive patrolling and reconnaissance to locate, fix, and destroy the enemy. It is often used to permit the local population to continue to remain in the area at the same time as the enemy is attacked.

5-70.   Companies are assigned areas of operation (AOs) within the battalion's area of operations. These can be contiguous, with boundaries between company AOs, or noncontiguous, with space between companies that is the responsibility of the battalion. Noncontiguous defense is often used where the location of the enemy is ill-defined, such as during stability operations. The weapons Company will often have its platoons attached to Infantry companies. These platoons and the company are employed as they would be in any defense with the addition of missions such as convoy security and acting as part of the cordon during cordon and search operations. It can also conduct mounted patrols and as a quick reaction force (QRF) to reinforce units in contact.

TACTICS

5-71.   The weapons company typically defends using one of four basic defensive tactics: defense of an AO, from a battle position, on a reverse slope, and in a perimeter. Detached weapons platoons conform to the scheme of maneuver of the Infantry company commander but will still fight from battle positions in support of the Infantry. Typical control measures for the defense are AOs, battle positions, phase lines, engagement areas, target reference points, decision points, and other movement and fire control measures. There are no set criteria for selecting the control measures.

DEFEND AN AO

5-72. An AO defense, Figure 5-2, uses control measures that provide the most freedom of action to a subordinate unit. It provides flexibility by allowing the subordinate unit to operate in a decentralized manner while still maintaining sufficient control to prevent confusion and to synchronize the higher unit's operation.

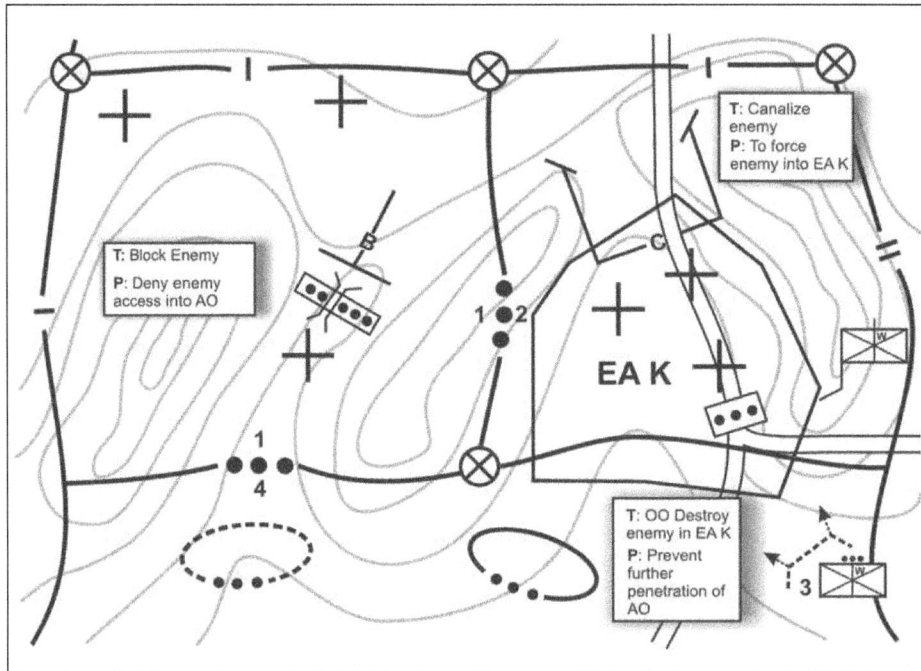

Figure 5-2. Defense of an area of operations.

Weapons Company's Disposition

5-73. A weapons company's disposition may consist of a company or platoon AOs and a series of mutually supporting battle positions. Positions are arrayed in depth. The strength of this defense comes from its flexibility. The weapons company defense normally orients on the enemy force and not on retaining terrain. It is effective because it forces the enemy to expose his flanks and critical command and control (C2) and mobility and protection assets through his own maneuver into the depth of the defense.

Platoon AOs

5-74. By assigning platoon AOs, the company may fight an AO defense very similar to a noncontiguous defense. This decentralized defense requires greater initiative and delegates more of the control to subordinate leaders. When required, subordinate units may disengage independently and move to another location within the AO to continue the fight. The company commander can control the rate of movement various ways, to include phase lines.

5-75. When fighting a weapons company defense with platoon AOs from battle positions, the goal is to defeat the attacker through the depth of his formation by confronting him with effective fires from mutually supporting battle positions as he attempts to maneuver around them. Observation posts, indirect fire targets, mines, and other obstacles cover gaps that, because of terrain masking or heavy woods, cannot be covered effectively by direct fire. Units remain in place except for local or internal movement to alternate or supplementary positions. If certain platoon positions become untenable during the battle, the platoon leader may withdraw his units to successive positions according to prepared plans and rehearsals. However, the platoon leader aggressively fights within his AO, moving his sections to bring the enemy under flank attack and re-taking lost positions. Some methods for fighting in AOs include--

- Allow the enemy to move into the engagement area and destroy him with massed fires.
- Engage the attacker at maximum range with fires from attack helicopters, field artillery, and mortars and then to engage with organic weapons systems positioned to deliver fires at maximum effective ranges from the flanks and rear. As the enemy closes, weapons systems may move to alternate or supplementary firing positions to continue firing and avoid being bypassed.

5-76.   The weapons company defense of an AO generally requires the company commander to be able to see and control the battle. It also requires good fields of fire to allow mutual support. If the terrain or the expected enemy course of action prevents this, the defense may be more effective if control is more decentralized and the platoons fight in AOs.

5-77.   A significant concern, particularly when fighting with platoon AOs within the company defense of an AO, is the enemy's ability to isolate a part of the weapons company and then fix, destroy, or bypass it. Without effective mutual support between battle positions and between adjacent platoons, this is likely to occur. Even with mutual support, responsive and effective indirect fire support is often critical to defending AOs.

DEFEND FROM A BATTLE POSITION.

5-78.   A defense from a battle position is a general location and orientation of forces on the ground from which units defend. The size of units occupying battle positions can from squad to battalion. The unit is located within the general area of the battle position. Security elements may be located forward and to the flanks of the battle position. Units defending from a battle position may not be tied in with adjacent units; thus, the requirement for all-round security is increased. When assigning battle positions, the company commander assigns sectors of fire and primary positions to his platoons to defend. Each position must contribute to the accomplishment of the company's assigned task and purpose within the higher commander's concept of the operation. A commander may also assign alternate, supplementary, and successive positions to platoons, depending on the situation. The leader occupying the battle position should also assign alternate, supplementary, and successive positions within the BP.

Engagements from a Battle Position

5-79.   Fighting from a battle position is a more centralized tactic and may also be more contiguous at the company level. Even so, it should not be a static defense. Battle positions should be positioned to achieve surprise and to allow maneuver forward, within, and between battle positions. A defense from battle positions is effective in concentrating combat power into an engagement area. It prevents the enemy from isolating one part of the company and concentrating his combat power in this area. Normally, subordinate platoons are assigned mutual supporting battle positions that cover the enemy's likely avenue of approach. These battle positions are located on terrain that provides cover and concealment.

Surprise

5-80.   A company commander's concept for using this method should concentrate on achieving surprise for each of the battle positions. This is accomplished by effective OPSEC and fire control. Counter reconnaissance, if the resources are available, prevents the enemy from locating the battle positions. By initiating fires from one battle position and waiting for the enemy to maneuver, other battle positions can then initiate fires on the enemy's flanks and rear. Fighting in this manner confuses the enemy and disrupts his C2.

Massed Fires

5-81.   When the terrain permits and the weapons company commander's concept focuses most of the enemy into the engagement area, the company may engage with massed fires from all of the platoon battle positions. Control of these fires through target reference points and other fire control measures reduces the possibility of multiple engagements of the same target. A disadvantage to this tactic is that if there are still uncommitted enemy forces outside the engagement area, they will know the locations of the BPs and will attempt to isolate and concentrate against them. To counter this threat, coordinated indirect fires on these enemy units reduce their effectiveness and ability to identify battle positions. The company commander must develop contingency plans to disengage from exposed battle positions and reorganize to continue the fight. This may involve displacing to alternate battle positions or disengaging to conduct counterattacks or spoiling attacks against identified enemy C2, mobility and protection, or sustainment assets.

Multiple Platoon Engagements

5-82.   Instead of one company engagement area, multiple platoon engagement areas may be identified to provide flexibility to the plan. The plan must clearly state which platoons must reorient fires into the alternate engagement area and when they must do so. This tactic is especially effective when operating in restrictive terrain or compartmented environment.

DEFEND ON A REVERSE SLOPE.

5-83.   An alternative to defending on the forward slope of a hill or a ridge is to defend on a reverse slope, Figure 5-3. In such a defense, the company is deployed on terrain that is masked from enemy direct fire and ground observation by the crest of a hill. Although some units and weapons may be positioned on the forward slope, the crest, or the counterslope (a forward slope of a hill to the rear of a reverse slope), most Infantry forces are on the reverse slope. However, weapons company units may be concentrated on the counterslope. The key to this defense is control of the crest by direct fire.

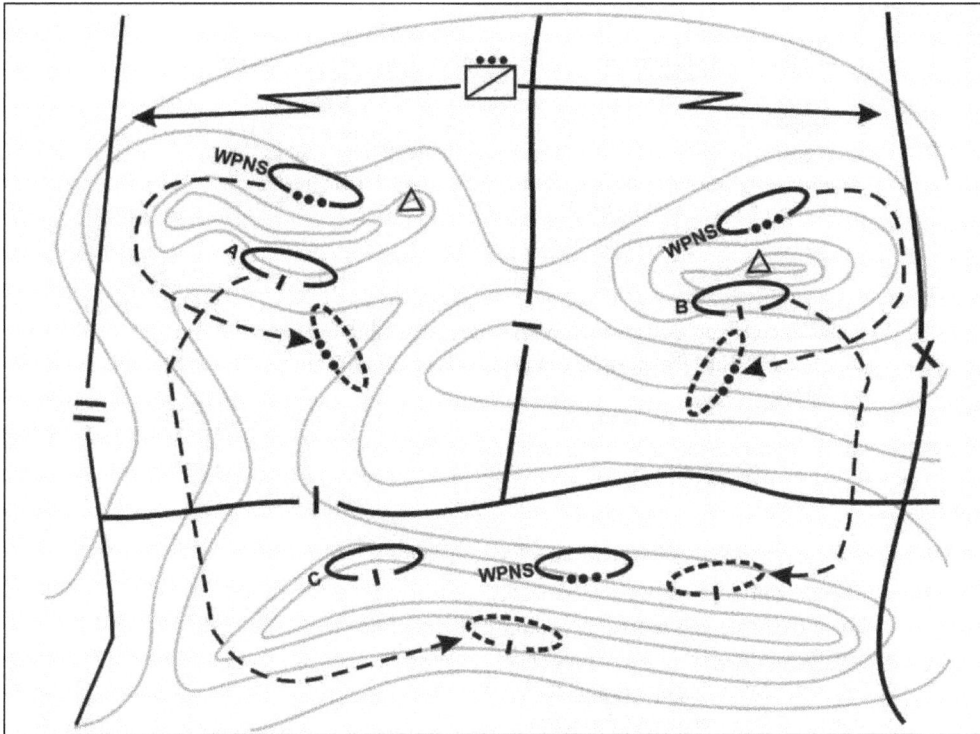

Figure 5-3. Defense from a reverse slope.

Advantages.

5-84. The following advantages generally apply when defending on a reverse slope:

- The crest protects the unit from direct fire. This is a distinct advantage if the attacker has greater weapons range and firepower than the defender. The reverse slope defense can eliminate or reduce the attacker's standoff advantage. It also makes enemy adjustment of his indirect fire more difficult since he cannot see his rounds impact. It keeps the enemy's second echelon from supporting his first echelon's assault.

- The enemy may be deceived and may advance to close contact before he discovers the defensive position. Therefore, the defender may gain the advantage of surprise.

- The defender can improve positions, build obstacles, and clear fields of fire without disclosing the location of the positions.

- The defender may use dummy positions on the forward slope to deceive the enemy.

- Resupply and evacuation (when under attack) may be easier when defending on a reverse slope.

- Enemy target acquisition and jamming efforts are degraded. Enemy radar, infrared sights, and thermal viewers cannot easily detect Soldiers masked by a hill. Radios with a hill between them and the enemy are less vulnerable to jamming and direction finders.

- Enemy use of close air support and attack helicopters is restricted. Enemy aircraft must attack defensive positions from the flank or from the rear, which makes it easier for friendly air defense weapons to engage them.

- A counterattacking unit has more freedom of maneuver since it is masked from the enemy's direct fire.

Disadvantages.

5-85.   The following disadvantages may apply when defending on a reverse slope.

- Observation of the enemy is more difficult. Soldiers in a reverse slope position can see forward no farther than the crest. This makes it hard to determine exactly where the enemy is as he advances, especially when visibility is poor. OPs should be placed forward of the topographic crest for early warning and long-range observation. Unmanned aircraft systems (UAS) and remote sensors can also be used.
- Egress from the position may be more difficult.
- Fields of fire are normally short but fires to the flank can increase the range.
- Obstacles on the forward slope can be covered only with indirect fire or by units on the flanks of the company unless some weapons systems are initially placed forward.
- If the enemy gains the crest, he can assault downhill. This may give him a psychological advantage.
- If observation posts are insufficient or improperly placed, the defenders may have to fight an enemy who suddenly appears in strength at close range.

Feasibility.

5-86.   A defense on a reverse slope may be effective when--

- The forward slope has little cover and concealment.
- The forward slope is untenable because of enemy fire.
- The forward slope has been lost or not yet gained.
- There are better fields of fire on the reverse slope.
- It adds to the surprise and deception.
- The enemy has more long-range weapons than the defender.

Use of the Weapons Company in the Reverse Slope Defense.

5-87.   The weapons company commander should consider the following while employing his company in a reverse slope defense:

- Weapons company's units may be employed on the forward slope and then displace to the rear.
- Forward Infantry unit positions should be within 200 to 500 meters of the crest of the defended hill or ridge and sited so they block enemy approaches and exploit existing obstacles. They should permit surprise fire on the crest and on the approaches around the crest. Weapons company units can provide fire support from the counterslope.
- Weapons such as the close combat missile systems can gain standoff distances by firing across the front or from the counterslope. The grenade machine guns can be fired from behind the counterslope in partial defilade or, with an observer, full defilade in an indirect mode.
- Emplace observation posts, including fire support team (FIST) personnel (if available), on the crest or the forward slope of the defended hill. At night, observation posts and patrol units should be increased to prevent infiltration. Weapon company units, especially the missile systems with thermal sights, may be employed at the observation posts.
- Position weapons units in depth or reserve where it can provide the most flexibility, support the forward units by fire, protect the flanks and the rear of the higher unit, and, if necessary, counterattack. It may be positioned on the counterslope to the rear of the forward units if that position allows it to fire and hit the enemy when he reaches the crest of the defended hill.
- Position the weapons company command post to the rear where it will not interfere with the supporting units or the employment of the reserve. The commander may have an observation post on the forward slope or crest and another on the reverse slope or counterslope. He uses the observation post on the forward slope or crest before the battle starts when he is trying to

determine the enemy's intentions. During the fight, he moves to the observation post on the reverse slope or counterslope.

- Indirect fire has to be coordinated with the battalion FSO. However, plan indirect fire well forward of, on, and to the flanks of the forward slope, crest, reverse slope, and counterslope.
- The battalion normally plans counterattacks. The plan focuses on driving the enemy off the crest by fire, if possible. The plan should also be prepared to drive the enemy off by fire and movement. The weapons company can support counterattacks from support by fire or attack-by-fire positions.

PERIMETER DEFENSE

5-88.   A perimeter defense, Figure 5-4, allows the defending force to orient in all directions. The weapons company uses the perimeter defense primarily in assembly areas, as a reserve, or as part of a larger force. In most instances, it would be difficult for a weapons company to establish a perimeter defense, assembly areas and reserve positions excluded, without Infantry augmentation. Ideally, the augmented weapons company would establish a perimeter defense on terrain that would enhance its long-range firepower. In terms of weapons emplacement, direct and indirect fire integration, and reserve employment, a commander conducting a perimeter defense considers the same factors as for any defense. As part of a larger force, the weapons company will usually cover the enemy's most likely high-speed avenues of approach. Some examples of using a perimeter defense include a firebase, a forward operating base, and a combat outpost. The weapons company might be ordered to execute a perimeter defense under a variety of conditions, including:

- When it must secure itself against terrorist or guerilla attacks. This tactic may also apply if the company must conserve or build combat power in order to execute operations.
- When it must hold critical terrain in areas where the defense is not tied in with adjacent units.
- When it has been bypassed and isolated by the enemy and must defend in place.
- When it conducts occupation of an independent assembly area or reserve position.
- When it is directed to concentrate fires into two or more adjacent avenues of approach.

5-89.   The following preparations are conducted during a perimeter defense:

- Preparing a perimeter defense is like preparing any other position defense, but the company must disperse in a circular configuration for all-round security (the actual shape depends on the terrain). The company must be prepared to defend in all directions.
- The commander assigns the weapons platoons to cover the most likely enemy avenues of approach. He prepares alternate and supplementary positions within the perimeter.
- If available, Infantry occupy positions to cover likely enemy dismounted avenues of approach.
- If available, snipers or designated marksmen should cover likely or suspected enemy positions or OPs. Snipers and designated marksmen may also be used to observe or overwatch areas where civilians congregate.
- If possible, hold a section or platoon in reserve. The company commander assigns a primary position to the rear of the platoon, covering the most dangerous avenues of approach.
- Prepare obstacles in depth around the perimeter.
- Plan direct and indirect fire as for any type of defense. Plan and use fire support from outside the perimeter when available.
- Counter enemy initial attacks by area fire weapons (artillery, mortars, grenade launchers) to avoid revealing the locations of fighting positions (rules of engagement (ROE) dependent).
- If the enemy penetrates the perimeter, the reserve occupies predetermined fire positions if possible and destroys the enemy, and then blocks the penetration. Even though the company's counterattack ability is limited, it must strive to restore its perimeter.

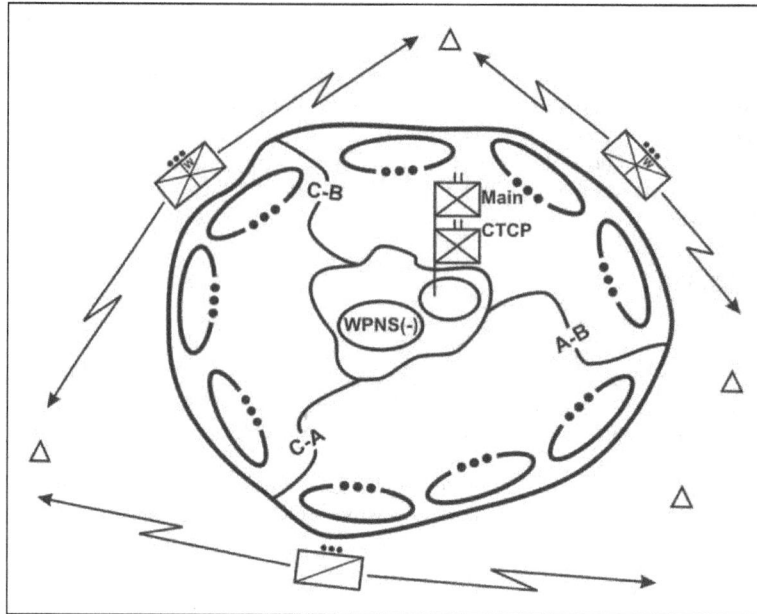

Figure 5-4. Perimeter defense.

OTHER EMPLOYMENT OPTIONS

5-90.   The weapons company may participate in a defense by operating as a battalion's security force, as part of the security force, and as a battalion reserve.

SECURITY FORCE.

5-91.   Battalion and brigade security forces normally conduct the tactical tasks of screen or guard. Defending battalions deploy security forces beyond the FEBA to provide early warning, to deny enemy observation of the MBA, to assist rearward passage of a covering force, and to deceive and disorganize the enemy. The security force commander places the security force where it can cover enemy avenues of approach into the defensive area. One or more weapons platoons can form part of the battalion's security force. The battalion commander positions the weapons company or platoon in areas that offer long-range observation and fields of fire on high-speed enemy avenues of approach. Their thermal sights and mobility make them an efficient asset in these operations. The other security elements, most often the scout platoon, report the direction and size of the enemy advance, and the weapons company units may then maneuver to engage. They can also support the withdrawal of the forward security units.

5-92.   Heavy weapons can destroy most types of enemy reconnaissance elements. The weapons unit is positioned so that it has good fields of fire, observation of the avenues of approach, and able to support the forward security units. The leader may have to designate supplementary positions if there are more mobility corridors than can be covered from one position.

Planning Considerations.

5-93.   The battalion S2 provides the results of his IPB in the form of the disposition, composition, capabilities, and the most probable course of action, with accompanying situation template, for the enemy's reconnaissance effort. The results of the terrain analysis, which includes LOS information, will be valuable when considering the tactical array or disposition of security forces. Weapons units can determine the LOS from maps or, if the digital map has been installed, from the Force XXI Battle Command, Brigade and Below (FBCB2) (FBCB2 LOS however does not account for vegetation and man-made structures).

5-94.   Leaders ensure their subordinates receive the appropriate control measures, which include the locations and graphics for the remainder of the security force. All security force elements should have common graphics to ensure a clear understanding of the situation (for example, phase lines, checkpoints, and target reference points to control the hand-off of targets). This includes confirmation of FBCB2 data. If each element in the security force uses different control measures, then the security force effort will be disjointed and ineffective.

5-95.   Security force elements observe named areas of interest (NAI) along the anticipated enemy avenues of approach. Upon detection of enemy targets, the platoon sends reports to the higher headquarters. The location and direction of travel are clarified by using the common control measures of the security force (for example, enemy armored personnel carrier at target reference point (TRP) 2 moving east to TRP 3). Security force elements use their optics equipment and observation devices to identify targets. This is especially useful when the elements of the security have difficulty detecting targets. The limitations to these methods are that the enemy may detect the laser signature and take evasive action as well as engage the source. Leaders closely monitor the situation and ensure their units positively identify targets to prevent fratricide.

5-96.   A weapons mix is selected based on the battalion's IPB, security force commander's guidance, and the platoon leader's own METT-TC analysis. Some major concerns are the type of reconnaissance vehicles expected and the fields of fire available. Close combat missile systems may not be an effective weapon system against reconnaissance vehicles in restrictive terrain because of tracking limitations. Since the Javelin is man-portable, it could be placed in a better position than the vehicle-mounted weapons. (Although all the weapons systems can be ground-mounted, time to remount these systems should be taken into consideration when deciding to dismount the systems.) The heavy machine guns can destroy most lightly armored reconnaissance vehicles such as BMPs and BRDMs.

Engagement

5-97.   Leaders monitor the situation to ensure they are aware of the locations of the remainder of the security force. They accept target hand over from the security element. They receive target information as to the type, location, and direction of enemy maneuver. Common control measures helps to clarify the information. Once targets are identified, they are tracked until the desired point of engagement, and then destroyed. There is always a risk of weapons systems being lost before the main battle when employing weapons elements during security operations.

Withdrawal.

5-98.   The security force normally attempts to conduct a rearward passage of lines during limited visibility. This requires detailed coordination. The withdrawal route and other control measures are provided to MBA forces before the passage of lines. The security force also can mark itself using IR markers, battlefield "VS" marking panels, chemlites or other tactical standing operating procedures (TSOP) markings to provide visual identification to the MBA forces. This identification, combined with rehearsals of the rearward passage, will improve night observation devices and reduce the likelihood of fratricide.

COMBAT OUTPOST

5-99.   A combat outpost is a reinforced OP capable of conducting limited combat operations. The commander uses a combat outpost when he wants to extend the depth of his security area, when he wants his forward OPs to remain in place until they can observe the enemy's main body, or when he anticipates that his forward OPs will be encircled by enemy forces. Combat outposts manned wholly or in part by weapons company units become in effect attack-by-fire positions located in the security zone. Units from the weapons company can provide long-range observation and fires, and can inflict casualties through the use of CAS, indirect fires, and direct fires. Besides causing casualties, the effective use of combat outposts occupied by weapons company units can confuse the enemy as to the location of the main defensive positions and make him deploy prematurely and thus reveal his scheme of maneuver. Weapons company units can further degrade the enemy threat by destroying priority targets such as C2 and recovery vehicles. The combination of long-range indirect and direct fires and other forces such as dismounted Infantry stay behind forces can be very effective. Weapons company units can also rapidly displace to reinforce threatened areas and to affect a passage of lines through the forward defensive units. Once the passage of lines is completed, these units will move to their previously assigned positions. The weapons company units do not want to become decisively engaged while in the security zone. The battalion commander has to weigh the advantages of adding depth to his engagement areas with the possibility of loosing all or some of his long-range mobile combat power.

5-100.   While the factors of METT-TC determine the size, location, and number of combat outposts established by a unit, a combat outpost must have sufficient resources to accomplish its designated missions, but not so much as to seriously deplete the strength of the main body. It is usually located far enough in front of the protected force to preclude enemy ground reconnaissance elements from observing the actions of the protected force.

RESERVE.

5-101.   The commander may decide to use his weapons units as his reserve, specifically when there is more than one mobility corridor the enemy is likely to use, negating the use of one unit battle position. When operating as the reserve, the weapons unit may perform a variety of missions to include these counterattack missions: Block a penetration from an attack-by-fire position. Occupy a battle position. Reinforce another unit's position. Destroy enemy mobility and protection or sustainment forces. The reserve is normally positioned in an assembly area to wait for orders to execute one of several preplanned contingency courses of action. The weapons company commander conducts rehearsals of all his contingency missions. During security operations, he receives the priority of the potential missions to ensure he can rehearse them with his subordinate leaders. Another method for the company is to have the company XO, with the platoon sergeants, rehearse the potential missions while the company is conducting the security operation. Full-up rehearsals may not always be possible.

5-102.   The factors of METT-TC determine the amount of preparation completed for each contingency mission assigned. The unit keeps the direct fire plan as simple as possible in each engagement area to reduce confusion.

5-103.   Weapons units may receive the mission to be prepared for a combination of the above roles. The battalion clarifies the priority of each contingency to focus their preparation. The execution of all of these missions may occur during limited visibility. IR markers are used to mark vehicle positions for rapid occupation. Any unit TRPs emplaced are set up for limited visibility before darkness (for example, heat the TRPs or use IR source markers as TRPs).

ENGAGEMENT AREA DEVELOPMENT

5-104.   The engagement area is where the company commander intends to destroy an enemy force using the massed fires of all available weapons. The success of any engagement depends on how effectively he can integrate the obstacle plan, the indirect fire plan, the direct fire plan, and the terrain within the engagement area to achieve the unit's tactical purpose. Beginning with an analysis of METT-TC factors, the development process covers these steps:

- Identify all likely enemy avenues of approach.
- Determine likely enemy schemes of maneuver.
- Determine where to kill the enemy.
- Emplace weapons systems.
- Plan and integrate obstacles.
- Plan and integrate indirect fires.

• Rehearse the execution of operations in the engagement area.

5-105.   Figures 5-5 through 5-10 are simplified examples of an engagement area development and do not necessarily show the requisite detailed requirements needed for a complete plan.

IDENTIFY LIKELY ENEMY AVENUES OF APPROACH.

5-106.   The following procedures and considerations, apply in identifying the enemy's likely avenues of approach.

• Conduct an initial reconnaissance. If possible, do this from the enemy's perspective along each avenue of approach into the AO or engagement area.

• Identify key and decisive terrain. This includes locations that afford positions of advantage over the enemy as well as natural obstacles and choke points that restrict forward and lateral movement.

• Determine which avenues will provide cover and concealment for the enemy while allowing him to maintain his tempo.

• Evaluate lateral routes adjoining each avenue of approach.

5-107.   In the example in Figure 5-5, avenues of approach 1 and 2 provide high-speed avenues of approach into the AO but they both narrow at the town and to the west. Avenue of approach 3 provides a concealed dismounted approach route to just east of the town. The following areas are decisive (D) and key (K) terrain features:

• D1: Blocks the two high-speed avenues of approach and is a choke point for all westward movement in the AO.

• K1: Covers avenue of approach 1 (AA1) and the southern part of the AO.

• K2: Reinforces D1 and is a choke point for further western movement into the AO.

• K3: Provides observation and long-range fires to the east.

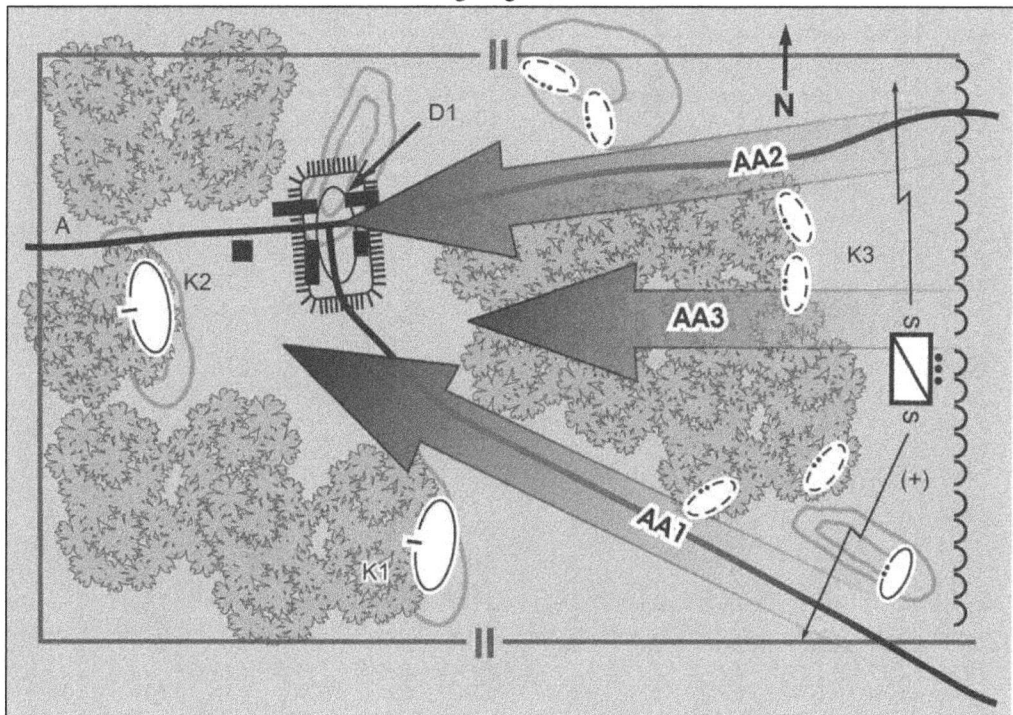

Figure 5-5. Likely enemy avenues of approach.

DETERMINE THE ENEMY SCHEME OF MANEUVER.

5-108.   The company commander can use the following procedures and considerations in determining the enemy's scheme of maneuver. Much of this information comes from the S2 and the operation plan (OPLAN)/FRAGO.

- Determine how the enemy will structure the attack. In what formation will he attack? How will he sequence his forces?
- Determine how the enemy will use his reconnaissance assets. Will he attempt to infiltrate friendly positions?
- Determine where and when the enemy will change formations and establish support-by-fire positions.
- Determine where, when, and how the enemy will conduct his assault and breaching operations.
- Determine where and when the enemy will commit follow-on forces.
- Determine the enemy's expected rates of movement.
- Assess the effects of the enemy's combat multipliers.
- Determine what reactions the enemy is likely to have in response to projected friendly actions.

5-109.   In Figure 5-6:

If enemy attacks along AA1, he will:

- Seize 1, the wood line at 2-3, K1, and wood line at 8.
- Capture D1.
- Capture K2 and 4.
- Continue along route A to the West.

If enemy attacks along AA2, he will:
- Seize wood line 5-6 and capture hill at 7.
- Capture D1.
- Capture K2 and 4.
- Continue along route A to the West.

If enemy attacks along AA3, he will:
- Seize woods 2-3-5-6.
- Capture D1.
- Capture K2 and 4.
- Continue along route A to the West.

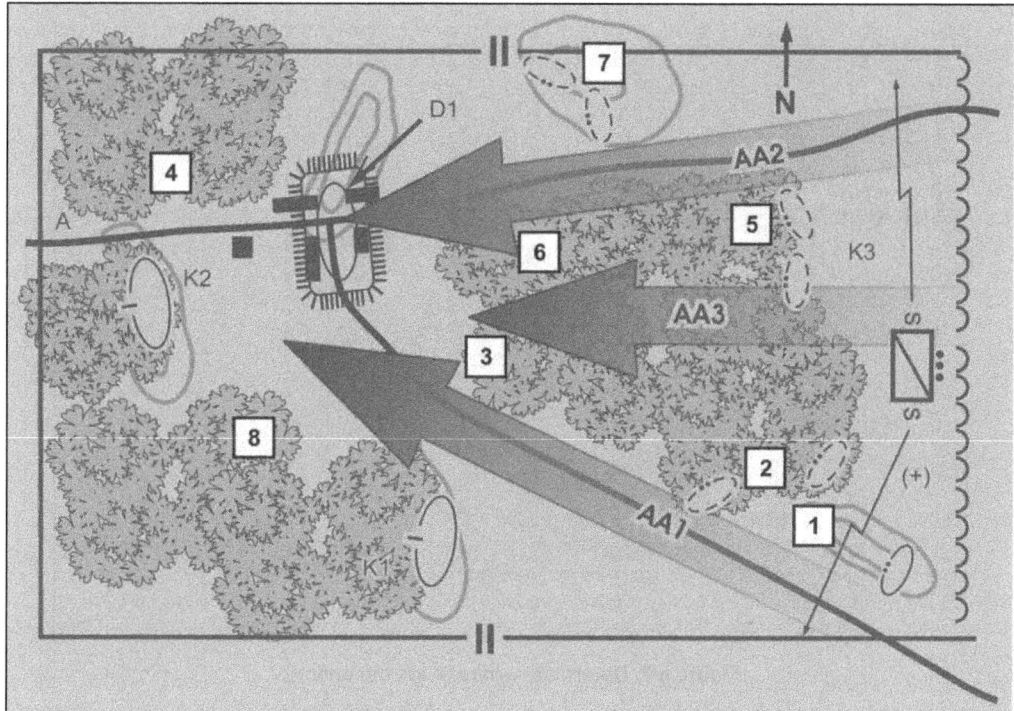

Figure 5-6. Enemy's scheme of maneuver.

DETERMINE WHERE TO KILL THE ENEMY.

5-110. The following steps apply in identifying and marking where the higher unit and company will engage the enemy.

- Identify direct fire control measures (DFCM), including TRPs, that match the enemy's scheme of maneuver, allowing the company to identify where it will engage enemy forces through the depth of the AO, how it will distribute fires, and identify unit sectors of fire.
- Identify and record the exact location of each TRP.
- Determine how many weapons systems, by type, must focus fires on each TRP to achieve the desired effects.
- Determine which platoons will mass fires on each TRP.
- Establish engagement areas around TRPs.
- Develop the direct fire planning measures necessary to focus fires at each TRP.
- Identify other control measures such as the trigger points and break points.
- In marking TRPs, use thermal sights to ensure visibility at the appropriate range under varying conditions, including daylight and limited visibility.

5-111. In Figure 5-7, TRPs 1 and 2 are used to initiate direct and indirect fires, TRP 3 is used to initiate and distribute fires from the scout and attached weapons platoon, TRP 4 is used to distribute fires along wood line, and TRPs 5 through 8 are used to distribute fires within engagement areas.

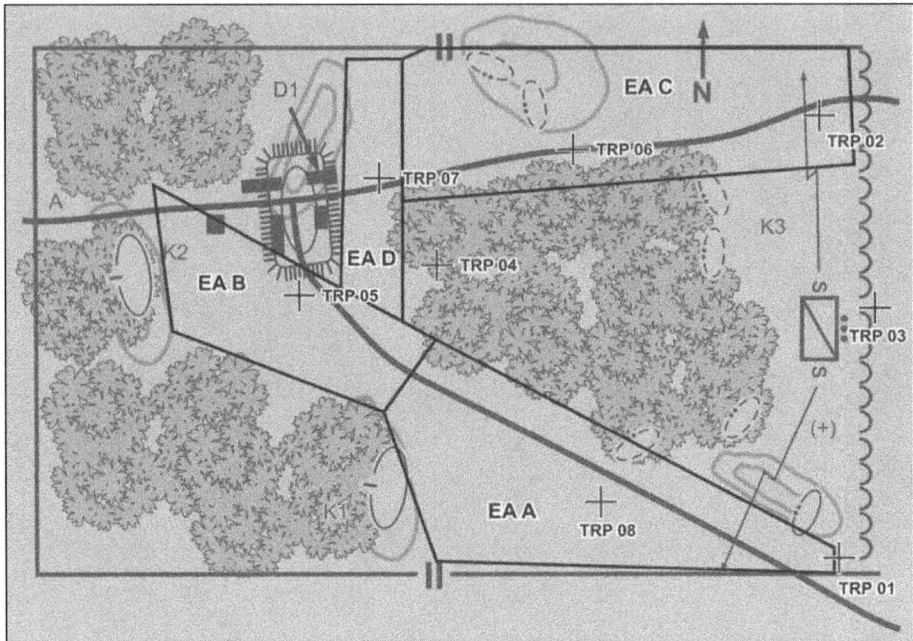

Figure 5-7. Determine where to kill the enemy.

EMPLACE WEAPONS SYSTEMS.

5-112. The following steps apply in selecting and improving battle positions and emplacing the company's weapons systems.

- Select tentative platoon battle positions. (When possible, select these while moving in the engagement area. Using the enemy's perspective enables the commander to assess survivability of the positions.)
- Conduct a leader's reconnaissance of the tentative battle positions.
- Drive the engagement area to confirm that selected positions are tactically advantageous.
- Confirm and mark the selected battle positions.
- Ensure that battle positions do not conflict with those of adjacent units and that they are effectively tied in with adjacent positions.
- Select primary, alternate, and supplementary fighting positions to achieve the desired effect for each TRP in the engagement area. If the terrain allows, select sites that permit hull down and hide positions.
- Ensure that platoon leaders, platoon sergeants, section leaders, and squad leaders position weapons systems to effectively cover each TRP with the required number of weapons systems (by type).
- Site and mark vehicle positions in accordance with unit SOP.

5-113. In the example in Figure 5-8, weapons are placed in the following battle positions as follows:

- BP1: (SE) Engage enemy in engagement area (EA) A. Be prepared to engage enemy in EAs B and D.
- BP2: (SE) Engage enemy in EA B. Be prepared to engage dismounted enemy south of TRP 04
- BP3: (ME) Engage enemy in EAs C and D. Be prepared to engage dismounted Infantry to north of TRP 04.

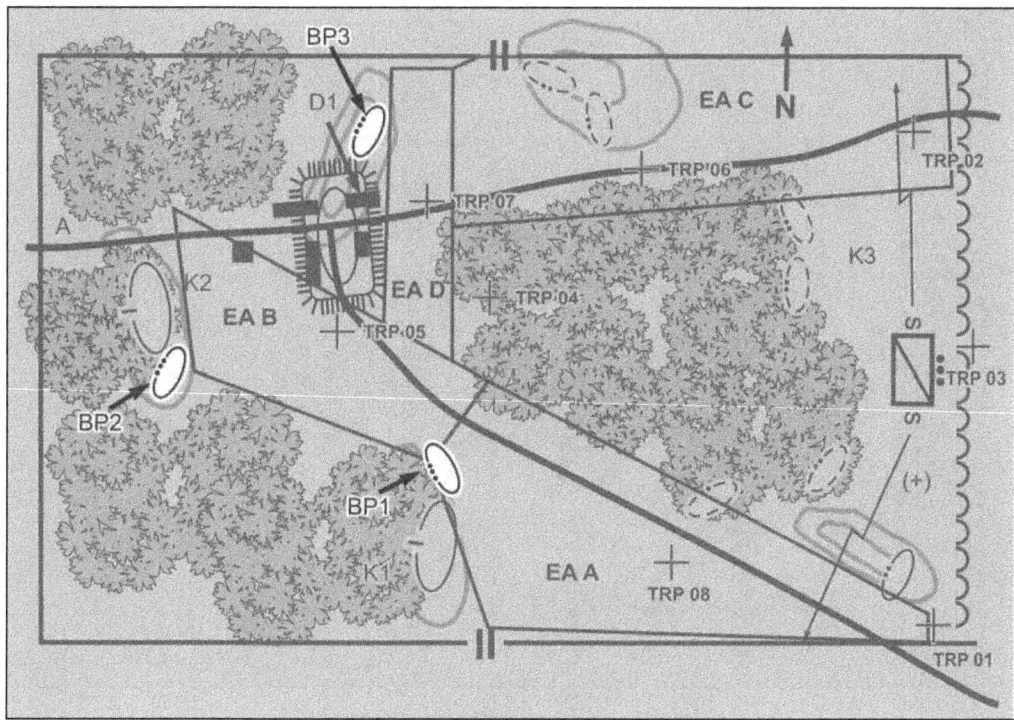

Figure 5-8. Emplace weapons systems.

PLAN AND INTEGRATE OBSTACLES.

5-114.   The following apply in planning and integrating obstacles in the weapons company defense.

- Understand the obstacle group intent.
- Coordinate with the engineers.
- Site and mark individual obstacle locations.
- Refine direct and indirect fire control measures.
- Identify lanes and gaps.
- Report obstacle locations and gaps to higher headquarters.

5-115.   Figure 5-9 shows an example obstacle plan.

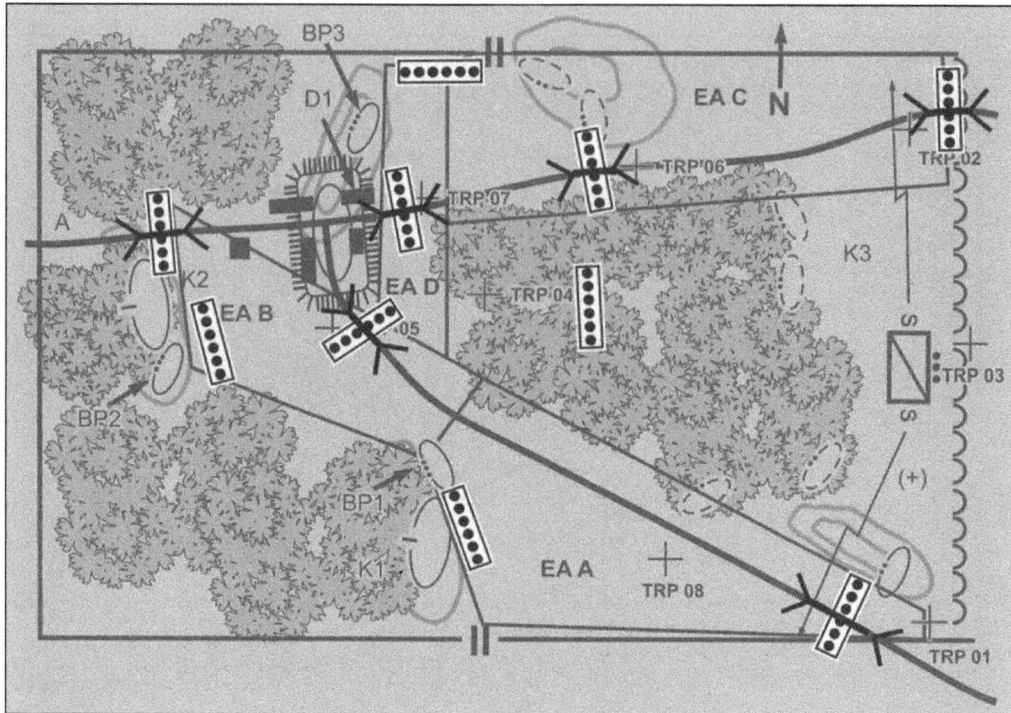

Figure 5-9. Plan and integrate obstacles.

PLAN AND INTEGRATE INDIRECT FIRES.

5-116. The following steps apply in planning and integrating indirect fires.

- Determine the purpose of fires and any essential task to be accomplished by fire support.
- Determine where that purpose can best be achieved.
- Establish the observation plan, with redundancy for each target. Observers include the FSO (if attached) as well as leaders of elements with fire support responsibilities.
- Establish triggers and observers.
- Obtain accurate target locations using lazing devices.
- Refine target locations to ensure coverage of obstacles.
- Adjust/register artillery and mortar targets.
- Plan FPFs.
- Request critical friendly zones (CFZ) for protection of maneuver elements and no-fire areas for protection of observation posts and forward positions.

5-117. Figure 5-10 shows planned indirect fires locations.

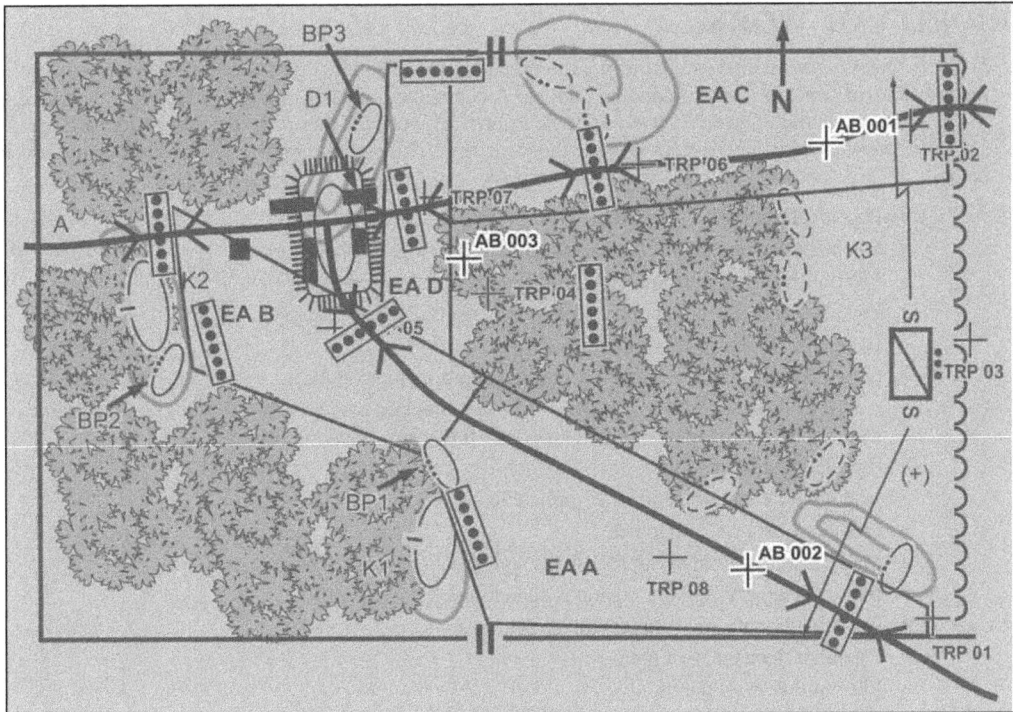

Figure 5-10. Plan and integrate indirect fires.

CONDUCT AN ENGAGEMENT AREA REHEARSAL.

5-118.   The purpose of this rehearsal is to ensure every leader and Soldier understands the plan and all elements are prepared to cover their assigned areas with direct and indirect fires. Although the weapons company commander has several options, the most common and most effective type of rehearsal is replicating the threat. The company commander should coordinate the rehearsal with the higher headquarters to ensure other units' rehearsals are not planned for the same time or location. The rehearsal should cover these actions:

- Rearward passage of security forces (as required).
- Closure of lanes (as required).
- Movement from the hide position to the battle position.
- Use of fire commands, triggers, and maximum engagement lines to initiate direct and indirect fires.
- Shifting of fires to refocus and redistribute fire effects.
- Emplacement of scatterable mines.
- Preparation and transmission of critical reports frequency modulation (FM) radio or FBCB2.
- Assessment of the effects of enemy weapons systems.
- Displacement to alternate, supplementary, or successive battle positions.
- Cross-leveling or resupply of Class V.
- Evacuation of casualties.

PRIORITY OF WORK

5-119.   This is a set method of controlling the preparation and conduct of a defense. SOP should describe the priorities of work to include individual duties. A commander changes priorities based on the situation. The leaders in the unit all should have a specific priority of work for their duty position. Although listed in sequence, several tasks may be performed at the same time. An example priority of work sequence is listed below:

- Post local security.
- Establish the company reconnaissance and surveillance operation.
- Position Javelins, machine guns, and Soldiers; assign sectors of fire.
- Position other assets (company command post (CP) and mortars).
- Designate final protective lines and FPFs.
- Clear fields of fire and prepare range cards and sector sketches.
- Adjust indirect fire FPFs. The firing unit fire direction center (FDC) should provide a safety box that is clear of all friendly units before firing any adjusting rounds.
- Prepare fighting positions.
- Install wire communications, if applicable.
- Emplace obstacles and mines.
- Mark (or improve marking for) TRPs and direct fire control measures.
- Improve primary fighting positions such as overhead cover.
- Prepare alternate and supplementary positions.
- Establish sleep and rest plan.
- Reconnoiter movements.
- Rehearse engagements and disengagements or displacements.
- Adjust positions and control measures as required.
- Stockpile ammunition, food, and water.
- Dig trenches between positions.
- Reconnoiter routes.
- Continue to improve positions...

SECTOR SKETCHES AND FIRE PLANS

5-120.   Weapons leaders prepare sector sketches based on their defensive plan. These sector sketches are based on range cards prepared for all crew-served weapons systems. The sector sketch allows the higher headquarters to determine the effectiveness of the direct fire plan. If necessary, the higher commander makes adjustments to the sectors and or position of his subordinates. Sector sketches also are useful for units occupying previously prepared defenses (example: a relief in place).

SECTION SECTOR SKETCH.

5-121.   Each section leader prepares a sector sketch to visually depict his section's fire plan. This information is found on the range card for the two squads. The section leader makes two copies of the sketch, keeping one and forwarding the other to his platoon leader. The sector sketch should provide the following information: Prominent terrain features in the sector of fire and the ranges to them. Each weapons squad's primary and secondary sectors of fire, TRPs, dead space, phase lines, break points (triggers), maximum engagement lines, obstacles, and indirect-fire targets. Also included is the distance and direction to all dead space and TRPs.

PLATOON SECTOR SKETCHES, AND PLATOON AND COMPANY FIRE PLANS.

5-122.   The platoon leader inspects the section sector sketches. He uses these sector sketches to prepare his platoon sector sketch and fire plan. He also makes two copies, keeping one and forwarding the other copy or digitally transmitting (if equipped) a copy of the sector sketch to his commander or higher headquarters. Using the section sector sketches, the platoon leader can prepare a platoon fire plan and engagement matrix. This matrix aids the platoon leader by detailing what TRPs each section can observe by position (primary, alternate, and supplementary). See Figure 4-8 in FM 3-20.151: The Mobile Gun System Platoon, for an example of a platoon fire plan. The company commander uses the platoons' fire plans to develop the company fire plan.

ADJACENT UNIT COORDINATION

5-123.   The goal of adjacent unit coordination is to ensure unity of effort in the accomplishment of the battalion mission. Items that adjacent units must coordinate include, but are not limited to, the following:

- Unit positions, including locations of command and control nodes.
- Locations of observation posts and patrols.
- Overlapping fires (to ensure that direct fire responsibility is clearly defined).
- Target reference points.
- Primary, alternate, and supplementary battle positions.
- Indirect fire and automated net control device (ANCD) information.
- Obstacles (location, orientation, and type).
- Exchange or confirm FBCB2 data.
- Air defense considerations, if applicable.
- Routes to be used during occupation and repositioning.
- Sustainment considerations.

Section IV. RETROGRADE OPERATIONS

Retrograde operations move friendly forces away from the enemy to gain time, preserve forces, place the enemy in unfavorable positions, or avoid combat under undesirable conditions. The enemy may force these operations or a commander may execute them voluntarily. In either case, the higher commander of the force executing the operation must approve the retrograde. Companies normally conduct retrogrades as part of a larger unit. The weapons company, along with the scout platoon, can greatly assist the execution of retrogrades by its maneuver advantages over the Infantry companies. It can move rapidly to a danger point and mass its fires onto an enemy that may be impeding the retrograde or attempting to conduct a maneuver to cut off the friendly force, such as an attack to the flank.

PURPOSE

5-124.   Retrograde operations accomplish the following.

- Resist, exhaust, and defeat enemy forces.
- Draw the enemy into an unfavorable situation.
- Avoid contact in undesirable conditions.
- Gain time.
- Disengage a force from battle for use elsewhere in other missions.
- Reposition forces, shorten lines of communication, or conform to movements of other friendly units.
- Secure more favorable terrain.

TYPES

5-125.   There are three types of retrograde operations: delay, withdrawal, and retirement.

DELAY

5-126.   This operation allows the unit to trade space for time, avoiding decisive engagement and safeguarding its elements. A delay is a series of defensive and offensive actions over subsequent positions in depth. It is an economy of force operation that trades space for time. While the enemy gains access to the vacated area (space), friendly elements have time to conduct necessary operations, while retaining freedom of action and maneuver. There are two types of delay missions: in an AO and forward of a specified line or position for a specified time. For either type of delay mission, the flow of the operation can be summarized as "hit hard, then move." Delay missions usually conclude in one of three ways: a defense, a withdrawal, or a counterattack. Planning options should address all three possibilities. A successful delay has three key components:

- The ability to stop or slow the enemy's momentum while avoiding decisive engagement.
- The ability to degrade the enemy's combat power.
- The ability to maintain a mobility advantage.

Weapons Company Role in Delay Operations

5-127.   The weapons company has a major subordinate role during retrograde operations. It can:

- With its long-range weapons and ability to mass fires, maintain the distance between the two forces and prevent decisive engagement, a key objective for the delay.
- Counter enemy threats through its rapid movement through the AO.
- Maneuver between the enemy and the rifle companies and, because of its armor, be protected from small arms fire.

5-128.   The battalion commander may task organize some of his Infantry companies by the attaching weapons platoons. Based on a METT-TC analysis, he may want to retain the bulk of the weapons company under battalion control to conduct attack or support by fire missions. Any attachments to the weapons company should have equal mobility.

5-129.   The area through which an Infantry battalion delays may be close terrain and not very trafficable to wheeled or armored vehicles. This will also affect the mobility of the vehicles in the weapons company.

WITHDRAWAL

5-130.   The commander uses this operation to break enemy contact, especially when he needs to free the unit for a new mission. Withdrawal is a planned operation in which a force in contact disengages from an enemy force. Withdrawals may or may not be conducted under enemy pressure. The two types of withdrawals are assisted and unassisted:

Assisted

5-131.   The assisting force occupies positions to the rear of the withdrawing unit and prepares to accept control of the operation. It can also assist the withdrawing unit with route reconnaissance, route maintenance, fire support, and sustainment. Both forces closely coordinate the withdrawal. After coordination, the withdrawing unit delays to a battle handover line, conducts a passage of lines, and moves to its final destination.

Unassisted

5-132. The withdrawing unit establishes routes and develops plans for the withdrawal and then establishes a security force as the rear guard while the main body withdraws. Sustainment and mobility and protection elements normally withdraw first followed by combat forces. To deceive the enemy as to the friendly movement, battalion may establish a detachment left in contact (DLIC) if withdrawing under enemy pressure. As the unit withdraws, the DLIC disengages from the enemy and follows the main body to its final destination.

5-133. Withdrawals are accomplished in three overlapping phases:

- Preparation. The commander dispatches quartering parties, issues warning orders, and initiates planning. Nonessential vehicles are moved to the rear.
- Disengagement. Designated elements begin movement to the rear. They break contact and conduct tactical movement to a designated assembly area or position.
- Security. A security force protects and assists the other elements as they disengage or move to their new positions. This is done either by a DLIC, which the unit itself designates in an unassisted withdrawal, or by a security force provided by the higher headquarters in an assisted withdrawal. As necessary, the security force assumes responsibility for the AO, deceives the enemy, and protects the movement of disengaged elements by providing overwatch and suppressive fires. The weapons company can provides this overwatch force. In an assisted withdrawal, the security phase ends when the security force has assumed responsibility for the fight and the withdrawing element has completed its movement. In an unassisted withdrawal, this phase ends when the DLIC completes its disengagement and movement to the rear.

5-134. In an unassisted battalion withdrawal, the DLIC may consist of an element from each company (under leadership of the company XO or a platoon leader), with the battalion S-3 as the overall DLIC commander. As an alternative, a company may serve as the DLIC for the rest of the battalion. The company commander has several deployment options. He can reposition elements across the entire battalion frontage. Another option is to position the company to cover only the most dangerous enemy avenues of approach; other avenues into the AO are covered with observation from additional security elements provided by the battalion such as the reconnaissance platoon.

5-135. In an assisted battalion withdrawal, the higher headquarters will normally provide a security element to maintain contact with and deceive the enemy while the battalion conducts its withdrawal. The security force establishes defensive positions behind the withdrawing unit and conducts preparations for a rearward passage of lines. The withdrawing force disengages from the enemy and conducts the rearward passage through the security force to assembly areas in the rear.

RETIREMENT

5-136. This operation is employed to move a force that is not in contact away from the enemy. Typically, the weapons company conducts a retirement as part of a larger force while another unit's security force protects their movement. A retiring unit organizes for combat but does not anticipate interference by enemy ground forces. Triggers for a retirement may include the requirement to reposition forces for future operations or to accommodate other changes to the current concept of operations. The retiring unit should move sustainment elements and supplies first, and then should move toward an assembly area that supports preparations for the next mission. Where speed and security are the most important considerations, units conduct retirements as tactical road marches.

This page intentionally left blank.

Chapter 6

Stability Operations

Stability operations are operations that restore, establish, preserve, or exploit security and control over areas, populations, and resources. In contrast to Civil Support operations, Stability operations are executed outside the United States. Stability operations involve a wide range of both coercive and cooperative actions that shape the political environment and respond to developing crises. Coercive military actions involve the application of limited, carefully prescribed force, or the threat of force, to achieve specific objectives. Cooperative actions are aimed at enhancing a government's willingness and ability to care for its people, or simply providing humanitarian relief following a natural disaster. Both of these types of operations are designed to help establish a safe and secure environment, facilitate reconciliation among local or regional adversaries, establish political, legal, social, and economic institutions, and facilitate the transition to legitimate local governance. Army forces engaged in stability operations establish or restore basic civil functions and protect them until the host nation is capable of providing these services themselves. Stability operations may occur in conjunction with offensive and defensive operations and are often diverse, continuous, noncontiguous and long-term. For more detailed information on stability operations, see FM 3-21.10 and FM 3-0.

Section I. OVERVIEW

Stability operations typically occur in conjunction with either offensive or defensive operations in foreign countries. They may be the decisive operation within a phase of a campaign or major combat operation. Although military forces set the conditions for success, the ultimate goal is to transition to where the other instruments of power predominate.

PURPOSES

6-1.   The purposes of stability operations are to assist foreign nations in a number of areas including to--

- Protect national interests.
- Promote peace and deter aggression.
- Satisfy treaty obligations or enforce agreements and policies.
- Reassure allies, friendly governments, and agencies.
- Maintain or restore order.
- Protect life and property.
- Demonstrate resolve.
- Prevent, deter, or respond to terrorism.
- Reduce the threat of conventional arms and weapons of mass destruction (WMD) to regional security.
- Protect freedom from oppression, subversion, lawlessness, and insurgency.
- Promote sustainable and responsive institutions.

TYPES

6-2.   Stability operations typically fall into five broad types that are neither discrete nor mutually exclusive. These are:

CIVIL SECURITY

6-3.   Protecting the populace from external and internal threats.

CIVIL CONTROL

6-4.   Regulating the behavior and activity of individuals and groups to reduce risk to individuals or groups and to promote security. Control channels the population's activity to allow for the provision of security and essential services while coexisting with a military force conducting operations. A curfew is an example of civil control.

PROVISION OF ESSENTIAL SERVICES

6-5.   Essential services include emergency life-saving medical care, the prevention of epidemic disease, provision of food and water, provision of emergency shelter from the elements, and the provision of basic sanitation (sewage and garbage disposal).

GOVERNANCE

6-6.   The provision of societal control functions that include regulation of public activity, rule of law, taxation, maintenance of security, control and essential services, normalizing means of succession of power.

SUPPORT TO ECONOMIC AND INFRASTRUCTURE DEVELOPMENT

6-7.   Direct and indirect military assistance to local, regional, and national economic and infrastructure development to provide an indigenous capacity and capability for continued economic and infrastructure development.

6-8.   Within each of these categories, units may be involved in a wide variety of missions. The actions they conduct within these missions will also vary. While certain actions may more likely be associated with a particular type of operation, many actions may be conducted within several or all of the operations. The characteristics of the Infantry weapons company may lend it to being assigned missions and actions that capitalize on their mobility, enhanced optics, weapons, communications, and transportation assets.

Section II. CAPABILITIES AND EMPLOYMENT

Stability operations are complex and demanding. The Infantry weapons company must master a wide variety of skills such as negotiating, establishing checkpoints and escorting convoys. This section includes employment considerations for some of the actions that could benefit from weapons company capabilities.

CAPABILITIES

6-9.   The Infantry weapons company is uniquely equipped with capabilities that can aid in the execution of many actions pertaining to stability operations. These additional capabilities may likely lead to assigning the weapons company specific actions that employ their unique assets and capitalize on their added contribution. Additional capabilities include, but are not limited to, weapons assets, transportation capability, increased mobility, increased observation with enhanced optics during limited visibility conditions, and increased communications assets. Examples of how these capabilities may be employed include--

- Weapons
    - -- Use in civil security, control and governance
    - -- Show of force
    - -- Protection of personnel, equipment and supplies
- Transportation
    - -- Assistance in food and water distribution in support of relief operations
    - -- Vehicle support for moving displaced civilians or other supplies
- Mobility
    - -- Mounted patrols
    - -- Rapid response to threats
    - -- Escorts
- Enhanced Optics
    - -- Security and Protection
    - -- Observation posts
    - -- Night operations
- Communications assets
    - -- Operations communications support
    - -- Communications relay assistance
    - -- Information distribution

EMPLOYMENT

6-10.   The weapons company commander may be required to perform a wide variety of actions to support stability operations. Depending on the type and nature of the overall mission, task requirements may come with specific execution guidelines. Rules of engagement (ROE) will often dictate conduct requirements while executing these actions. Regardless of the specific missions and actions assigned to the weapons company, units should keep in mind that the ultimate goal is to restore, establish, preserve, or exploit security and control to an area or population and its resources. The weapons company will often be assigned missions that capitalize on its unique capabilities. Some of the more common actions that employ these capabilities include the following. For a more detailed explanation see FM 3-21.10, FM 3-21.20, FM 3-21.11 and FM 3-21.91:

ESTABLISH AN OBSERVATION POST

6-11.   Constructing and operating observation posts (OP) is a high-frequency task for Infantry units and subordinate elements whenever they must establish area security. Each OP is established for a specified time and purpose. Some OPs are overt (clearly visible) and deliberately constructed. Others are covert and designed to observe an area or target without the knowledge of the local population. Each type of OP must be integrated into supporting direct and indirect fire plans and into the overall observation plan. Based on mission, enemy, terrain, troops, time, civilians (METT-TC) factors, deliberate and overt OPs may include specialized facilities such as--

- Observation towers.
- Ammunition and fuel storage areas.
- Power sources.
- Supporting helipads.
- Billeting, food service, and sanitation areas.

6-12.   During establishment of OPs, Infantry weapons companies will not only capitalize on the increase in limited visibility operations but also the use of heavy weapons assets. The optics for the Improved Target Acquisition System (ITAS), the target acquisition system (TAS) an integrated day/night sight, and Javelin's command launch unit (CLU) may be used to enhance the unit's observation ability during daylight or limited visibility conditions. This proves to be a tremendous asset for establishing observation posts. The weapons systems provide for defensive measures and, in the case of overt OPs, help establish a sense of deterrence for aggressive behavior. Weapons may be either vehicular or ground-mounted depending on the type and permanence of the OP. Additionally, since the weapons company has more heavy weapons than vehicles, the capability exists to ground mount and vehicle mount weapons simultaneously. However, leaders must take into account the time needed to collect ground-mounted systems in the event of a quick displacement.

ACT AS A MOUNTED QUICK REACTION FORCE

6-13.   A quick reaction force (QRF) is a designated organization for any immediate response requirement that occurs in a designated area of operation. In contrast to a unit designated as a reserve, a QRF is not committed to support one particular mission but rather is on-call to respond to a multitude of contingencies within an operational area. An Infantry weapons company is uniquely equipped to act as a mounted QRF. It has organic vehicles for rapid mobility and protection, a mix of automatic heavy weapons for firepower, communications assets for operational control, and the ability to better operate in limited visibility conditions. However, these units are limited in their ability to conduct dismounted operations once arriving at the site. If transportation is available, an Infantry element may be attached to the mounted QRF...

ESCORT A CONVOY

6-14.   This mission requires a unit to provide a convoy with security and close-in protection from direct fire while on the move. If given this mission, Infantry rifle companies must be augmented with additional transportation assets. On the other hand, Infantry weapons companies with their organic vehicles have the mobility and firepower to perform this mission without augmentation.

6-15.   In any escort operation, the basic mission of the convoy commander (and, as applicable, the convoy security commander) is to establish and maintain security in all directions and throughout the length of the convoy. He must be prepared to move the security force to fit the situation. Several factors apply, including convoy size, organization, and composition. Sometimes, he positions the security elements, such as platoons, to the front, rear, or flanks of the convoy. He may also disperse the combat vehicles throughout the convoy body. The convoy commander often organizes the convoy security into three distinct elements: advance guard, close-in protective group, and rear guard.

6-16.   The weapons company is well equipped to react to contact while performing a convoy escort mission. Contact usually occurs in the form of an ambush, often executed at a hasty obstacle. The safety of the convoy rests on the speed and effectiveness with which escort elements can execute appropriate actions on contact. Based on the factors of METT-TC, portions of the convoy security force might be designated as a reaction force. This element performs its normal escort duties, such as conducting tactical movement or occupying an assembly area, unless enemy contact occurs. Upon contact, it performs a reaction mission given by the convoy commander. The mix of weapons systems gives the convoy commander the option of creating a mix of vehicular mounted heavy weapons based on METT-TC conditions.

ESTABLISH A CORDON

6-17.   The establishment of a cordon is normally in conjunction with a cordon and search mission unless task organized with Infantry platoons. Due to the number of resources required for an effective cordon and search, the mission is often given to a battalion size element. In this respect, the weapons company will most likely be given all or part of the task of establishing the cordon. The inherent characteristics of the company make it ideal for establishing the cordon. Infantry rifle companies will often perform the search with the weapons company and other elements providing the cordon for security and protection.

6-18.   The cordon and search mission centers on an objective area with a limited degree of information regarding the exact location of what is sought, usually personnel, equipment, weapons etc. A cordon and search usually, but not always, takes a large amount of time due to the unknown nature of actual locations of personnel or items.

6-19.   In establishing a cordon, two cordons may be established: the outer cordon to focus on isolating the objective from outside, and the inner cordon to focus on keeping individuals from escaping the objective area. However, both cordon elements must focus both inward and outward for security purposes. Emplacement of these cordon elements may occur simultaneously or sequentially. Although more difficult to control, the use of limited visibility aids in the establishment and security of the cordon. The weapons company enhanced optics greatly assist with this task. Figure 6-1 shows an example of the establishment of inner and outer cordon.

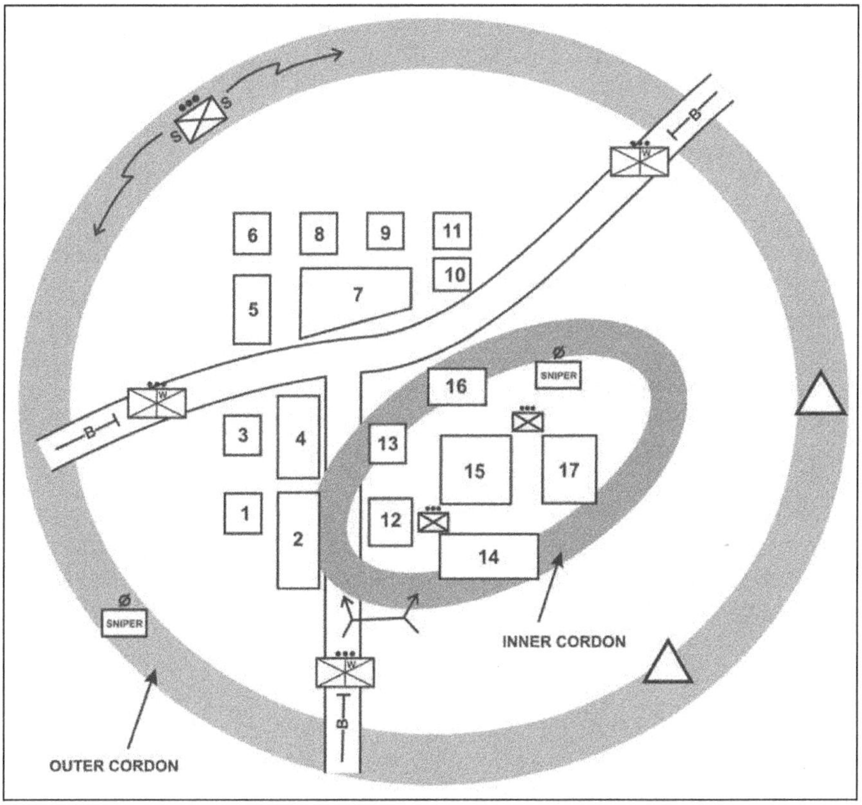

Figure 6-1. Establishment of a cordon.

Outer Cordon

6-20.   The outer cordon is an integral part of the security element in any cordon and search operation. It requires detailed planning, effective coordination, and meticulous integration and synchronization to achieve the combined arms effects. Both lethal and nonlethal effects should be considered by the commander.

6-21.   Each subordinate outer cordon element (traffic control point or blocking position) must have a designated leader and a clear task and purpose. Units and elements to consider for establishing the outer cordon include--

- Weapons company.
- Assault platoons.
- Weapons squads.
- Sniper teams.

6-22.   The security element of the outer cordon may include the following:

- Vehicle mounted platoons or sections.
- Interpreter(s).
- Detainee security teams.
- Crowd control teams.
- Observation posts.
- Traffic control points or blocking positions.
- Host nation security forces (military or police).
- Aviation.
- Dismounted platoons or squads.
- Female search teams.

Inner Cordon

6-23.   The inner cordon may be under the control of the security element of the search element. It is normally tasked with the following actions:

- Preventing exfiltration or reposition of threat forces.
- Serving as a support by fire force for search teams.
- Maintaining communications with the search element.
- Understanding the marking system and control measures.
- Seizing supporting structures in built-up areas to overwatch target area buildings

ESTABLISH A CHECKPOINT

6-24.   A common mission during stability operations is a vehicle or traffic checkpoint. In recent operations, checkpoints have been used so often that through repetitive execution units can perform them virtually like battle drills.

Purposes

6-25.   Checkpoints may be established to--

- Obtain intelligence.
- Identify enemy combatants or seize illegal weapons.
- Disrupt enemy movement or actions.
- Deter illegal movement.
- Create an instant or temporary roadblock.
- Control movement into the area of operations or onto a specific route.
- Demonstrate the presence of US or peace forces.
- Prevent smuggling of contraband.
- Enforce the terms of peace agreements.
- Serve as an OP, patrol base, or both.

Types

6-26.   Checkpoints may be established for many reasons including one or more of the purposes listed above. Based on the purpose for establishing the checkpoint and METT-TC conditions checkpoints may be established using one of the common types listed below.

- Deliberate Checkpoints.
    -- Permanent or semipermanent.
    -- May be classified as heavy or light traffic.
    -- Used to protect an operating base, well-established main supply route, critical intersections.
    -- Complete or random searches.
- Hasty Checkpoints.
    -- Used only for a short, set period.
    -- Employed during the conduct of a patrol.
    -- Only uses transportable materials.
    -- Can be quickly positioned where needed.
    -- May be conducted when specific intelligence indicates that a checkpoint hinders the enemy's freedom of movement at a specific time and place.

6-27.   Many checkpoint operations require a highly mobile unit for employment. The organic vehicles in a weapons company suit it perfectly for these type checkpoint operations.

Secure a Route

6-28.   This task is a combined arms operation normally conducted with engineer support. The Infantry weapons company might be tasked to assist in route security and to provide overwatch support. Route clearance may achieve one of several tactical purposes.

- To clear a route for the initial entry of the battalion into an area of operations.
- To clear a route ahead of a planned convoy to ensure that belligerent elements have not emplaced new obstacles since the last time the route was cleared.
- To secure the route for use as a main supply route.

6-29.   While Infantry rifle companies are sometimes tasked for any portion of this mission, the weapons company portion will often be to provide security for the route rather than assist in route clearance. Depending on METT-TC, security may be performed in a combination of ways. Often security procedures resemble those of a convoy escort but may also include setting up static or mobile overwatch positions. The weapons company is both mobile and equipped with heavy weapons for overwatching fires making it ideally suited for this mission.

Conduct a Patrol

6-30.   Patrolling is also a high-frequency task during stability operations. Patrols help to add security, aid in information gathering and provide for a strong presence in an operation area. Security and presence patrols usually occur in urban areas and leaders must be aware of the ROE and the purpose of the patrol.

6-31.   Urban terrain provides multiple opportunities for attack against patrols in the stability environment. The locations of enemy firing points can be concealed by building characteristics, vehicles, civilian population, and noise. The patrol must therefore have a through understanding of reactionary procedures based on their standing operating procedure (SOP), METT-TC and ROE. An attack is normally initiated on a patrol only when the attacker has an open escape route. This emphasizes the need react quickly and if conditions exist that call for aggressive action.

6-32.   US forces are deployed increasingly in combat operations in urban areas and in support of stability operations missions all around the world. The Infantry weapons company would conduct these patrols to show force and lend confidence and stability to the local population of the host nation. Rarely should a commander use a presence patrol where enemy contact is likely. Although the weapons company will be a mounted element, it may be employed with or without dismounted troops. Either way, vehicular-based personnel are not precluded from interfacing with the local populace. The presence patrol is a primary means by which leaders collect information about the area of operations (AO). Interface with local civilians provides much of the valuable information. The presence patrol is often used to--

- Confirm or supervise an agreed cease-fire.
- Gain information.
- Cover gaps between OPs or checkpoints.
- Show a stability force presence.
- Reassure isolated communities.
- Inspect existing or vacated positions of former belligerents.
- Escort former belligerents or local populations through trouble spots.

6-33.   Infantry weapons units may find themselves conducting frequent patrols during stability operations. Leaders should consider the following if assigned a patrolling mission:

- Organize and orient vehicle gunners and commanders to maintain all-round security
- Rehearse battle drills
- Plan alternate routes, civilian traffic, and roadblocks
- Plan actions for disabled or destroyed vehicles
- Configure vehicles for optimal observation and select weapons systems for firepower
- Consider positioning of weapons
- Harden unarmored vehicles
- Establish a communications plan
- Secure external gear to prevent theft and inspect it to ensure it is not flammable
- Plan for heavy civilian vehicle and pedestrian traffic
- Conduct a map reconnaissance and identify likely chokepoints, ambush sites and overpasses.
- Plan primary and alternate routes to avoid potential hazards

SUPPORT RELIEF OPERATIONS

6-34.   Providing support during relief operations in a foreign country is very similar to conducting civil support operations in the US. Both involve using the Army to respond with a wide array of capabilities and services to aid authorities in the following types of actions.

- Protecting public health.
- Restoring public order.
- Assisting in disaster recovery.
- Alleviating large-scale suffering.
- Protecting critical infrastructure.

6-35.   Examples of how these capabilities may be employed include--

- Transportation
  -- Assistance in food, fuel, water, clothing and blanket distribution
  -- Vehicle support for personnel and other supplies
  -- Medical evacuation assistance
- Mobility
  -- Transport capability to remote areas
  -- Assistance in rapid assessments of large areas
  -- Assistance with verbal or written information distribution

- Enhanced Optics
  - -- Security
  - -- Search and rescue
  - -- Personnel and civil disturbance control
- Communications assets
  - -- Operations communications support
  - -- Communications relay assistance
  - -- Information distribution

CONTROL CROWDS

6-36.   Hostile crowds or disturbances pose a threat to US troops that are conducting relief operations. Commanders must consider the effects of mob mentality, the willingness of enemies to manipulate media, and the ease with which a small, isolated group of Soldiers can be overwhelmed by masses of people. The police forces of each state and territory are normally responsible for controlling crowds involved in mass demonstrations, industrial, political and social disturbances, riots, and other civil disturbances. The prime role of US troops in the control of unlawful assemblies or demonstrations is to support and protect the police, innocent bystanders, and property. The troops will only use force as a last resort to disperse the crowd or prevent its advancing past a given point or line.

6-37.   Often, isolating a hostile crowd from peaceful civilians and key facilities is a sufficient means to control the disturbance. This isolation should prevent reinforcement of demonstrators and prevent the disturbance from moving. Although complete isolation is probably unlikely, roadblocks, checkpoints, or even a cordon can help. As stated earlier, the Infantry weapons company is ideally suited to conduct these missions. They may be required to employ them to varying degrees based on the immediate situation and other METT-TC factors. Unit SOPs, the ROE and agreements with civil authorities will all play a part in determining what action can and will be taken in response to large crowds and riots.

Section III. ESCALATION OF FORCE

During the conduct of stability operations, a myriad of complex circumstances, actions and events can evolve sometimes making the mission demanding and difficult to control. Units must not only understand specific task procedures but also the overall mission purpose. Circumstances may often arise that call for the use of force, whether slight, lethal or anywhere in between. The determination of what type and how much force to use can be confusing if all personnel are not trained on the proper execution of employing force during stability operations. Escalation of force (EOF) is the process of determining force level(s) to be used in reaction to a particular incident. The quick determination of what type of force should be applied within those guidelines remains with the leaders and individuals confronted with any particular incident.

OVERVIEW

6-38.   EOF is a term used to describe a process that friendly forces use in making a determination of a level of response and the response itself to an incident. An incident may be presented in a variety of ways that involve some form of contact with a threat or a potential threat to friendly forces. EOF centers on the use of a proportionate amount of force needed to achieve a desired effect without endangering friendly personnel. If the desired effect is not achieved, the EOF process includes a graduating the response by increased means of force until the desired effect is met. It is not a step-by-step process but rather a range of options. Its purpose is to provide a common concept basis that helps enable Soldiers to make quick decisions to protect themselves and other unit members, while preventing unnecessary deaths and collateral damage during the application of force.

6-39. EOF supports, but is different than, ROE. ROE are directives issued by a competent military authority to delineate the circumstance and limitations under which its own naval, ground and air forces will initiate and/or continue combat engagement with other forces encountered.

6-40. Key EoF concepts include--

- Leaders and Soldiers must continually train and rehearse EOF procedures
- Soldiers are never limited in actions of self-defense
- All Soldiers must understand how EOF supports ROE and the difference between the two
- Leaders must plan and prepare for EOF prior to an operation
- Units must be resourced with the proper equipment and intelligence information to implement EOF
- Leaders and Soldiers must understand EOF principles and possible strategic impacts of EOF incidents

6-41. The ultimate goal is to properly train and equip Soldiers at all levels to apply EOF principles to prevent unnecessary deadly force engagements. This will build and reinforce a positive image of military forces with the local Nationals and other noncombatants.

GUIDELINES AND PRINCIPLES

6-42. All uses of force should be necessary, proportional and reasonable in intensity, duration and magnitude based on the perceived threat. The general guidelines for the employment of EOF are:

- De-escalate the incident. When time and circumstances permit, the forces committing hostile acts or demonstrating hostile intent should be warned and given the opportunity to withdraw or cease their threatening actions.
- Determine the necessity of employing force. When a hostile act occurs, or when hostile intent is demonstrated, a determination of the use of force may be made and force applied while the force continues the acts or intent.
- Act in proportionality. The use of force in self-defense is often a sufficient response to hostile acts or demonstrations of hostile intent. Such use of force may exceed the means and intensity of the hostile act or intent but the nature, duration and scope of force used should not exceed what is required.
- When time and circumstances allow, use a gradual EOF with the means available.
- If use of deadly force is warranted, always get a positive identification of the target and use aimed fire.

6-43. Below is list of EOF principles in the form of graduated measures for use in response to hostile acts or demonstrations of hostile intent. These principles may be printed on a Soldiers card for individual reference. There is no requirement to use all the measures in order. Each circumstance will often be unique and the selection of type of force applied may graduate with some or all of the measures listed while others may require the immediate use of deadly force. EOF principles do not apply to declared hostile forces.

- Display a visual warning such as a sign, spotlight, or laser.
- Sound an audible warning, for example, shout, or use a bullhorn or air horn.
- Show weapon and demonstrate the intent to use it.
- Block access using a physical barrier or spike strips, for example.
- Physically detain the person.
- Fire a warning shot, if authorized.
- Fire disabling shots at tires or engine block, for example.
- Engage with deadly force.

6-44. Units will often prepare a leader's card with EOF measures and procedures outlined for reference. However, all personnel should be trained and familiar with the procedures since events often require the application of a quick decision. An example of a leaders EOF card is shown below in Figure 6-2.

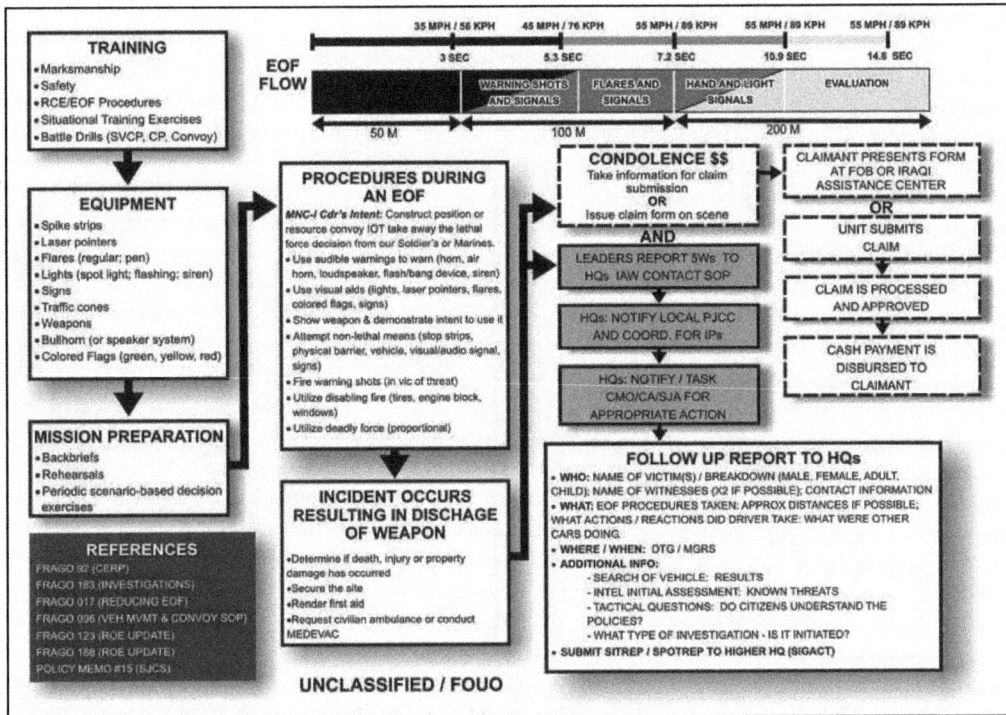

Figure 6-2. EOF leader's card.

6-45. The following situation is an example of the use of EOF. Since each situation is unique within its own operational context, this example is an application of how EOF may be used and not how it must be employed:

SITUATION: A platoon from the weapons company has been tasked to provide a four-vehicle roadblock on a high-speed avenue of approach, in support of a Cordon and Search mission. During the conduct of the operation, one of the guards identifies a vehicle traveling at an unusually slow speed coming towards the cordon from the north.

ACTION: The vehicle arrives at the alert line

REACTION: A guard attempts to use hand and arm signals to stop the vehicle

ACTION: Vehicle passes the alert line, and speed bumps

REACTION: A guard uses visual and audio tools i.e. lasers, floodlights, bullhorns, sirens, etc. in an attempt to stop the vehicle

ACTION: Vehicle ignores the signals and drives over the stop sticks

REACTION: Guards escalate to disabling shots and/or deadly force. It is reasonable to assume this driver has shown hostile intent; therefore, deadly force is authorized.

This page intentionally left blank.

Chapter 7

Civil Support Operations

Civil support operations are actions that assist domestic civil authorities in providing essential supplies and services to control disease and alleviate suffering, restoring civil order, or helping people and communities recover from disasters. The ultimate goal of civil support operations is to meet the immediate crisis, and then to transfer responsibility quickly and efficiently back to the appropriate civilian authorities. For more information on Civil Support Operations see FM 3-21.20, The Infantry Battalion.

Section I. OVERVIEW

The US military provides civil support based on a DoD directive for military assistance to civil authorities. Such a directive normally addresses both natural and manmade disasters. It can direct military aid in civil disturbances, counterdrug and counterterrorism activities, law enforcement, and management of consequences associated with weapons of mass destruction (WMD).

PURPOSES

7-1.   The US active duty military is limited by the Posse Comitatus Act (PCA) and other legislation in the actions it can take in within the US and its territories. Under PCA, Army forces do not conduct stability operations within the United States, but we do conduct civil support operations. Normally, for US armed forces to conduct offensive and defensive operations inside the US and its territories, the President must do two things. First, he must identify a significant armed force that threatens the territorial integrity of the US. Second, he must declare a national emergency.

7-2.   Only then can jointly commanded Army forces conduct, in accordance with (IAW) Chapter 4, *Offensive Operations* and Chapter 5, *Defensive Operations*, offensive and defensive Homeland Security missions.

7-3.   The fundamental rule in employing military forces in civil support operations is to recognize that civil authorities have the primary authority and responsibility for domestic operations. When so authorized, Army forces conduct civil support operations, providing Army resources, expertise, and capabilities in support of the lead agency. This expertise and capability is limited to supporting civil authorities and law enforcement agencies, and to preventing civil disturbance. Civil support may include circumstances that require the conduct of offensive and defensive operations in order to return the affected population to a state of normalcy.

7-4.   Significant legal and constitutional issues arise when military forces are committed to combat operations within the US. Differences exist between the actions that active duty forces, federalized reserve component forces, and National Guard forces are authorized to perform. Commanders and leaders at all levels must ensure they clearly understand the guidelines and rules of engagement established by the President and his legal representatives.

7-5.   Leaders must keep their Soldiers informed on the situation and on guidance from higher headquarters. The Infantry company will encounter various units and organizations classified by certain titles under US Code that may affect command and control relationships. Civil authorities may need to be told what each can and cannot do.

- National Guard, in its role as the state militia, can be called to respond as state active duty (SAD) under the command of the governor.
- Title 32 says that National Guard on full time status can be moved from SAD to Title 32.
- Title 10 applies to Active duty military units, including active Guard and Reserve.
- Title 14 applies to the US Coast Guard.

7-6.   In disaster relief, the Infantry weapons company becomes a force provider. As such, it supplements the efforts and resources of state and local governments, and possibly those of nongovernmental organizations, within the United States. During civil support operations, the US military responds in support of civilian agencies and may receive guidance and instructions from civil authorities through their assigned chain of command. These include responding to civil emergencies or major disasters. A presidential declaration of an emergency or disaster usually precedes the Army's commitment to civil support operations, but in cases of extreme emergency, it may follow the initial actions. Regardless of the relationship between the civil authorities and the military, the fundamental elements and responsibilities of military command do not change. A representative of the civil authority does not, except in some specific and rare circumstances, exercise command over military forces.

7-7.   The US Constitution mandates that the civilian government is responsible for preserving public order. However, the Constitution also allows military forces to protect federal and civilian property and functions. The Posse Comitatus Act restricts the use of the military in civilian law enforcement except in the role of supporting or technical assistance.

7-8.   Federal military forces remain under the military chain of command while supporting civil law enforcement. The supported law enforcement agency coordinates Army force activities under appropriate civil laws and interagency agreements. Army and Air National Guard units that have not been federalized can assist civil authorities when active duty federal units cannot under the provisions of the Posse Comitatus Act.

TYPES

7-9.   Civil support involves using the Army to respond with a wide array of capabilities and services to aid civil authorities in the following types of actions:

- Protecting public health.
- Restoring public order.
- Assisting in disaster recovery.
- Alleviating large-scale suffering.
- Protecting critical infrastructure.

Civil support operations are varied and unpredictable. The Infantry weapons company must adaptable to a wide variety of unconventional actions that may arise during civil support operations. This section includes employment considerations for some of the actions that could benefit from weapons company capabilities.

CAPABILITIES

7-10.   In contrast to an Infantry rifle company, the weapons company is uniquely equipped with additional capabilities that may aid in the execution of certain civil support actions. While the mission remains the same, these additional capabilities may lead to assigning specific actions to the weapons company that employ their unique assets. Additional capabilities include, but are not limited to, increased transportation capability, increased mobility, increased assets in observation with enhanced optics during limited visibility conditions, and increased communications assets. Examples of how these capabilities may be employed include--

- Transportation
  -- Assistance in food, fuel, water, clothing and blanket distribution
  -- Vehicle support for personnel and other supplies
  -- Medical evacuation assistance
- Mobility
  -- Transport capability to remote areas
  -- Assistance in rapid assessments of large areas
  -- Assistance with verbal or written information distribution
- Enhanced Optics
  -- Security
  -- Search and rescue
  -- Personnel and civil disturbance control
- Communications assets
  -- Operations communications support
  -- Communications relay assistance
  -- Information distribution

EMPLOYMENT

7-11.   The weapons company commander cannot predict the exact actions his unit might have to perform during civil support operations. Infantry units must often perform nonstandard actions during national and local emergencies. Civil support operations respond to requests for help with protection and restoration. Typically, these include riots or widespread disorder; forest and grassland fires; hazardous material releases; and floods, storms, hurricanes, tornados, and earthquakes.

7-12.   State, local, and federal authorities are responsible for restoring essential services in the case of a disaster. Army forces may support their efforts. Disaster relief focuses on recovery of critical infrastructure after a natural or manmade disaster. Both humanitarian and disaster relief normally occur simultaneously. The most common civil support actions the Infantry weapons company may encounter include--

- Search and rescue of survivors.
- Recovery of human remains.
- Disposal of animal carcasses.
- Disinfection and sanitation.
- Debris and trash removal.
- Riot and civil disturbance control.

- Police augmentation.
- Food and ice distribution.
- Fuel distribution.
- Contamination containment.
- Personnel movement and control.
- Key facilities protection.
- Vital services assessment.
- Medical triage and treatment.
- Emergency fire fighting.
- Emergency flood control.
- Hazard identification.
- Water purification and distribution.
- Temporary shelter construction and administration.
- Transportation support.
- Power generation.
- Communications support.
- Clothing and blanket distribution.
- Information distribution.
- Medical evacuation coordination.
- Operations coordination.
- Observation posts.
- Checkpoints and roadblocks.

7-13.   Since the actions the weapons company may be required to perform during civil support operations vary widely, a detailed discussion of employment of weapons company capabilities in support of possible actions is not warranted. Leaders and authorities will analyze the missions to be performed with the units available to perform them and assign actions to individual units that will best accomplish the mission. The weapons company must remain flexible and adaptive in their response to the missions they may be assigned during civil support operations. While the unit will often be selected for missions that employ their enhanced mobility, visibility, communications and transportation assets, leaders and personnel must also realize they may be assigned other actions that do not necessarily capitalize on those capabilities. For a further discussion of these actions see FM 3-21.10 and FM 3-21.20.

Chapter 8

Tactical Enabling Operations

The commander conducts tactical enabling operations to assist the planning, preparation, and execution of any of the four types of military operations. Tactical enabling operations are either shaping or sustaining. This chapter describes how the weapons company commander conducts tactical enabling operations independently or as part of the battalion.

Section I. RECONNAISSANCE

Reconnaissance is any mission undertaken to get information about the activities and resources of enemy forces or the physical characteristics of a particular area, using visual observation or other methods. Successful reconnaissance is a focused collection effort, aimed at gathering timely and accurate information about the enemy and the terrain in the area of operations. All commanders have the requirement to gain the information he needs to ensure the success of his mission. The weapons company may conduct reconnaissance operations to gather information for his unit, other units, or as directed by a higher headquarters. For a more detailed discussion of reconnaissance operations, see FM 3-20.98. This section discusses reconnaissance efforts in which the weapons company may be involved.

TYPES

8-1.   In addition to reconnaissance performed as part of another type of operation, three types of reconnaissance missions are conducted as distinct operations. These are the route, zone and area reconnaissance. The weapons company may often conduct a route reconnaissance for themselves or elements within the battalion. The weapons company, because of their inherent mobility, may be assigned to a zone or area reconnaissance mission. If involved in a zone or area reconnaissance, it will often be as a part of a larger scale mission rather than a separate mission of their own and may be attached to a reconnaissance unit. A brief explanation of the three types follows.

ROUTE RECONNAISSANCE

8-2.   A route reconnaissance is a directed effort to get detailed information on a specific route as well as on all terrain where the enemy could influence movement along that route. Route reconnaissance might be oriented on a specific area of movement, such as a road or trail, or on a more general area, like an axis of advance.

ZONE RECONNAISSANCE

8-3.   A zone reconnaissance is a directed effort to get detailed information about all routes, terrain, enemy forces, and obstacles, including areas of chemical, biological, radiological or nuclear (CBRN) contamination, within specified boundaries. The company may be a part of a zone reconnaissance when the enemy situation is vague, or when information about cross-country trafficability is needed. As in route reconnaissance, the commander's intent as well as mission, enemy, terrain, troops, time, civilians (METT-TC) dictates the company's actions.

AREA RECONNAISSANCE

8-4.   An area reconnaissance is a directed effort to get detailed information about the terrain or enemy activity within a prescribed area. The area can be any location that is critical to the unit's operations. Examples include easily identifiable areas covering fairly large spaces such as towns or military installations; terrain features such as ridge lines, wood lines, or choke points; or single points such as bridges or buildings. As with the zone reconnaissance, the weapons company may be involved in an area reconnaissance as a part of a larger operation and my be attached to another unit for this mission.

RECONNAISSANCE IN FORCE

8-5.   A reconnaissance in force is a deliberate combat operation designed to discover or test threat strength, disposition, and reaction, or to obtain other information. It is conducted when the threat is known to be operating within an area, but adequate intelligence cannot be obtained by other means. It is an aggressive reconnaissance, conducted as an offensive operation in pursuit of clearly stated information requirements. The overall goal of the operation is to determine threat weaknesses that can be exploited. The weapons company cannot conduct a reconnaissance in force independently. It can, however, participate in such an operation as part of a robust combined arms force. During a reconnaissance in force, the weapons company may be tasked to conducts zone, area, or route reconnaissance, or may conduct screening operations in support of the unit conducting a reconnaissance in force.

OPERATIONS

8-6.   In planning for route, zone, or area reconnaissance, the company commander determines the objective of the mission, and identifies whether the reconnaissance will orient on the terrain or on the enemy force. He provides the company with clear guidance on the objective of the reconnaissance. In a force-oriented reconnaissance operation, the critical task is to find the enemy and gather information on him; terrain considerations of the route, zone, or area are a secondary concern. The company is generally able to move more quickly in a force-oriented reconnaissance than in a terrain-oriented reconnaissance.

8-7.   To be most effective, reconnaissance must be continuous and conducted before, during, and after operations. Before an operation, the company focuses its reconnaissance effort to confirm or deny a possible course of action. After an operation, the company normally reconnoiters so it can maintain contact with the enemy, collect information for upcoming operations, and provide force protection and security.

8-8.   Situations in which the company may conduct reconnaissance before or after an operation include--

- Reconnaissance by a quartering party of an assembly area and the associated route to it.
- Reconnaissance before an offensive operation.
- Reconnaissance to probe enemy positions for gaps prior to an attack or infiltration.
- Reconnaissance to locate and/or observe enemy forward positions.
- Reconnaissance to locate bypasses around obstacle belts or to determine the best locations and methods for breaching operations.
- Reconnaissance of choke points or other danger areas in advance of the remainder of the company.
- Reconnaissance of defensive positions or engagement areas prior to the conduct of the defense.
- Reconnaissance as part of security operations to secure friendly obstacles, clear possible enemy observation posts (OP), or cover areas not observable by stationary OPs.
- Reconnaissance to maintain contact with adjacent units.
- Reconnaissance to maintain contact with enemy elements.

METHODS

8-9.   Infantry weapons companies involved in reconnaissance missions may conduct them in one of two ways. They often will be conducted through the employment of a patrol but certain types may also be accomplished through the use of a reconnaissance by fire.

RECONNAISSANCE BY PATROL

8-10.   Most reconnaissance is accomplished through the employment of patrols. (For a discussion of reconnaissance patrol operations see Section V.)

RECONNAISSANCE BY FIRE

8-11.   The focus of reconnaissance by fire is on the key terrain that dominates danger areas, on built-up areas that dominate the surrounding terrain, and on uncleared wooded areas. The reconnaissance by fire can be a planned or ordered action. The battalion commander may direct the company to execute reconnaissance by fire when enemy contact is expected, or when contact has occurred but the enemy situation is vague. Rules of engagement (ROE) will often dictate opportunities to use or not to use reconnaissance by fire. The platoon then conducts tactical movement, occupying successive overwatch positions until it makes contact with the enemy or reaches the objective.

8-12.   At each overwatch position, the leader must plan and develop direct fire control measures (DFCM) and fire support coordination measures (FSCM). Then he either requests indirect fires or employs direct fires on likely enemy locations. This forces the enemy force to return direct fire or to move, thus compromising its positions. The weapons leader then uses fire commands to control the fires of his unit. The machine guns can provide a heavy volume of fire at long range. If appropriate targets are sighted, then the close combat missile systems may also be used. The weapons leader usually observes and corrects the fires of his unit.

8-13.   A disciplined enemy force might not return fire, or might move if it determines that the pattern or type of fires employed will lethal. The leader must analyze the situation and direct the use of appropriate fires on suspected positions.

Section II. SPECIAL-PURPOSE OPERATIONS

This section discusses three special-purpose operations including passage of lines, relief in place, and linkup.

PASSAGE OF LINES

8-14.   Passage of lines occurs when one unit moves through the stationary positions of another, as part of a larger force. The weapons company participates in a passage of lines as part of the battalion. If it is part of the stationary force, the company occupies firing positions and assists the passing unit. If it is part of a passing unit, the company executes tactical movement through the stationary unit. A passage may be forward or rearward, depending on whether the passing unit is moving toward (forward) or away from (rearward) an enemy unit or area of operations.

PASSAGE LANES

8-15.   The passage should facilitate transition to follow-on missions through the use of multiple lanes or lanes wide enough to support doctrinal formations for the passing units.

USE OF DECEPTION

8-16.   The unit can use deception techniques, such as smoke (previously coordinated with the stationary unit and approved by the commander), to enhance security during the passage.

BATTLE HANDOVER

8-17.   The controlling higher commander must clearly define the battle handover criteria and procedures to be used during the passage. His order should cover the roles of both the passing unit and the stationary unit and the use of direct and indirect fires. He also specifies the location of the battle handover line (BHL) as part of the unit's graphic control measures. For a forward passage, the BHL is normally the line of departure (LD) for the passing force; in a rearward passage, it is normally a location within the direct fire range of the stationary force. In general, a defensive handover is complete when the passing unit is clear and the stationary unit is ready to engage the enemy. Offensive handover is complete when the passing unit has deployed and crossed the BHL.

OBSTACLES

8-18.   The passing and stationary units must coordinate obstacle information to include the locations of enemy and friendly obstacles, existing lanes and bypasses, and guides for the passage.

AIR DEFENSE

8-19.   Air defense coverage is imperative during the high-risk passage operation. The stationary unit normally is responsible for providing air defense, allowing the passing unit's air defense assets to move with it.

SUSTAINMENT RESPONSIBILITIES

8-20.   Responsibility for sustainment actions, such as vehicle recovery or casualty evacuation in the passage lane, must be defined clearly for both passing and stationary units.

COMMAND AND CONTROL

8-21.   To enhance command and control during the passage, the weapons company co-locates a command and control element with a similar element from the stationary or moving unit (as applicable).

OPERATIONAL CONSIDERATIONS

8-22.   Detailed reconnaissance and coordination are critical in ensuring that the passage of lines is conducted quickly and smoothly. The commander usually conducts all necessary reconnaissance and coordination for the passage. At times, he may designate the executive officer (XO), first sergeant, or a platoon leader to conduct liaison duties for reconnaissance and coordination. The following items of information are exchanged or coordinated. An asterisk indicates items that should be confirmed by reconnaissance.

- Unit designation and composition, including type and number of passing vehicles.
- Passing unit arrival time(s).
- Location of attack positions or assembly areas.*
- Current enemy situation.
- Stationary unit's mission and plan (to include OP, patrol, and obstacle locations).*
- Location of contact points, passage points, and passage lanes (NOTE: The use of global positioning system (GPS) waypoints will simplify this process and speed the passage.).*

- Guide requirements.
- Order of march.
- Anticipated and possible actions on enemy contact.
- Supporting direct and indirect fires, including location of any restrictive fire lines (RFLs).*
- CBRN conditions.
- Available support assets and their locations.*
- Communications information (to include frequencies, digital data, and near and far recognition signals).
- Chain of command, including location of the BHL.
- Additional procedures for the passage.
- Vulnerability of concentrated vehicles and decreased maneuverability.

FORWARD PASSAGE OF LINES

8-23.   In a forward passage, the passing unit first moves to an assembly area or an attack position behind the stationary unit. Designated liaison personnel move forward to link up with guides and confirm coordination information with the stationary unit. Guides then lead the passing elements through the passage lane.

8-24.   As the passing unit, the weapons company conducts tactical movement to maximize its battle space within the limitations of the passage lane. Radio traffic is kept to a minimum. Disabled vehicles are bypassed. The company holds its fire until it passes the BHL. Once clear of passage lane restrictions, the company conducts tactical movement in accordance with its orders.

REARWARD PASSAGE OF LINES

8-25.   Because of the increased chance of fratricide during a rearward passage, coordination of recognition signals and direct fire restrictions are critical. The passing unit contacts the stationary unit while it is still beyond direct fire range, and conducts coordination as discussed previously. RFLs and near recognition signals are emphasized.

8-26.   As the passing unit, the weapons company then continues tactical movement toward the passage lane. Weapons are oriented on the enemy, and the company is responsible for its security until it passes the RFL. Ideally, the passing unit moves through the passage lanes without stopping or stopping only long enough to pick up guides. The company then moves quickly through the passage lane to a designated location behind the stationary unit.

RELIEF IN PLACE

8-27.   A relief in place occurs when one unit assumes the mission of another unit. It may occur during offensive operations or during defensive operations, preferably during periods of limited visibility. There are two methods by which to conduct a relief in place:

- Simultaneous. All elements are relieved simultaneously.
- Sequential. The relief takes place one element at a time (by individual vehicle or by groups of vehicles).

8-28.   The weapons company follows the same procedures for a relief in place during combat as does an Infantry company (Chapter 8, FM 3-21.10).

8-29.   Often during stability operations and civil support operations, a relief in place is referred to as a transfer of authority. In addition to the normal responsibilities of a relief, commanders must also deal with civilians or coalition partners. The departing unit often develops a continuity book that includes lessons learned, details about the populace, village and patrol reports, updated maps, and photographs; anything that helps follow-on units master the environment. For more detail on relief in place during stability and civil support operations, see FM 3-05.401 and FM 3-90.

LINKUP

8-30.   A linkup is an operation that entails the meeting of friendly ground forces (or their leaders or designated representatives). The company conducts linkup activities independently or as part of a larger force. Within a larger unit, the company may lead the linkup force.

8-31.   Linkup may occur in, but is not limited to, the following situations.

- Advancing forces reaching an objective area previously secured by air assault, airborne, or infiltrating forces.
- Units coordinating a relief in place.
- Cross-attached units moving to join their new organization.
- A unit moving forward with a fixing force during a follow-and-support mission.
- A unit moving to assist an encircled force.
- Units converging on the same objective during the attack.
- Units conducting a passage of lines.

8-32.   The weapons company follows the same procedures for a linkup operation as an Infantry company (Chapter 8, FM 3-21.10).

Section III. SECURITY OPERATIONS

Security operations are conducted to provide early and accurate warning of enemy operations, to provide the protected force with time and maneuver space to react to the enemy and to develop the situation to allow a commander to employ the protected force effectively. Units may conduct these operations to the front, flanks, or rear of the higher force. The weapons company can conduct security operations as an independent force or subordinate to another element. (For additional information on security operations, refer to FM 17-95.)

TYPES

8-33.   The four types of security operations are screen, cover, guard, and area security. Screen, guard, and cover entail deployment of progressively higher levels of combat power and provide increasing levels of security for the main body. Area security preserves a higher commander's freedom to move his reserves, position fire support assets, conduct command and control operations, and provide for sustainment operations. A weapons company can conduct screen operations. It participates in cover, guard, and area security missions as part of a larger element or with significant augmentation.

8-34.   All forces have an inherent responsibility to provide for their own local security. Local security includes observation posts, local security patrols (mounted and dismounted), perimeter security, and other measures taken to provide close-in security for the force.

PLANNING CONSIDERATIONS

8-35.   Security operations require the commander assigning the security mission and the security force leader to address a variety of special operational factors.

AUGMENTATION OF SECURITY FORCES

8-36.   When a weapons unit conducts a screen, guard, or area security mission, the unit may receive additional combat, and sustainment elements. Attachments may include, but are not limited to, the following:

- A scout platoon or squad.
- A mortar section.
- An engineer element.

ENEMY-RELATED CONSIDERATIONS

8-37.   Security operations require the weapons element to deal with a varying set of enemy considerations. For example, the array of enemy forces (and the tactics that enemy commanders use to employ them) may be different from those for other tactical operation the unit conducts. Additional enemy considerations can influence security operations including the following:

- The presence or absence of specific types of forces on the battlefield, including:
  -- Insurgent elements (not necessarily part of the enemy force).
  -- Enemy reconnaissance elements of varying strength and capabilities (at divisional, regimental, or other levels).
  -- Enemy security elements.
  -- Enemy stay-behind elements or enemy elements that have been bypassed.
- Possible locations that the enemy will use to employ his tactical assets, including:
  -- Reconnaissance and infiltration routes.
  -- OP sites for surveillance or indirect fire observers.
- Availability and anticipated employment of other enemy assets, including:
  -- Surveillance devices, such as radar devices or unmanned aircraft systems (UAS).
  -- Long-range rocket and artillery.
  -- Helicopter and fixed-wing air strikes.
  -- Elements capable of infiltration.
  -- Mechanized forward detachments.

INITIATION OF THE SECURITY OPERATION

8-38.   The time by which the screen or guard must be established influences the unit's method of deploying to the security area as well as the time it begins the deployment.

RECONNAISSANCE OF THE SECURITY AREA

8-39.   The weapons company commander conducts a thorough analysis of the factors of METT-TC to determine the appropriate methods and techniques for the unit to use in accomplishing this mission. The weapons company commander should make every effort to conduct his own reconnaissance of the security area that he expects the unit to occupy, even when the operation is preceded by a reconnaissance by other battalion elements.

MOVEMENT TO THE SECURITY AREA

8-40.   In deploying elements to an area for a stationary security mission, the weapons company commander must resolve the competing requirements of establishing the security operation quickly to meet mission requirements while providing the necessary level of local security in doing so. Two methods can be used to move to the security area:

Tactical Road March

8-41.   If enemy contact is not expected or when time is critical, the unit can conduct a tactical road march to a release point (RP) behind the security area to occupy their initial positions. This method of deployment is faster than a movement to contact, but less secure.

Movement to Contact

8-42.   If time is not critical and either enemy contact is likely or the situation is unclear, the weapons element conducts an approach march from the LD to the security area. This method is slower than a tactical road march, but it is more secure.

LOCATION AND ORIENTATION OF THE SECURITY AREA.

8-43.   The higher commander determines the location, orientation, and depth of the security area in which he wants the security force to operate. The security force commander conducts a detailed analysis of the terrain in the security area. He then establishes his initial dispositions. This is usually a screen line (even for a guard mission) as far forward as possible and on terrain that allows clear observation of avenues of approach into the area of operations (AO). The initial screen line is shown as a phase line and sometimes represents the forward line of own troops (FLOT). As such, the screen line may be a restrictive control measure for movement. This requires the security force commander to conduct all necessary coordination if he decides to establish observation posts (OPs) or to perform any reconnaissance forward of the FLOT.

INITIAL OP LOCATIONS.

8-44.   The weapons company commander may deploy OPs to ensure effective surveillance of the AO or of named area of interests (NAI). He designates initial OP locations on or behind the screen line. He should assign the OPs with specific orientation and observation guidance, including, at a minimum, the primary orientation for the surveillance effort during the conduct of the screen. Once set on the screen line, the surveillance elements report their locations. The element that occupies each OP always retains the responsibility for changing the location in accordance with tactical requirements and the commander's intent and guidance for orientation.

SPECIAL REQUIREMENTS AND CONSTRAINTS.

8-45.   The security force commander must specify any additional considerations for the security operation, including, but not limited to, the following:

- All requirements for observing NAIs, as identified by the battalion or brigade.
- Any additional tactical actions or missions that the unit must perform.
- Engagement and disengagement criteria for the subordinate elements.

INDIRECT FIRE PLANNING.

8-46.   The security force commander conducts indirect fire planning to integrate artillery and mortar assets into the security mission. If mortars are attached, a wide area may require him to position mortar assets where they can provide effective coverage of the enemy's most likely axis of attack or infiltration routes. The fire support officer (FSO) assists him in planning artillery fires.

POSITIONING OF COMMAND AND CONTROL AND SUSTAINMENT ASSETS.

8-47.   The security force commander normally positions himself where he can observe the most dangerous enemy axis of attack or infiltration route, with the XO (or the person identified as second in command) positioned on the second most critical axis or route. The XO positions the company command post (if used) in depth and, normally, centered in the AO. This location allows the XO to provide control of initial movement, to receive reports from the screen or guard elements, and to assist the commander in more effectively facilitating command and control. Unit trains are positioned behind masking terrain, but they remain close enough for rapid response. The trains are best sited in depth and along routes that afford good lateral mobility. Patrols may be required to cover gaps between the OPs. The security force commander tasks elements to conduct either mounted or dismounted patrols, as required.

COORDINATION.

8-48.   The security force commander must conduct adjacent unit coordination to ensure there are no gaps in the screen or guard and to ensure smooth execution of the unit's rearward passages of lines (if required). Additionally, he must coordinate for the unit's follow-on mission.

SUSTAINMENT CONSIDERATIONS.

8-49.   The security force commander's primary considerations for sustainment during the security operation is coordinating and conducting resupply of the unit, especially for Class III and V supplies, and casualty evacuation. In addition to normal considerations, however, the security force commander may acquire other responsibilities in this area, such as arranging sustainment for attached elements or coordinating resupply for a subsequent mission. The unit's support planning can be further complicated by a variety of factors. To prevent these factors from creating tactical problems, the unit may receive requested logistical support, such as additional medical evacuation vehicles, from the higher headquarters.

FOLLOW-ON MISSIONS.

8-50.   The complexities of security missions, combined with normal operational requirements (such as troop-leading procedures, engagement area development, rest plans, and sustainment activities), can easily rob the security force commander of the time he needs for planning and preparation of follow-on missions. He must address these competing demands in his initial mission analysis to ensure that the unit and its leaders can adequately meet all requirements for current and future operations. If possible, the security force commander can shift his focus to preparing for follow-on missions once preparations for the security mission are complete (or satisfactorily under way). Another technique is to task the XO, with support personnel and vehicles, to prepare for follow-on missions. The XO and this element can handle such operational requirements as reconnaissance, selection of firing positions, coordination, and development of follow-on engagement areas and battle positions. The drawback to this technique is that the XO and those with him are unavailable for the current fight.

SCREEN

8-51.   A screen primarily provides early warning. It observes, identifies, and reports enemy actions to the main defense. A screen provides the least amount of protection of any security mission. Generally, a screening force fights only in self-defense; however, it may engage enemy reconnaissance elements within its capability. It does not want to become decisively engaged. If the area to be screened is large, the weapons company may have the combat power to develop the situation. Using the weapons company for the screening mission however, provides the screen with long-range fires and the mobility to mass these fires. Terrain is a key factor with long-range fields of fire providing an advantage to the weapons company while close terrain making it less effective.

PURPOSES.

8-52.   A screen is appropriate to cover gaps between forces, the exposed flanks or rear of stationary and moving forces, or the front of a stationary formation. It is used when the likelihood of enemy contact is remote, the expected enemy force is small, or the friendly main body needs only a minimum amount of time once it is warned to react effectively. Units accomplish a screen primarily by establishing a series of OPs and conducting patrols to ensure adequate surveillance of the assigned AO. Purposes of a screen include the following:

- Prevent enemy ground elements from passing through the screen undetected or unreported.
- Maintain continuous surveillance of all avenues of approach into the AO under all visibility conditions.
- Destroy or repel enemy reconnaissance elements within its capability without violating the commanders' intent.
- Locate the lead elements of each enemy advance guard force and determine their direction of movement.
- Maintain contact with enemy forces and report any activity in the AO.
- Impede and harass the enemy within capability while displacing.
- Maintain contact with the enemy main body and any enemy security forces operating on the flanks of friendly forces.

STATIONARY SCREEN.

8-53.   The weapons company commander assigns surveillance responsibility to its platoons and attached elements. He designates locations of OPs, which should be in depth through the AO. Weapons squads within the unit normally man the OPs. The commander identifies the enemy's likely axes of attack or infiltration routes. If necessary, he identifies additional control measures (such as NAIs, phase lines, target reference points (TRP), or checkpoints) to assist in movement control and in tracking of enemy elements. The unit conducts mounted and limited dismounted patrols to reconnoiter areas that cannot be observed from OPs. Once the enemy is detected from an OP, the screening force may engage him with indirect fires. This prevents the enemy from penetrating the screen line and does not compromise the location of the OP. Within its capability, the screening force may destroy enemy reconnaissance assets with direct fires if indirect fires cannot accomplish the task. The screening force also impedes and harasses other enemy elements, primarily through the use of indirect fires. If enemy pressure threatens the security of the screening force, the unit normally reports the situation and requests permission to displace to a subsequent screen line, conduct a passage of lines, or execute a follow-on mission.

MOVING SCREENS.

8-54.   A weapons company can conduct a moving screen to the flanks or rear of the main body force. Its mobility permits it to move and establish a series of OPs to protect the flank or rear of the Infantry battalion. The movement of the screen is keyed to time and distance factors associated with the movement of the friendly main body.

Moving Flank Screen.

8-55.   Responsibilities for a moving flank screen begin at the front of the main body's lead combat element and end at the rear of the protected force. In conducting a moving flank screen, the company either occupies a series of temporary OPs along a designated screen line or, if the protected force is mounted and moving too fast, continues to move while maintaining surveillance and preparing to occupy a designated screen line. There are four basic methods of controlling movement along the screened flank. The screening force may use one or more of these methods as the speed of movement of the protected force changes or contact is made.

Alternate Bounds by Individual OP.

8-56.   This method is used when the protected force is advancing slowly and enemy contact is likely along the screen line. Designated elements of the screening force move to and occupy new OPs as dictated by the enemy situation and the movement of the main body. Other elements remain stationary, providing overwatch and surveillance, until the moving elements establish their new positions; these elements then move to new positions while the now-stationary elements provide overwatch and surveillance. This sequence continues as needed. The method of alternate bounding by individual OP is secure but slow.

Alternate Bounds by Unit.

8-57.   This method is used when the protected force is advancing slowly and enemy contact is likely along the screen line. Designated elements of the screening force move and occupy new positions as dictated by the enemy situation and the movement of the main body. Other elements remain stationary, providing overwatch and surveillance, until the moving elements establish their new positions; these elements then move to new positions while the now-stationary elements provide overwatch and surveillance. This sequence continues as needed. The method of alternate bounding by unit is secure but slow. Because of the mix of weapons at the section and platoon level, the weapons company may use this method if the threat has both armored and motorized or dismounted Infantry.

Successive Bounds.

8-58.   The screening element uses this method when the total tactical environment is being developed and enemy contact is possible. During this time, the main body makes frequent short halts during movement. Each subordinate unit of the screening force occupies a designated portion of the screen line each time the main body stops. When main body movement resumes, the subordinate units move simultaneously, retaining their relative position as they move forward.

Continuous Marching.

8-59.   This method is used when the main body is advancing rapidly at a constant rate and enemy contact is not likely. This can occur if the Infantry battalion is mounted. The screening force maintains the same rate of movement as the main body while at the same time conducting surveillance as necessary. Stationary screen lines are planned along the movement route, but the screening force occupies them only as necessary to respond to enemy action.

Moving Rear Screen.

8-60.   A moving rear screen may be established to the rear of a main body force conducting an offensive operation or between the enemy and the rear of a force conducting a retrograde operation. In either case, movement of the screen is keyed to the movement of the main body or to the requirements of the enemy situation; the weapons company commander normally controls the moving rear screen by moving to a series of pre-designated phase lines.

GUARD

8-61.   A guard force protects the friendly main body either by fighting to gain time (while simultaneously observing the enemy and reporting pertinent information) or by attacking, defending, or delaying the enemy to prevent him from observing the main body and engaging it with direct fires. There are three types of guard operations (advance, flank, and rear guard). They can be conducted in support of either a stationary or a moving friendly force. The guard force differs from a screening force in that it contains sufficient combat power to defeat, repel, or fix the lead elements of an enemy ground force before they can engage the main body with direct fires. In addition, the guard force normally deploys over a narrower front than does a comparably sized screening force, allowing greater concentration of combat power. The guard force routinely engages enemy forces with both direct and indirect fires, and it normally operates within range of the main body's indirect fire weapons. With its firepower and range, the weapons company may be designated to conduct a guard mission but the battalion commander has to weigh the benefits of the increased firepower for the guard force and the possibility of loosing a portion of his weapons company.

PURPOSES.

8-62.   The purposes of the guard, in addition to those listed in the earlier discussion of the screen, include the following:

• Destroy or repel all enemy reconnaissance elements.
• Fix and defeat enemy security elements.
• Cause the enemy main body to deploy, then report its direction of travel to the friendly main body commander.

TYPES.

8-63.   The following paragraphs describe the operational considerations for a weapons company conducting advance, flank, or rear guard:

Advance Guard.

8-64.   An advance guard for a stationary force is defensive in nature. The weapons company defends or delays in accordance with the intent of the higher commander. An advance guard for a moving force is offensive in nature. The weapons company normally conducts an offensive advance guard mission during a movement to contact as part of a battalion. Its role is to maintain the freedom of maneuver of the main body by providing early warning of enemy activity and by finding, fixing, and destroying enemy reconnaissance and security elements.

Flank Guard.

8-65.   A flank guard protects an exposed flank of the main body. A flank guard is similar to a flank screen except that both OPs and defensive positions are planned. The weapons company may conduct a moving flank guard during an attack or a movement to contact. In conducting a moving flank guard, the weapons company normally occupies a series of pre-designated battle positions along the protected flank. It must maintain orientation both to the front (to perform its overwatch role and to maintain its own security) and to the protected flank. It must also maintain a sufficient distance from the main body to prevent the enemy from engaging the main body with long-range direct fires before early warning can be sent.

Rear Guard.

8-66.   The rear guard protects the rear of the main body. This may occur during offensive operations when the main body breaks contact with the enemy or during retrograde operations. Rear guards may be deployed behind either moving or stationary main bodies. The rear guard for a moving force displaces to successive battle positions along phase lines as the main body moves. During retrograde operations, the rear guard normally deploys its elements across the entire AO behind the main body's forward maneuver units.

STATIONARY GUARD.

8-67.   As noted, a stationary guard mission is, at least initially, defensive in nature. The guard force normally employs OPs to accomplish all surveillance requirements of the guard mission. The weapons company is prepared to conduct actions against the enemy's main body and security elements as well as his reconnaissance forces. The following paragraphs describe considerations for the weapons company commander in operations involving specific enemy elements:

Actions against Main Body and Security Elements.

8-68.   Once contact is made with an enemy main body or security force, the guard force attacks, defends, or delays in accordance with the enemy situation and the intent of the commander of the protected force (main body).

Actions against Reconnaissance Elements.

8-69.   When it must execute counterreconnaissance tasks, the weapons company normally task-organizes into surveillance elements that normally occupy a screen line and attack elements. Surveillance elements may include the scout platoon. Each element has specific responsibilities but must be prepared to work effectively with the other to ensure success of the operation. The weapons company commander must assign clear responsibilities for surveillance of identified avenues of approach and designated NAIs. The surveillance element is tasked with detecting, reporting, and maintaining contact with the enemy in the assigned area.

MOVING FLANK GUARD.

8-70.   Many of the considerations for a moving flank screen apply to the execution of a moving flank guard. However, unlike a moving flank screen, which occupies a series of OPs, the flank guard force plans to occupy a series of defensive positions. In conducting a moving flank guard, the weapons company either occupies a series of temporary battle positions along the protected flank or, if the protected force is moving too quickly, continues to move along the protected flank. During movement, the weapons company maintains surveillance to the protected flank of the higher unit while preparing to occupy designated battle positions based on enemy activity or on the movement of the protected force. There are three basic methods of controlling movement along the guarded flank. The methods are similar to the methods for controlling movement along a screened flank, except that the weapons company and its platoons occupy pre-designated battle positions instead of OPs. The three methods are--

- Alternate bounds by unit.
- Successive bounds by unit.
- Continuous marching.

8-71.   The lead element of a moving flank guard must accomplish three tasks. It must maintain contact with the protected force, reconnoiter the flank guard's axis of advance, and reconnoiter the zone between the protected force and the flank guard's advance. The remainder of the flank guard marches along the axis of advance and occupies battle positions to the protected flank as necessary.

LOCAL SECURITY

8-72.   A weapons company is responsible for maintaining its own security at all times. It does this by deploying mounted and dismounted OPs and patrols to maintain surveillance and by employing appropriate operations security (OPSEC) measures. In addition to maintaining security for its own elements, the unit may implement local security, if augmented, for other units as directed by the higher commander. Examples of such situations include, but are not limited to, the following:

- Provide security for engineers as they emplace obstacles or construct survivability positions in the unit's battle position (BP).
- Secure pickup zone (PZ) and landing zones (LZ).
- Establish mounted or dismounted OPs to maintain surveillance of enemy infiltration and reconnaissance routes.
- Conduct mounted or dismounted patrols to cover gaps in observation and to suppress possible enemy OPs from surrounding areas.

Section IV. OPERATIONS WITH AIRBORNE, AIR ASSAULT, AND SPECIAL OPERATIONS FORCES

Weapons companies may often find themselves operating with other units including airborne, air assault and special operations forces. The nature of these operations can be complementary to both the weapons company and the other forces. While the weapons company may assist in an airborne or air assault mission, aviation assets may assist the weapons company in a mission of its own. Special operations forces (SOF) may use the weapons company to assist in a raid while the weapons company may need to capitalize on intelligence from SOF units in order to conduct a separate mission. Regardless, weapons unit leaders must be prepared to work alone side these forces in combined arms operations.

AIRBORNE AND AIR ASSAULT FORCES

8-73.   Weapons company elements may conduct operations in support of or in conjunction with airborne or air assault forces. The nature of these operations may be varied including operations at PZs, LZs, or drop zones (DZ), or may include the company itself being air lifted in an air assault operation.

PICK-UP AND DROP ZONES

8-74.   Whether the operation is in support of an airborne or an air assault operation, weapons company involvement will most likely be constituted with similar missions. Some drop zones can be very large in nature and security of these areas concentrates on the high-speed avenues of approach. Weapons companies are ideally suited to cover these avenues. The use of a weapons company in these roles implies that most likely the PZ or DZ is in territory occupied by friendly forces and the weapons company would be able to move to the zone for the security mission. If the DZ is occupied by enemy forces, security would most likely be conducted by the airborne forces into the zone.

LANDING ZONES

8-75.   LZs are often in enemy territory. Weapons company involvement in these missions would most likely not security, but as a part of the assault force itself. In this situation, first-in elements would be ground forces that can quickly assemble on the LZ and provide security for the following elements. Weapons company elements would then be brought in via sling load with ground forces providing security during their assembly.

AIRLIFTING VEHICLES

8-76.   The rotary wing aircraft used for airlifting vehicles is the CH-47D. Weapons company vehicles that are sling loaded into a LZ will normally be a follow-on unit with security maintained from initial forces on the ground. It is important to note, however, that the vehicles will not be fully ready for combat until post-landing preparations have been accomplished. Sling loaded vehicles will not have a main gun mounted, glass will be taped and certain other sling load preparations will have been performed on the vehicle. Upon landing, slings will need to be secured from the vehicle and the vehicle driven to a place with additional cover and concealment rather than the openness of the LZ. Main weapon systems will be stored inside the vehicle for air transport. Whether or not a main gun is mounted prior to leaving the LZ is a commanders METT-TC decision. As always during LZ operations, time on the LZ itself should remain at a minimum.

SPECIAL OPERATIONS FORCES

8-77.   In today's complex operational environment, interoperability and integration between friendly units are a necessity in order to achieve battlefield success. Historically, SOF operated independently from conventional forces. SOF operations were typically separated from conventional unit missions largely by space and time. Planning was conducted independently and missions varied. Modern day conflicts are now more often characterized by SOF and conventional units occupying the same operational area. Combining the various forms of Infantry with special operations elements is a combat multiplier. Such operations can take advantage of the firepower and mobility of the weapons company while the weapons company itself takes advantage of SOF characteristics such as information gathering. Special operations forces provide Infantry units with force multipliers, especially in information operations, effects, and intelligence. The Infantry units provide the additional forces sometimes required for SOF to accomplish their mission.

WEAPONS COMPANY AND SOF COMBINED OPERATIONS

8-78.   Modern conflicts have been increasingly marked with incidents of conventional forces (CF) and SOF interoperation and integration. CF units find themselves operating along side SOF units, often supporting each other in a common mission. These type operations may include CF operating with SOF A-Teams, civil affairs teams, and tactical psychological operations teams. Examples of integration for combined operations include--

- Cordon and Search mission – SOF generally does not have the manpower to complete this mission on their own. The weapons company is ideally suited to provide a cordon for a SOF operation.
- Checkpoints in support of SOF – SOF units may use the weapons company to establish checkpoints in order to support a particular mission.
- Crowd control – psychological operations (PSYOP) teams and CF units may work together to influence crowds or local citizens in order to gain or maintain control in urban environments.

For more information regarding integration with SOF see FM 3-12.10.

COORDINATION

8-79.   When operating with or near SOF, the weapons company commander should coordinate, at a minimum, the following with the SOF unit leader:

- Command and control (C2) relationship.
- Communication information (frequencies, call signs, challenge and passwords, emergency signals and codes).
- Safehouse locations.
- Number and types of vehicles.
- Control measures being used.
- Battle handover criteria.
- Liaisons.
- Sustainment plans.
- Contingency plans for mutual support.

8-80.   For a complete Quick Reference Checklist for CF and SOF integration and interoperability see USSOCOM Pub 3-33.

Section V. BREACHING OPERATIONS

Breaching operations are conducted when a unit cannot bypass the obstacles with maneuver. Units should always try to bypass enemy obstacles. If the situation demands that the obstacles be reduced, then units should try to bypass the obstacles, destroy or repel the defending enemy forces, and then reduce the obstacles. Only as a last resort should commanders try to breach into an obstacle that is actively defended. For breaching operations, the weapons company may be part of the support force with an element attached to the assault force to provide additional firepower on the far side of the breach. For more detail on breaching operations, see FM 3-21.10, and FM 5-7-30.

FUNDAMENTALS

8-81.   Suppress, obscure, secure, reduce and assault (SOSRA) are the five breaching fundamentals. These fundamentals always apply, but their importance may vary based on the specific METT-TC conditions.

SUPPRESS

8-82.   Suppression is a tactical task that focuses direct and indirect fires on enemy personnel, weapons, or equipment to prevent effective fires on friendly forces. The purpose of suppression during breaching operations is to protect forces while they move to, reduce and maneuver through an obstacle. It is the key to a successful breaching operation. The weapons company often plays a critical role during the suppression mission.

OBSCURE

8-83.   Obscuration protects forces conducting obstacle reduction and the passage of assault forces. Obscuration hampers enemy observation and target acquisition, and it conceals friendly activities and movement.

SECURE

8-84.   Those actions in which friendly forces eliminate the enemy's ability to interfere with obstacle reduction and passage of combat units through a lane created during the reduction.

REDUCE

8-85.   Reduction is the creation of lanes through or over an obstacle to allow an attacking force to pass.

ASSAULT

8-86.   A breaching operation is not complete until friendly forces have assaulted to destroy the enemy on the far side of the obstacle and battle handover with follow-on forces has occurred.

ORGANIZATION

8-87.   A commander organizes friendly forces to accomplish the five breaching fundamentals. This requires him to organize support, breach, and assault forces with the necessary assets to accomplish their roles.

SUPPORT FORCE

8-88.   The support force's primary responsibility is to eliminate the enemy's ability to interfere with a breaching operation. Suppression depends on the commander massing enough direct fires to protect the breach force. The weapons company is ideally suited to be the support force element. The support force must--

- Isolate the reduction area with fires.
- Mass and control direct and indirect fires to suppress the enemy and to neutralize any weapons that can fire on the breach force.
- Control obscuring smoke to prevent enemy-observed direct and indirect fires.

8-89.   The support force should be provided with assets to reduce the impact of unexpected obstacles or scatterable minefields on their approach to and occupation of support-by-fire positions. Failure to provide reduction assets can greatly affect the synchronization of the entire breaching operation. As a technique, a unit may create a reserve that supports the decisive operation throughout the operation. Initially, the reserve can support the support force until it seizes support by fire (SBF) positions. Then, the reserve shifts priority to the breach or assault force. If possible, the support force should follow a covered or concealed route to the SBF position, take up its assigned sectors of fire and observation, and begin to engage the enemy.

8-90.   Observation is critical. Artillery observers with the support force may initially bring indirect fires on enemy positions to fix and suppress the enemy. The support force adjusts the indirect fire-delivered obscuring smoke to protect the breach and assault forces as they approach the reduction area. When allocating resources to the support force, consider possible personnel and equipment losses as the assault force fights its way into its SBF position. To increase the survivability of the support force, the commander may request a designation of the SBF(s) as a critical friendly zone (CFZ). A CFZ is an area, usually a friendly unit or location, which the maneuver commander designates as critical to protect an asset whose loss would seriously jeopardize the mission. Covered by target acquisition sensors, the CFZ supports counterfire operations by providing the most responsive submission of targets to the fire support system when rounds impact inside the CFZ.

BREACH FORCE

8-91.   The breach force helps in the passage of the assault force by creating, proofing (if necessary), and marking lanes. The breach force might be a combined-arms force. It includes reduction assets, enough maneuver forces to provide additional suppression, and local security and engineers (if available). The breach force applies portions of the following breaching fundamentals as it reduces an obstacle. The role of the weapons company will most likely be near side security/suppression until the obstacle is reduced enough to allow travel.

ASSAULT FORCE

8-92.   While the breach is in progress, the assault force assists the support force, or follows the breach force while it maintains cover and dispersion. Once a lane is cleared through the obstacle, the assault force moves through the breach. It secures the far side of the obstacle by physical occupation and/or continues the attack in accordance with the commander's intent. Once the far side is secured, elements of the weapons company can move forward to support the assault force.

Section VI. PATROLS

A patrol is a detachment sent out by a larger unit to conduct a combat, reconnaissance, or security mission. A patrol's organization is temporary and specifically matched to the immediate task. Because a patrol is an organization, not a mission, it is not correct to speak of giving a unit a mission to "*Patrol*."

OPERATIONS

8-93.   Commanders send patrols out from the main body to conduct specific tactical tasks with an associated purpose. Upon completion of that task, the patrol leader reports to the commander and describes the events that took place, the status of the patrol's members and equipment, and any observations.

8-94.   The senior officer or noncommissioned officer (NCO) is designated as the patrol leader. This temporary title defines his role and responsibilities for that mission. The patrol leader may designate an assistant, normally the next senior man in the patrol, and any subordinate element leaders he requires.

8-95.   A weapons company patrol element may consist of a unit as small as a single squad. Squad and platoon size patrols are common. For larger combat tasks, such as a raid, the patrol may consist of a company or company (-) element.

8-96.   The leader of any patrol, regardless of the type or the tactical task assigned, has an inherent responsibility to prepare and plan for possible enemy contact while on the mission. Patrols are never administrative. They are always assigned a tactical mission. On his return to the main body, the patrol leader must always report to the commander. He then describes the patrol's actions, observations, and condition.

TYPES

8-97.   The planned action determines the type of patrol and the weapons company commander determines the units weapons mix based on an analysis of the factors of METT-TC. The two main types of patrols are combat and reconnaissance. Regardless of the type of patrol, the unit needs a clear task and purpose.

COMBAT PATROL

8-98.   A combat patrol provides security and harasses, destroys, or captures enemy troops, equipment, or installations. When the commander gives a unit the mission to send out a combat patrol, he intends for the patrol to make contact with the enemy and engage in close combat. A combat patrol always tries to escape detection while moving, but of course discloses their location to the enemy in a sudden, violent attack. For this reason, the patrol normally carries a significant amount of weapons and ammunition. It may carry specialized munitions. A combat patrol collects and reports any information gathered during the mission, whether related to the combat task or not. The three types of combat patrols are a raid, an ambush and a security patrol. Both the raid and ambush are characterized by surprise, avoidance of detection until the attack is initiated, and short but violent action.

Raid

8-99.   As stated in the discussion of offensive operations, a raid is a limited-objective form of attack that entails a penetration of hostile terrain with a high expectation of encountering enemy resistance. A raid is not intended to hold territory and is always accompanied by a planned withdrawal to a friendly location upon the completion of the assigned mission. It is an offensive operation with a specific purpose. The weapons company may participate in the conduct a raid along with other forces or conduct an independent raid.

8-100.   During a raid conducted with other ground forces, the weapons company is best suited to establish security and isolate the objective. In this role, they are able to respond to external enemy support or interference from outside the objective area but also able to respond with heavy weapons inside the objective if needed. As an independent force, the weapons company may conduct a raid using its direct fire weapons to attack an objective and obtain a specific outcome, e.g. the destruction of an observation post. Since speed is an important aspect of a raid, the mobility of the weapons company make it well suited to conduct a raid where the distance to the objective is considerable. Unit vehicles will not only get them to the objective quickly but will also provide for a rapid withdrawal.

8-101.   Raids are also common offensive actions conducted in a region where stability operations are ongoing. Most often in these instances, raids are used to obtain personnel, equipment or information. These raids usually have detailed information on the location of the persons or items sought and hostile contact is expected during the operation. As always, standing operating procedures (SOP), ROE and METT-TC will play a part in determining how these type raids will be conducted.

Role.

8-102.   The weapons company conducts raids to accomplish a number of missions, including the following:

- Destroy specific command and control locations.
- Destroy logistical areas.
- Destroy vehicle assembly or staging areas.
- Isolate the objective.
- Support the withdrawal of the assault force.
- Confuse the enemy or disrupt his plans (feint).
- Obtain information concerning enemy locations, dispositions, strength, intentions, or methods of operation.
- Capture of personnel (threat or captured prisoners)
- Capture of weapons, caches or equipment

Ambush

8-103.   An ambush is a surprise attack, from concealed positions, on a moving or temporarily halted enemy. It may take the form of an assault to close with and destroy the enemy, or it may be an attack-by-fire only, executed from concealed positions. An ambush does not require that ground be seized or held. Although the execution of an ambush is offensive in nature, the unit may be directed to conduct an ambush in a wide variety of situations. It may stage the ambush during offensive or defensive operations, as part of the higher unit's sustaining operations, or during retrograde operations. OPSEC is critical to the success of an ambush. The unit must take all necessary precautions to ensure that it is not detected during movement to or preparation of the ambush site. The unit must also have a secure route of withdrawal following the ambush.

Role.

8-104.   The weapons company, or elements of the weapons company is well equipped to conduct an ambush. The ambush is generally conducted to reduce the enemy force's overall combat effectiveness. Destruction is the primary reason for conducting an ambush. Other reasons for an weapons company to participate in ambushes are--

- To confuse the enemy or disrupt his plans.
- To isolate enemy units in the kill zone.
- To destroy vehicles and personnel with accurate, long range, and high volume fires.
- To harass the enemy.
- To capture the enemy.

Task Organization.

8-105.   The unit is normally task-organized into assault, support, and security forces for the execution of the ambush. Elements of the weapons company can be employed in any of the three forces.

- The assault force executes the ambush. It may employ an attack-by-fire, an assault, or a combination of those techniques to destroy the ambushed force.
- The support force fixes the enemy force and prevents it from moving out of the kill zone, allowing the assault force to conduct the ambush. The support force generally uses direct fires in this role; however, it may also be responsible for calling for and adjusting indirect fires to assist in fixing the ambushed force.
- The security force provides protection and early warning to the ambush patrol and secures the objective rally point or assault position. It isolates the ambush area both to prevent the ambushed enemy force from moving out of the ambush site and to keep enemy reaction forces from reaching the site. The security force may also be responsible for securing the unit's withdrawal route.

Security Patrol

8-106.   A security patrol is sent out from a unit location during a halt, when the unit is stationary, to search the local area, to detect any enemy forces near the main body, and to engage and destroy them within the capability of the patrol. Weapons company units may be assigned a mounted security patrol mission. This type of combat patrol is normally sent out by units operating in close terrain with limited fields of observation and fire. Although this type of combat patrol seeks to make direct enemy contact and to destroy enemy forces within its capability, the patrol should try to avoid decisive engagement. A security patrol detects and disrupts enemy forces that are conducting reconnaissance of the main body or that are massing to conduct an attack. Security patrols are normally away from the main body of the unit for limited periods, returning frequently to coordinate and rest. They do not operate beyond the range of communications and supporting fires from the main body, especially mortar fires.

RECONNAISSANCE PATROL

8-107.   A reconnaissance patrol collects information or confirms or disproves the accuracy of information previously gained. The intent for this type of patrol is to avoid enemy contact and accomplish its tactical task without engaging in close combat. With one exception (presence patrols), reconnaissance patrols always try to accomplish their mission without being detected or observed. Because detection cannot always be avoided, a reconnaissance patrol carries the necessary arms and equipment to protect itself and break contact with the enemy. A reconnaissance patrol travels light, that is, with as few personnel and as little arms, ammunition, and equipment as possible. This increases stealth and cross-country mobility in close terrain. Regardless of how the patrol is armed and equipped, the leader always plans for the contact. For more information on types of reconnaissance patrols, see FM 3-21.10. Weapons company elements may be assigned or involved in any of the following types of reconnaissance patrol missions:

- Route reconnaissance patrols
- Area reconnaissance patrols
- Zone reconnaissance patrols
- Point reconnaissance patrols
- Leader's reconnaissance patrols
- Presence patrols (Unique to stability or civil support operations)
- Tracking patrols
- Contact patrols

Chapter 9

Direct Fire Control

The integration of direct fires into the scheme of maneuver is essential to success on the battlefield. While individual elements may be well rehearsed in their particular tasks relating to the mission, effective direct fire engagements do not happen without careful planning, coordination and control. All direct fires in a particular engagement area must be well synchronized to enhance combat effectiveness and protect friendly troops. Effective direct fires are the unique contribution of maneuver forces to the combined arms team, and fire and movement are complementary components of maneuver. Although the weapons company is a maneuver unit, a large portion of the weapons company mission is directed toward the direct fire support of other maneuvering friendly forces. The weapons company commander should be well aware of all direct fire control measures and how the direct fires of his subordinate elements fit into the battalion direct fire plan.

COMMANDER'S ROLE IN COA DEVELOPMENT

9-1.   As the owner of much of the Infantry battalions direct fire heavy weapons, the weapons company commander should be ready to act as a participating member of the battalion-planning cell if requested by the battalion commander. In this role, he would be the principal advisor on employment of his company heavy weapons in mission support during course of action (COA) development. He would not only advise on how best to support the mission with heavy weapons, but also suggest any additional fire control measures that would help facilitate operations. During COA development and mission execution, commanders should take into consideration the fire control principles that will ultimately increase the effectiveness of direct fires.

PRINCIPLES

9-2.   When planning and executing direct fires, all company commanders and subordinate leaders in an Infantry battalion must know how to apply several fundamental principles. The purpose of these direct fire control principles is not to restrict the actions of subordinates, but to help the company accomplish the primary goal of any direct fire engagement: to eliminate the enemy by *acquiring first and shooting first*. Applied correctly, these principles give subordinates the freedom to respond rapidly upon acquisition of the enemy. This discussion focuses on the following principles.

- Mass the effects of fire.
- Destroy the greatest threat first.
- Avoid target overkill.
- Employ the best weapon for the target.
- Minimize friendly exposure.
- Plan and implement fratricide avoidance measures.
- Plan for extreme limited visibility conditions.
- Develop contingencies for diminished capabilities.

MASS FIRES

9-3.   The Infantry units must mass its direct fires to achieve decisive results. Whether a battalion or company mission, or whether in a primary or supporting role, the principle of massing fires remains the same. Massing entails focusing direct fires at critical points and distributing the effects. Random application of fires is unlikely to have a decisive result. For example, concentrating the company's fires at a single target may ensure its destruction or suppression; however, that fire control option will fail to achieve the decisive result on the remainder of the enemy formation or position. The weapons company commander will often have his platoons in a supporting role such as in a support by fire position. He must integrate his fires with those of the maneuvering unit to achieve a combined mass effect of direct fires.

9-4.   The weapons company masses its fires by positioning its units so that more than one platoon can fire into an engagement area. Through the use of control measures such as target reference points (TRP), the commander can distribute their fires and, in turn, his platoon leaders distribute the fires within their assigned area. Use of engagement criteria and control measures such as engagement lines, the commander can destroy the enemy with sudden, distributed, and simultaneous fires from multiple platoons. Careful analyses of time-distance factors between positions can also allow the leaders to displace units in time to reinforce a threatened area and affect the outcome of the battle.

DESTROY GREATEST THREAT FIRST

9-5.   The order in which Infantry units engage enemy forces is in direct relation to the danger these forces present. The threat posed by the enemy depends on his weapons, range, and positioning. Presented with multiple targets, a unit must initially concentrate direct fires to destroy the greatest threat, and then distribute fires over the remainder of the enemy force. The weapons company with long-range direct fire capabilities will often be the first to engage an approaching enemy unit and will concentrate on attacking the greatest threat first such as tanks and other heavy weapons vehicles.

9-6.   The commander establishes a priority for targets. This may be part of the tactical standing operating procedure (TSOP) or is revised based on the mission and threat. For example, bridging equipment may become a priority target when the Infantry battalion is defending a river crossing.

AVOID TARGET OVERKILL

9-7.   Use only the amount of fire required to achieve necessary results. Target overkill wastes ammunition and is not tactically sound. To the other extreme, the company cannot have every weapon engage a different target because the requirement to destroy the greatest threats first remains paramount. The help avoid target overkill, leaders should use robust fire control measures. If the target is not burning or showing obvious signs of destruction however, it is often difficult to determine whether a target has been destroyed.

EMPLOY BEST WEAPON FOR TARGET

9-8.   Using the appropriate weapon for the target increases the probability of rapid enemy destruction or suppression; at the same time, it conserves ammunition. The Infantry weapons company has a variety of weapons with which to engage the enemy. Target type, range, and exposure are key factors in determining the weapon and ammunition that should be employed, as are weapons and ammunition availability and desired target effects. Careful planning and analysis will enable the weapons company commander to select the best weapons to mount on the vehicles and allow him to array his forces based on the terrain, enemy, and achieve the desired effects from all his direct fire engagements. A given weapons system can have its own priority of fires and engage different targets in sequence. Although the specific mission and threat dictates the use of specific weapons, close combat missile systems and machine guns are most often employed using the guidelines in the following paragraphs:

   • Close combat missile systems provide long-range direct fire capable of destroying armored vehicles and fortifications. They have a limited high explosive effect on Infantry. Their primary disadvantages are a relatively slow flight time for the missile and the number of missiles that can be carried are limited. Specifically, Javelins have a fire-and-forget and both it and some versions of the tube-launched, optically-tracked, wire-guided (TOW) missile have top attack capability.

- Grenade machine guns and heavy caliber machine guns are very effective against dismounted Infantry and lightly armored vehicles and can also provide area suppression or be used for reconnaissance by fire. The amount of ammunition is limited and may not be effective against more heavily armored vehicles.

MINIMIZE FRIENDLY EXPOSURE

9-9.   Units increase their survivability by exposing themselves to the enemy only to the extent necessary to engage him effectively. Natural or manmade defilade provides the best cover from antitank guided missiles (ATGM) and other large caliber direct fire munitions. Although armored, weapons company vehicles are vulnerable to direct fires from weapons larger than small arms and to indirect fires. The weapons company commander must select positions that minimize their exposure by constantly seeking effective available cover, trying to engage the enemy from the flank, remaining dispersed, displacing to and firing from multiple positions, and limiting engagement times.

PLAN AND IMPLEMENT FRATRICIDE AVOIDANCE MEASURES

9-10.   The company commander must work proactively to reduce the risk of fratricide and noncombatant casualties. He must plan and use the numerous tools to assist him in this effort: identification training for combat vehicles and aircraft, the unit's weapons safety posture, the weapons control status (WCS), and recognition markings. Knowledge and employment of applicable rules of engagement (ROE) are the primary means of preventing noncombatant casualties. Digital tracking systems and control measures also decrease the chance of fratricide.

PLAN FOR EXTREME LIMITED VISIBILITY CONDITIONS

9-11.   The Infantry weapons company is uniquely equipped to adapt to limited visibility conditions. The night sights for close combat missile systems not only allow for engagements during limited visibility conditions but also may be used as a night observation device for security missions. At night, limited visibility fire control equipment enables the weapons company to engage enemy forces at nearly the same ranges that are applicable during the day. However, obscurants such as dense fog, heavy rain, heavy smoke, and blowing sand can reduce the capabilities of thermal and IR equipment. The company commander develops contingencies for limited visibility conditions. Although a decrease in acquisition capabilities has little effect on area fire, point target engagements are likely to occur at decreased ranges. Firing positions, whether offensive or defensive, typically must be adjusted closer to the area or point where the commander intends to focus fires. Another alternative is the use of visual or IR illumination when there is insufficient ambient light for passive light intensification devices.

PLAN FOR DIMINISHED CAPABILITIES

9-12.   Leaders initially develop plans based on their units' maximum capabilities; they make backup plans for implementation in the event of casualties, weapon damage, or failure. While leaders cannot anticipate or plan for every situation, they develop plans for what they view as the most probable occurrences. Building redundancy into these plans, such as having two systems observe the same sector, is an invaluable asset when the situation (and the number of available systems) permits. Designating alternate sectors of fire and supplementary firing positions provides a means of shifting fires if adjacent elements become unable to fire.

PROCESS

9-13.   To bring direct fires against an enemy force successfully, commanders and leaders continuously apply the four steps of the fire control process. At the heart of this process are two critical actions: rapid, accurate target acquisition and the massing of fires to achieve decisive results on the target. Target acquisition consists of detecting, identifying, and locating the enemy in sufficient detail to permit the effective employment of weapons. Massing entails focusing fires at critical points and then distributing the fires for optimum effect. The four steps are--

- Identify probable enemy locations and determine the enemy scheme of maneuver.
- Determine where and how to mass (focus and distribute) fires.
- Orient forces to speed target acquisition.
- Shift fires to refocus or redistribute their results.

9-14.   Planning and coordination at the battalion and between the weapons and rifle company commanders is required for an effective operation. For example, if a rifle company is attacking an objective it is vitally important for the weapons company units in a support by fire role to understand where and when the maneuver commander plans to focus and mass his direct fires. He must also be aware of all control measures and know when and where to refocus or redistribute those fires in synchronization with the maneuver company operation. For a complete discussion of the four steps in the fire control process refer to FM 3-21.10

PLANNING CONSIDERATIONS

9-15.   The company commander plans direct fires as part of the troop-leading procedures. Determining where and how the company can and will mass fires are essential steps as the commander develops his concept of the operation.

OVERVIEW

9-16.   After identifying probable (or known) enemy locations, the commander determines points or areas where he will focus his combat power. His situational understanding (SU), or vision, of where and how the enemy will attack or defend helps him determine the volume of fires he must focus at particular points to have a decisive result. In addition, if he intends to mass the direct fires of more than one platoon, he must establish a means for distributing those fires effectively.

- Based on where and how he wants to focus and distribute direct fires, the commander can establish the weapons ready postures for company elements as well as triggers for initiating fires. He must evaluate the risk of fratricide and establish controls to prevent it. Fratricide prevention measures include designation of recognition markings, weapons control status (WCS), and weapons safety posture.
- Having determined where and how he will mass and distribute direct fires, the company commander orients platoons so they can rapidly and accurately acquire the enemy. The commander anticipates how the enemy will fight. He gains this anticipation through a detailed war-game of the selected course of action. With this war game, he determines probable requirements for refocusing and redistributing fires and for establishing other necessary controls. Also during the troop-leading procedures, the company commander plans and rehearses direct fires (and the fire control process) based on his analysis.
- The company commander continues to apply planning procedures and considerations throughout execution. When necessary, he must also apply effective direct fire standing operating procedures (SOP).

STANDING OPERATING PROCEDURES

9-17. A well-rehearsed direct fire SOP enhances direct fire planning and ensures quick, predictable actions by all members of the company. The commander bases the various elements of the SOP on the capabilities of his force and on anticipated conditions and situations. SOP elements should include standard means for focusing fires, distributing their results, orienting forces, and preventing fratricide. He should adjust the direct fire SOP whenever changes to anticipated and actual factors of mission, enemy, terrain, troops, time, civilians (METT-TC) become apparent.

Focus Fires

9-18. One technique is to establish a standard respective position for TRPs in relation to friendly elements and then to consistently number the TRPs such as from left to right. This allows leaders to quickly determine and communicate the location of the TRPs.

Distribute Fires

9-19. Two useful means of distributing the results of the company's direct fires are engagement priorities and target array. Engagement priorities, by type of enemy vehicle or weapon, are assigned for each type of friendly weapon system. The target array technique helps in distribution by assigning specific friendly elements to engage enemy elements of approximately similar capabilities.

Orient Forces

9-20. A standard means of orienting friendly forces is to assign a primary direction of fire, using a TRP, to orient each element on a probable (or known) enemy position or likely avenue of approach. To provide all-round security, the SOP can supplement the primary direction of fire with sectors using a friendly-based quadrant. The following sample SOP elements show the use of these techniques.

The front (center) platoon's primary direction of fire is TRP 2 (center) until otherwise specified; the platoon is responsible for the front two quadrants.

The left flank platoon's primary direction of fire is TRP 1 (left) until otherwise specified; the platoon is responsible for the left two friendly quadrants (overlapping with the center platoon).

The right flank platoon's primary direction of fire is TRP 3 (right) until otherwise specified; the platoon is responsible for the right two friendly quadrants (overlapping with the center platoon).

Prevent Fratricide

9-21. The SOP must address the most critical requirement of fratricide prevention. It must direct subordinate leaders to inform the commander, adjacent elements, and subordinates whenever a friendly force is moving or preparing to move. One technique is to establish a standing WCS of WEAPONS TIGHT, which requires positive enemy identification prior to engagement. The SOP must also cover means for identifying dismounted Infantry squads and other friendly dismounted elements. Techniques include using armbands, medical heat pads, or an IR light source, as well as detonating a smoke grenade of a designated color at the appropriate time.

CONTROL

9-22. Acquiring the enemy is a precursor to direct fire engagement. Leaders must expect the enemy to use covered and concealed routes effectively when attacking and to make best use of flanking and concealed positions in the defense. As a result, the company may not have the luxury of a fully exposed enemy that it can easily see. The acquisition of the enemy often depends on visual recognition of very subtle indicators such as exposed antennas, reflections from the vision blocks of enemy vehicles, small dust clouds, or smoke from vehicle engines or ATGM or tank fires. Because of the difficulty of target acquisition, the company commander must develop surveillance plans to assist the company in acquiring the enemy.

CONTROL MEASURES

9-23.   Fire control measures are the means by which leaders control direct fires. Application of these concepts, procedures, and techniques help the unit acquire the enemy, focus fires on him, distribute the results of the fires, and prevent fratricide. At the same time, no single measure is enough to control fires effectively. At company level, fire control measures are effective only if the entire unit has a common understanding of what they mean and how to employ them. Table 9-1 lists terrain-based and threat-based fire control measures.

Table 9-1. Common fire control measures.

Terrain-Based Fire Control Measures	Threat-Based Fire Control Measures
Target reference point Engagement area Sector of fire Direction of fire Terrain-based quadrant Friendly based quadrant Maximum engagement line Restrictive fire line Final protective line	Fire patterns Target array Engagement priorities Weapons ready posture Engagement criteria Weapons control status Rules of engagement Weapons safety posture Engagement techniques

9-24.   Commanders use terrain-based fire control measures to focus and control fires on a particular point, line, or area rather than on a specific enemy element. Threat-based fire control measures are used to focus and control direct fires by directing the unit to engage a specific enemy element rather than to fire on a point or area. A complete detailed discussion of each of these measures can be found in FM 3-21.10.

COMMANDS

9-25.   Fire commands are oral orders issued by the commander and his subordinate leaders to focus and distribute fires as required to achieve the desired results against an enemy force. Fire commands allow leaders, in the already confusing environment of close combat, to articulate their firing instructions rapidly and concisely using a standard format. Unit fire commands include these elements:

Alert

9-26.   The alert specifies the units that are directed to fire. It does not require the leader who initiates the command to identify himself. Examples of the alert element (call signs and code words based on unit SOP) include--

GUIDONS (all subordinate elements)
RED (1st platoon only)

Weapon or Ammunition (Optional)

9-27.   This element identifies the weapon and ammunition to be employed by the alerted units. Leaders may designate the type and number of rounds to limit expenditure of ammunition. Examples of this element include--

JAVELIN
MACHINE GUN

Target Description

9-28.   Target description designates which enemy forces are to be engaged. Leaders may use the description to focus fires or achieve distribution. Example target descriptions include--

TROOPS IN TRENCH
BUNKER
PCs

Orientation

9-29.   This element identifies the location of the target. The location of the target might be designated in any of several ways, for example--

Closest TRP   TRP 13
Clock direction   ONE O'CLOCK
Terrain quadrant   QUADRANT ONE
Friendly quadrant   LEFT FRONT
Target array   FRONT HALF
Tracer on target   ON MY TRACER
Laser pointer ON MY POINTER

Range (Optional)

9-30.   The range element identifies the distance to the target. Announcing range is not necessary for systems that have range finders or that employ command-guided or self-guided munitions. For systems that require manual range settings, leaders have a variety of means for determining range, including--

Predetermined ranges to TRPs or phase lines.
Handheld rangefinders.
Range stadia.
Mil reticles.

Control (Optional)

9-31.   The company commander may use this optional element to direct desired target results, distribution methods, or engagement techniques. Subordinate leaders may include the control element to supplement the company commander's instructions and achieve effective distribution. Examples of information specified in the control element include--

Target array - FRONT HALF
Fire pattern –FRONTAL
Terrain quadrant - QUADRANT 1
Engagement priorities - M203 ENGAGE BUNKERS;
MACHINE GUNS ENGAGE TROOPS
Engagement technique – ALTERNATING
Target effect - AREA

Execution

9-32.   The execution element specifies when direct fires should be initiated. The company commander may engage immediately, delay initiation, or delegate authority to engage. Examples of this element include--

>   FIRE
>   AT MY COMMAND
>   AT YOUR COMMANDAT PHASE LINE ORANGE

Chapter 10

Fire Support, Mobility, Protection, and Other Support

Full combat potential is only achieved by the combined integration of all available combat arms and maneuver support assets into the maneuver unit's mission plan. This often includes attachments to the weapons company, detachments of weapons company platoons to other units, and other surrounding units. Commanders must evaluate all available assets and effectively employ them to not only quickly and decisively obtain mission success, but to achieve it with the least amount of friendly causalities as possible. Based on the mission, higher command establishes specific command and support relationships between surrounding and supporting units. Each commander must understand the command and support relationships between his company and these units (FM 3-21.10). This chapter reviews other combat elements that the Infantry weapons company is most likely to work with such as fire support, engineers, air defense, chemical, biological, radiological or nuclear (CBRN) and Army aviation units.

FIRE SUPPORT

10-1.   Fire support is the collective and coordinated use of indirect fire weapons and armed aircraft in support of the battle plan. Fire support assets include mortars, field artillery cannons and rockets, and close air support (CAS). Desired results from fire support assets can be achieved through a combination of both lethal and nonlethal means. The integration of fire support assets is critical to the success of the company. The Infantry battalion fire support officer (FSO) plans fires (in coordination with the plans developed by the Infantry battalion S-3) to support the Infantry battalion commander's concept of the operation. The company FSOs plan company fire support, and the company commander approves his plan. Fire support planning is the process of analyzing, allocating, and scheduling fire support assets.

INDIRECT FIRE CAPABILITIES

10-2.   Indirect fire assets include 60-mm, 81-mm, and 120-mm mortars as well as 105-mm and 155-mm cannon artillery. Each system has a variety of projectiles, fuzes, ranges, and sustained rate of fire (FM 3-21.10).

AIR FIRE SUPPORT

10-3.   Infantry company operations might be supported by attack aircraft including Army helicopters or ground attack fighters of the Air Force, Navy, or Marines. However, next to Army aviation, the Air Force most commonly provides sorties for the close-in fight. This type air power is typically CAS but can also be joint air attack team (JAAT) operations. Though JAAT missions might be flown in or near the company area of operations (AO), they are more complex than pure CAS, requiring higher-level command and control (C2). For attack helicopter operations with Infantry units see FM 3-21.10.

FIRE SUPPORT TEAM

10-4.   The weapons company link to artillery, mortar and tactical air support is provided by the fire support team (FIST). The Infantry weapons company has a dedicated FIST associated with them that are normally attached to the company from the Fires Support Platoon in the battalion headquarters. The weapons company FIST consists of an FSO, a fire support sergeant, a fire support specialist, and a radio operator. Infantry rifle company FIST contain six additional personnel (three radio-telephone operators and three forward observers) that form forward observer (FO) teams (one FO and one radio operator) that are normally sent to the rifle platoons. The weapons company four man FIST will normally be positioned near the weapons company commander. The mission of the fire support team is to provide fire support for the weapons company through fire support planning, fire support coordination, target location, calls for indirect fire, battlefield information reporting, and emergency control of CAS.

FIRE SUPPORT PLANS AND COORDINATION

10-5.   At all levels, leaders plan fire support and maneuver concurrently. Infantry battalions typically plan fire support from the top down, and refine plans from the bottom up. The commander develops guidance for fire support tasks, purposes, and results. The fire support planner determines the method for accomplishing each task. Individual units then incorporate assigned tasks into their fire support plans. In addition, units tasked to initiate fires refine and rehearse their assigned tasks. The company commander refines his unit's assigned portion of the battalion fire support plan, ensuring that the designated targets will achieve the intended purpose. He also conducts rehearsals to prepare for the mission and, as specified in the plan, directs the company to execute its assigned targets. Leaders must understand basic fire support terms to effectively plan and employ fire support assets. A complete list of terms and definitions associated with fire support planning and coordination can be found in FM 3-21.10.

FIRE SUPPORT PREPARATION

10-6.   Although the Infantry battalion and brigade commanders establish target tasks and purposes and allocate appropriate fire support assets, the maneuver company commanders are the one who must ensure execution of the fire support plan and assigned targets. Often this responsibility is given to the Infantry rifle companies while the platoons of the Infantry weapons company are in a supporting role themselves. Execution of a portion of the indirect fire plan may become the responsibility of the Infantry weapons company commander while operating pure or task organized with a specific company mission. The weapons company commander has his company FSO to assist in fire support planning and preparation. The successful execution of his plan demands thorough preparation that focuses on the key areas covered in the following paragraphs:

Observation Plan

10-7.   As stated, the Infantry weapons company does not have dedicated forward observer teams attached down to the platoon level. When required, company or platoon personnel will function as their own observers for indirect fire support. Often this responsibility will fall on the platoon leader or platoon sergeant. The weapons company is unique in the fact that often they are given missions that place them in positions with good observation. Additionally, they have eight Improved Target Acquisition System (ITAS) within the company, which are equipped with the target acquisition system (TAS), the optical sighting system for the weapon. This integrated day/night sight may be used to enhance the unit's observation ability during daylight or limited visibility conditions. Other systems, such as the ground/vehicle laser locator designator or similar device provides enhanced execution of fires by allowing first round fire-for-effect capability. In developing the observation plan, the commander must ensure that both primary and alternate observation is available to cover all targets and to determine whether the desired target results have been achieved. The plan provides clear, precise guidance for the observers. Perhaps the most important aspect of the plan is positioning. An observer's positions must allow him to see the trigger for initiating fires as well as the target area and the enemy force on which the target is oriented; this is done to help the observer determine if the target results have been achieved. The observation plan must also include contingency plans that cover limited visibility conditions and backup communications.

Battle Damage Assessment

10-8.   Battle damage assessment (BDA) is the timely and accurate estimate of damage resulting from the application of lethal or nonlethal military force against a target. BDA is primarily an intelligence responsibility but requires coordination with maneuver and fire support observers to be effective. Commanders use BDA to get a series of timely and accurate snapshots of their effects on the enemy. This helps determine when or if the targeting objectives are being met. BDA also helps determine if restrike is necessary.

Rehearsals

10-9.   The company commander is responsible for involving his FSO in company and battalion level rehearsals. The weapons company commander must ensure that he and his FSO are clear on the execution of the company fire support plan and that it fits with the battalions plan. Company rehearsals are necessary to ensure that personnel responsible for executing indirect fires are clear on how, when and where to employ fires in the plan. The company FSO may be used to reinforce this portion of the mission rehearsal. The commander must also ensure that the company's primary and backup communications systems adequately support the plan.

Target Adjustment

10-10.   In preparation for a defense mission, target adjustments may be made to confirm target location and ensure first round effects during execution. Adjustment of fires may normally be conducted as time and situation permit for targets such as an engagement area development.

Tactical and Technical Triggers

10-11.   The two types of triggers associated with a target are tactical and technical. The company commander develops a tactical trigger for each target and then he or his FSO develop the technical trigger. A tactical trigger is the maneuver related event or action that causes the commander to initiate fires. This event can be friendly or enemy based. The tactical trigger is usually determined during course of action (COA) development. The technical trigger is the mathematically derived solution for firing the indirect fires based on the tactical trigger to ensure that the indirect fires arrive at the correct time and location to achieve the desired results. Triggers can be marked using techniques similar to those for marking Target reference points (TRP).

10-12.   When selecting the tactical trigger the commander must ensure that either he, or the designated observer, is able to observe the enemy forces or event that is designated as the trigger. For example, "*When enemy forces occupy their defensive positions vicinity Objective Brown.*" The tactical trigger may also be friendly event or time driven; for example, "*When Charlie company crosses phase line Bowen*" or "*at 0900.*"

10-13.   Several factors govern the selection and positioning of the technical trigger. Critical factors are the enemy's likely locations or rate of travel, and the time required for the enemy force to move from the technical trigger to the target area. Using this information, the commander can then select the technical trigger location based on the following considerations:

- The amount of time required to initiate the call for fire.
- The time needed by the fire support element to prepare for and fire the mission.
- The time required to clear the fires.
- Any built-in or planned delays in the firing sequence.
- The time of flight of the indirect fire rounds.
- Possible adjustment times.

Ceasing or Shifting of Fires

10-14.   As in trigger planning for the initiation of fires, the commander must establish triggers for ceasing or shifting fires based on battlefield events such as the movement of enemy or friendly forces. One technique is the use of a minimum safe line (MSL) when a friendly element, such as a breach force, is moving toward an area of indirect fires. As the element approaches the MSL, observers call for fires shift or cease, allowing the friendly force to move safely in the danger area.

Clearance of Fire

10-15.   The maneuver commander has the final authority to approve (clear) fires and their results within his zone or AO. Although he may delegate authority to coordinate and clear fires to his FSO, the ultimate responsibility belongs to the company commander. Normally, the FSO helps the commander by making recommendations on the clearance of fires.

Fire Support Execution Matrix

10-16.   As a tool in fire support planning and execution, the company commander may develop a graphic summary outlining the critical elements of the fire support plan and the company's role. The commander incorporates this information into his own execution matrix or into a separate fire support execution matrix, similar to the battalion's fire support execution matrix. The company fire support execution matrix is similar and should include, as a minimum, the following information for each target:

- Target number and type, to include final protective fire (FPF) designation.
- Allocated fire support asset and munitions type.
- Observer and backup observer.
- Trigger.
- Target purpose.
- Target grid.
- Priority of fire.
- Priority targets.
- Fire support coordination measures (FSCMs).

Maneuver Commander's Intent

10-17.   The company commander ensures the FSO clearly understands the intent and desired results for maneuver and fire support. He identifies the role of fire support in the concept of operations (when, where, what, and why) by explaining in detail the concept of the fires supporting the scheme of maneuver, and tasks and desired results for fire support to the FSO.

- Providing this level of guidance is not easy. Artillery fires are not instantaneous, and planning must allow for this lag time. It takes several minutes to process targets of opportunity and deliver fires in the target area. While war-gaming the maneuver, the company commander refines the critical targets or engagement areas, priority of targets, priority of engagement, sequence of fires, triggers, and results desired. He then can see when and how to synchronize direct and indirect fires to destroy the enemy and protect the force.
- The company commander normally designates the company's decisive operation to have priority of fires. This prioritizes requests when two or more units want fires at the same time. He also designates where to place obscuration or illumination, suppressive fires, and preparation fires.

FIRE SUPPORT PLANNING

10-18.   While the company commander develops and refines the tactical plan, he also develops the fire support plan. The FSO concurrently helps develop and refine fire support. Targets are placed in the fire support planning channels as soon as possible in order for processing at the battalion Fires Cell or battery fire direction center (FDC). For a complete description of the fire planning process, see FM 3-21.10. Regardless of the planning method used, the company fire support plan should include--

- Target number and location.
- A description of the expected target.
- Primary and alternate persons responsible for shooting each target.
- The amount of result required and purpose.
- Radio frequency and call sign to use in requesting fires.
- When to engage the target.
- Priority of fires and shifting of priority.

Other Planning Considerations

10-19.   While not unique in themselves to the Infantry weapons company, there are some considerations during fire support planning that may have a unique effect on weapons company mission planning and execution. The following paragraphs include some of these considerations for the commander:

Special Munitions

10-20.   Obscuration fires use smoke and white phosphorous (WP) ammunition to degrade the enemy by obscuring his view of the battlefield. (High explosive ammunition may also obscure his view with dust and fires, but the unit should not rely on it as the primary means.) Because smoke is subject to changes in wind direction and terrain contours, its use must be coordinated with other friendly units affected by the operation. Used properly, obscuration fires can--

- Slow enemy vehicles to blackout speeds.
- Obscure the vision of enemy direct fire weapon crews.
- Reduce accuracy of enemy-observed fires by obscuring observation posts (OP) and command posts (CP).
- Cause confusion and apprehension among enemy Soldiers.
- Limit the effectiveness of the enemy's visual command and control signals.

10-21.   Screening fires are closely related to obscuration fires; they also involve the use of smoke and WP. However, screening fires mask friendly maneuver elements to disguise the nature of their operations. Screening fires may assist in consolidation by placing smoke in areas beyond the objective. They may also be used to deceive the enemy to believe that a unit is maneuvering when it is not. Screening fires require the same precautions as obscuration fires.

10-22.   The weapons company has no organic mortars. Therefore, smoke support must come from external mortars, artillery and smoke pots. Smoke pots are a primary means of producing small-area screening smoke. A smoke platoon is required for long-term, large-area obscuration. If attached, the smoke platoon can provide both hasty smoke and large-area smoke support for tactical operations in the main battle area.

10-23.   Weapons company commanders need to carefully plan the use of obscuration or screening fires because their effects may adversely affect mission execution of his or other friendly troops. Hot obscuration fires such as WP munitions may degrade both the day and night visibility of weapon sights if placed improperly. Other obscurants such as smoke munitions and smoke generators may obscure day sights while still allowing use of thermal night sights.

10-24.   Special munitions may be used for illumination. These may be scheduled or on-call missions. Illumination from indirect fires may need to be adjusted to illuminate areas of suspected enemy movement or to orient moving units. There are two types of illumination, infrared (IR) and white light, that may be used based on availability and mission, enemy, terrain, troops, time, civilians (METT-TC) conditions.

Observer Positions

10-25.   To ensure that indirect fire can be called on a specific target, observers are designated and in the proper position. As the company plans indirect fire targets to support the operation and passes these down to the platoon, observers are positioned to observe the target and the associated trigger line or TRP. As already mentioned the Infantry weapons company has no dedicated observer teams in the platoons. Therefore, indirect fires will often be initiated by the company FSO. However, any Soldier can perform this function as long as he understands the mission and has the communications capability and training. Once the target has been passed to the platoon or included by the platoon in the fire support plan, the platoon leader must position the observer and make sure he understands the following in precise terms:

* The nature and description of the target he is expected to engage.
* The terminal results required (destroy, delay, disrupt, limit, and so on) and purpose.
* The communications means, radio net, call signs, and FDC to be called.
* When or under what circumstances targets are to be engaged.
* The relative priority of targets.
* The method of engagement and method of control to be used in the call for fire.
* Purpose and location of target; observers (primary and alternate); trigger; communications; and the resource providing the fires.

Final Protective Fires

10-26.   These are immediately available planned fires that block enemy movement, especially dismounted Infantry approaching defensive lines or areas. These areas are integrated with defensive plans. The pattern of FPF plans may be varied to suit the tactical situation. They are drawn to scale on the target overlay. The size of the FPF is determined by the number and type of weapons used to fire on it. The company commander is responsible for the precise location of FPFs. The company FSO--

* Reports the desired location of the FPF to the supporting FDC.
* Adjusts indirect fire on the desired location, by weapon.
* Transmits the call to fire FPF to the supporting FDC.

10-27. The leader (normally the company commander or a platoon leader) in whose area the FPF is located has the authority to call for the FPF. The FPF has the highest priority of any target assigned to a fire support means. The FPF is only fired when required to repel the enemy's assault. Premature firing wastes ammunition and allows the enemy to avoid the impact area.

Rehearsals and Execution

10-28. Once the company has developed and coordinated the fire support plan, it rehearses the plan. As the company rehearses the maneuver, it rehearses the fire plan. The target list is executed as the maneuver is conducted; fires are requested (though not actually executed by the firing units) just as they would be during the operation. Under ideal circumstances, an FPF can be adjusted during the rehearsal. Rehearsals on the terrain reveal any problems in visibility, communications, and coordination of the fire support plan. Conduct rehearsals under degraded conditions (at night and in mission-oriented protective posture (MOPP) 4) to make sure the company can execute the plan in all circumstances.

- If time or conditions prohibit full-scale rehearsals, key leaders can meet, preferably at a good vantage point, and brief back the plan. They can use a sand table to show it on the terrain. Each participant explains what he does, where he does it, and how he plans to overcome key-leader casualties. The fire support plan execution is integral to this process and is rehearsed in exactly the same way.
- The company executes the fire plan as it conducts the operation. It fires targets as required and makes adjustments based on enemy reactions. Priority targets are cancelled as friendly units pass them or they are no longer relevant to the maneuver.

Communications

10-29. The FSO can monitor three of four possible radio voice nets and three digital nets. The company's mission and priority determine the specific nets. The commander and company FSO should ensure that all communication channels, assignments and networks are available and understood by all elements. These networks should be tested as part of the mission rehearsal.

Echelonment Of Fires

10-30. Fires support planning should include the concept of echelonment of fires. This concept takes into account the available fire support assets, their accuracy and lethal zones and orchestrates a time to fire, shift fire or cease fire of each specific system. These fires are also planned and executed in conjunction with the direct fire plan as discussed in Chapter 9 of this manual. For a complete explanation of echelonment of fires, see FM 3-21.10.

10-31. Company commanders will often find themselves as the observer (and executor) of battalion fires. Understanding the concept of echelonment of fires is critical for the indirect fire plan to be effectively synchronized with the maneuver plan. The purpose of echeloning fires is to maintain constant fires on a target while using the optimum delivery system up to the point of its risk-estimate distance (RED) in combat operations or minimum safe distance (MSD) in training. Echeloning fires provides protection for friendly forces as they move to and assault an objective, allowing them to close with minimal casualties. It prevents the enemy from observing and engaging the assault by forcing the enemy to take cover, allowing the friendly force to continue the advance unimpeded.

10-32.   The concept behind echeloning fires is to begin attacking targets on or around the objective using the weapons system with the largest RED-combat (or MSD-training). As the maneuver unit closes the distance, that is, crosses the RED line for that specific munition en route to the objective, the fires cease, shift, or switch to a different system such as to the 81- or 60-mm mortar. This triggers the engagement of the targets by the delivery system with the next largest RED-combat (or MSD-training). The length of time to engage the targets is based on the rate of the friendly force's movement between the RED-combat (or MSD-training) trigger lines. The process continues until the system with the least RED-combat (or MSD-training) ceases fires and the maneuver unit is close enough to eliminate the enemy with direct fires or make its final assault and clear the objective.

10-33.   The RED for combat (or MSD training) take into account the bursting radius of particular munitions and the characteristics of the delivery system. It associates this combination with a probability of incapacitation for Soldiers at a given range. The RED-combat (or MSD-training) is defined as the minimum distance friendly troops can approach the effects of friendly fires without 0.1 percent or more probability of incapacitation. A commander may maneuver their units into the RED-combat area based on the mission. However, he is making a command decision to accept the additional risk to friendly forces.

MOBILITY

10-34.   The combat engineer company of the Infantry brigade combat team (IBCT) is tailored to fight as part of the combined arms team in the IBCT. It focuses on mobility but also provides limited countermobility and survivability engineer support. Only one engineer company is organic to the IBCT. Depending on the mission and other METT-TC conditions, the Infantry weapons company may have or need support from engineer assets. These assets may be a supporting engineer element such as a sapper squad to aid in mobility, countermobility, and survivability.

ORGANIZATION

10-35.   The engineer company can be augmented according to the mission with units with brigades at echelons above the IBCT. Augmentation provides additional engineer capability and functions.

Engineer Company

10-36.   The IBCT engineer company is assigned and executes engineer missions that are identified by the brigade combat team (BCT) commander. Their employment depends on the BCT commander's analysis of METT-TC. The engineer company commander may receive augmentation from other engineer units. He directs his unit in the execution of mission support to the BCT. The engineer company is self-sufficient for mobility purposes.

Engineer Platoon

10-37.   An engineer platoon (Sappers) might be task-organized to a battalion or company, based on the BCT commander's analysis of METT-TC. The engineer platoon can be employed to accomplish almost any engineer mission. However, the engineer platoon lacks organic sustainment assets and has minimal C2 depth and combat systems. Thus, it will most likely require augmentation or external support to conduct continuous operations over a sustained period of time (more than 48 hrs). The engineer platoon might also require some augmentation to conduct combined-arms tasks such as breaching operations. The engineer platoon may receive augmentation from its engineer company or other units as required.

Sapper Squad

10-38.   A sapper squad might be task organized to a company. It executes engineer tasks to support the company mission. Task organization is based on the battalion commander's analyses of METT-TC. The squad is the smallest engineer element that can be employed with its own organic C2 assets and as such can accomplish tasks such as reconnaissance, manual breaching, demolitions, or route clearance as part of a platoon or company mission. The sapper engineer may receive augmentation of engineer equipment such as a small emplacement excavator or other specialized engineer equipment based on METT-TC.

MISSIONS

10-39.   The tactical missions of combat engineers correspond to those of IBCT Infantry units. Combat engineer units can operate in restrictive terrain such as forests, jungles, mountains, and urban areas. Because of their austere nature, IBCT engineers have limited tactical mobility. To compensate for this, IBCT engineers train to operate in a decentralized manner. Like their supported maneuver force, they are very well suited to operate under conditions of limited visibility.

10-40.   The mobility, countermobility, and survivability tasks performed by combat engineers fall primarily within the *Maneuver and Movement* or *Protection* warfighting function (WFF). Table 10-1 shows the main tasks included in each of these categories. A combat engineer platoon or squad might be attached to a company depending on METT-TC. Engineers also provide general (construction) and geospatial engineering. Engineers also conduct reconnaissance (see FM 3-34.170) which may support or enable each of the three engineer functions of combat, general, and geospatial engineering. Combat engineers are also prepared to fight as Infantry.

Table 10-1. Combat engineer focus.

Mobility	Countermobility	Survivability
Breach obstacles. Clear minefields. Clear routes. Cross gaps (expedient). Construct combat roads or trails.	Construct obstacles to turn, fix, block, or disrupt enemy forces.	Construct crew-served weapons and vehicle fighting positions.

CAPABILITIES

10-41.   The IBCT combat engineer company was designed with a focus on mobility support. For the weapons company this may include route reconnaissance or clearance and obstacle reduction support among other missions. They may also identify potential enemy counterattack routes and support to establishment of countermobility measures such as scatterable mines to protect the force. IBCT engineers train in Infantry skills and are able to move undetected when close to the enemy. For a complete listing of weapons and engineer assets see FM 3-21.10 and FM 5-7-30.

PROTECTION

10-42.   Air defense assets may operate in and around the Infantry weapons company AO. However, the company is unlikely to receive task-organized air defense assets. Therefore, the company conducts its own air defense operations. It relies on disciplined, passive air defense measures and the ability to engage aerial platforms actively with organic weapons systems. Troops should be familiar with air defense assets, capabilities, operational procedures, as well as self-defense measures.

SYSTEMS, ORGANIZATION, AND CAPABILITIES

10-43. The man-portable Stinger and the vehicle-mounted Stinger (then called the *"Avenger"*), Figure 10-1, might be used in and adjacent to the company AO. A maneuver battalion might be task organized with an air defense platoon equipped with four Avengers.

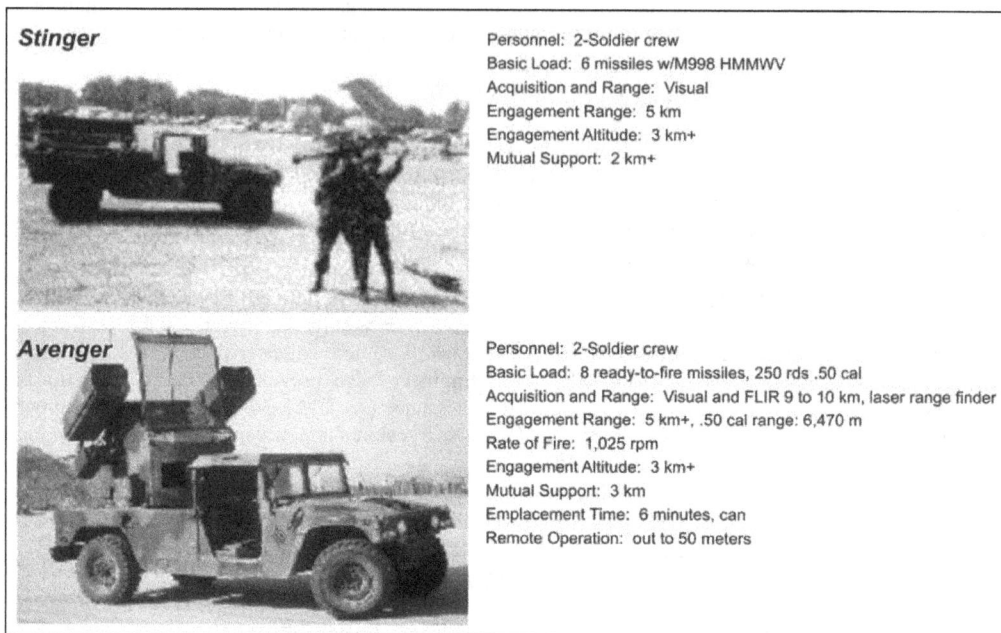

Stinger

Personnel: 2-Soldier crew
Basic Load: 6 missiles w/M998 HMMWV
Acquisition and Range: Visual
Engagement Range: 5 km
Engagement Altitude: 3 km+
Mutual Support: 2 km+

Avenger

Personnel: 2-Soldier crew
Basic Load: 8 ready-to-fire missiles, 250 rds .50 cal
Acquisition and Range: Visual and FLIR 9 to 10 km, laser range finder
Engagement Range: 5 km+, .50 cal range: 6,470 m
Rate of Fire: 1,025 rpm
Engagement Altitude: 3 km+
Mutual Support: 3 km
Emplacement Time: 6 minutes, can
Remote Operation: out to 50 meters

Figure 10-1. Stinger, man-portable, mounted on a HMMWV.

EMPLOYMENT

10-44. In offensive situations, man-portable Stingers and Avengers accompany the main attack. They may maneuver with the battalion's lead companies, orienting on low-altitude air avenues of approach. When the unit is moving or in a situation that entails short halts, the Stinger gunners can dismount to provide air defense when the unit reaches the objective or pauses during the attack. In the defense, man-portable Stinger and the vehicle-mounted Stinger might be used in and adjacent to the company AO. A maneuver battalion might be task-organized with an air defense platoon equipped with four Avengers.

10-45. The term weapons control status (WCS) describes the relative degree of control in effect for air defense fires. It applies to all weapons systems. The WCS is coordinated between the airspace-controlling agency and brigade and disseminated when required. For more information on WCS, see FM 3-21.10.

OTHER SUPPORT

10-46. Other support includes at the least CBRN support, Army aviation support, other attack helicopters, unmanned aircraft,

CHEMICAL, BIOLOGICAL, RADIOLOGICAL, OR NUCLEAR SUPPORT

10-47.   CBRN weapons can cause casualties, destroy or disable equipment, restrict the use of terrain, and disrupt operations. They might be used separately or in combination to supplement conventional weapons. The company must be prepared to fight on a CBRN-contaminated battlefield. The commander designates principal CBRN defense trainers and advisors on CBRN defense operations and CBRN equipment maintenance. These trainers include a CBRN defense officer, a CBRN noncommissioned officer (NCO), and an enlisted alternate. The commander ensures all personnel in his command can operate and perform maintenance on all organic CBRN equipment. CBRN assets within the Infantry company are limited. To survive on a contaminated battlefield, the company must practice the fundamentals of CBRN defense, avoidance, protection, and decontamination. (For more on CBRN, see FM 3-21.10 or FM 3-11.)

ARMY AVIATION

10-48.   Army aviation is an asset available to the BCT and can be requested by the Infantry battalion. Requests from the Infantry weapons company go through the battalion. These requests are processed and integrated by the air defense airspace management/brigade aviation element cell at the BCT. Army aviation can be used for command and control, reconnaissance, medical evacuation (MEDEVAC), movement of troops and supplies, direct fire support, and as maneuver units. Air assault helicopter operations deliver assault elements of an Infantry company to locations on or near tactical objectives.

OTHER ATTACK HELICOPTERS

10-49.   Other Attack helicopters are employed as integral parts of the joint and combined arms team and might be provided by US Marine or Navy assets. They are aerial attack systems also suited for situations calling for a quick response if available.

UNMANNED AIRCRAFT SYSTEMS

10-50.   The Weapons company commander should consider support from unmanned aircraft systems (UAS) as he plans, coordinates, and executes operations. UAS can increase the situational awareness of commanders through intelligence, surveillance, reconnaissance, and communications relay. They are capable of locating and recognizing enemy forces that contrast with their surroundings, locating and confirming the position of friendly forces, and the presence of noncombatant civilians, etc. The RQ-11 Raven is the most common UAS used at the battalion and company level.

10-51.   A primarily use of UAS is for surveillance and reconnaissance. UAS can provide surveillance to the front, flanks, and rear of weapons company units during movement. They can survey planned attack and support by fire positions prior to their occupation. They can also provide reconnaissance along high-speed avenues of approach into the battalion or company AO and provide time for the weapons company to deploy and counter the threat. UAS can also provide reconnaissance along secondary avenues of approach that may not have coverage by ground units.

Capabilities of UAS

10-52.   UAS currently bring numerous capabilities to Army units, providing near real time reconnaissance, surveillance, and target acquisition. They can be employed on the forward line of friendly elements, on the flanks, or in rear areas. Employed as a team, UAS and manned systems provide excellent reconnaissance and attack resolution. Some UAS can be fitted with laser designators to mark targets and others may be armed. Other capabilities currently provided are:

- Support target acquisition efforts and lethal attacks on enemy reconnaissance and advance forces.
- Assist in route, area, and zone reconnaissance.
- Locate and help determine enemy force composition, disposition, and activity.

- Maintain contact with enemy forces from initial contact through battle damage assessment.
- Provide target coordinates with enough accuracy to enable an immediate target handover, as well as first-round fire-for-effect engagements.
- Provide or enhance multispectrum sensor coverage of the AO.
- Provide extended three-dimensional vantage, both in distance and time, at critical decision points in difficult terrain.
- Perform decoy, demonstration, feint, and deception operations.
- Support mission duration beyond those of manned systems.
- Provide digital connectivity, allowing for rapid product dissemination.

Limitations of UAS

10-53.   While UAS are an excellent force multiplier, they have limited effectiveness in locating enemy forces that are well covered or concealed. Tactical unmanned aircraft (UA), such as Shadow and Raven, are not well suited for wide area searches. Rather, employing UA as part of an overall collection plan takes advantage of their capabilities. Other limitations include--

- Vulnerability to enemy fire.
- Weather restrictions (cloud cover, turbulence, and others).
- Must maintain line of sight to ground control stations.
- Limited frequencies for UAS control.
- Air space command and control issues.
- Limited sensor field of view.
- Limited detection capability in highly vegetated areas.
- Unique Class III/V Requirements.
- Assembly Area survivability.

RQ-11 Raven

10-54.   The weapons company has the RQ-11 Raven, a small, man-portable, hand-launched, unmanned aircraft system used for reconnaissance, surveillance, and remote monitoring. The operator can launch and recover the Raven in minutes from unprepared terrain without special equipment. He can either control it remotely from the ground control unit, or he can set it up to fly completely autonomous missions using global positioning system (GPS) waypoint navigation. If the operator selects the "Home" command, the Raven will immediately return to its launch point.

Capabilities

- Expendability.
- Day and night imagery and operations.
- Low noise signature.
- Portability.
- Interchangeable payloads and components.
- Hand launched auto-landing or manual recovery.
- Auto navigation using military Py code GPS.
- Manual navigation and flight modes.
- Quick assembly (less than three minutes).
- Man-portable or backpack portable.
- Reusable (100 or more flights).
- Climbs to operational altitude in 1 to 2 minutes.

Limitations

- More difficult to launch in zero wind conditions. Mounted launch or launch from atop building or terrain is an option.
- Winds less than 20 knots increase battery use, which decreases system endurance, and can cause uncommanded altitude deviations.
- Extreme heat and cold reduces endurance and degrades system performance. Overheating can cause ground control unit failure.
- Night front-looking or side-looking camera only.
- Fragile components.

This page intentionally left blank.

Chapter 11

Sustainment Operations

The role of sustainment support in any military unit is to sustain the force for continuous combat operations. Within the Infantry battalion, sustainment at the company level is provided by the forward support company (FSC) from the brigade support battalion (BSB) and the battalion headquarters and headquarters company (HHC) under the staff supervision of the battalion executive officer (XO), HHC commander, S-1, and S-4. At the company level, the company commander has ultimate responsibility for sustainment. The XO and the first sergeant are the company's primary sustainment operators; they work closely with the battalion staff to ensure they receive the required support for the company's assigned operations.

Sustainment operations for the Infantry weapons company mirrors that of the Infantry rifle company as discussed in FM 3-21.10 with few minor changes. This chapter briefly discusses the elements of sustainment operations and identifies those aspects unique to the Infantry weapons company.

Section I. PLANNING CONSIDERATIONS

Infantry company commanders, as well as the battalion S-4, make plans and key decisions concerning sustainment. The battalion S-4, company XO, company first sergeant, company supply sergeant, platoon sergeants, and squad leaders implement these plans. Platoon leaders plan and relay support requirements for mission accomplishment to the company headquarters where it is consolidated and passed on to the battalion. Unit standing operating procedures (SOP) address planning, implementation, and responsibilities in detail and standardize as many routine sustainment operations as possible.

OVERVIEW

11-1.   The Infantry company plans, prepares, and executes its portion of the sustainment plan. Concurrent with other operational planning, the company develops and refines its sustainment plan during troop-leading procedures. Rehearsals are normally conducted at both battalion and company levels to ensure a smooth, continuous flow of materiel and services. The company's sustainment responsibilities follow:

- Determine requirements.
- Report status.
- Request support.
- Receive support.
- Distribute.

11-2.   Army Health System support in the Infantry weapons company is a critical sustainment function. The battalion medical platoon provides the Army Health System (AHS) support that includes Health Service Support (HSS) and Force Health Protection (FHP). The battalion medical platoon provides direct support (DS) support to the Infantry weapons company with a combat medic and habitually positions a ground ambulance team/crew with the company. Nonmedical personnel performing first-aid procedures assist the combat medic in his duties. First aid is administered by an individual (self-aid/buddy aid) and enhanced first aid by the combat lifesaver (CLS).

- Self-aid and buddy aid. Each individual Soldier is trained to be proficient in a variety of specific first-aid procedures. These procedures include aid for chemical casualties with particular emphasis on lifesaving tasks. This training enables the Soldier or a buddy to apply first aid to alleviate a life-threatening situation.
- Combat lifesaver. The CLS is a nonmedical Soldier selected by his unit commander for additional training beyond basic first-aid procedures. A minimum of one individual per squad, crew, team, or equivalent-sized unit should be trained. The primary duty of this individual does not change. The additional duty of the CLS is to provide enhanced first aid for injuries based on his training before the combat medic arrives. Combat lifesaver training is normally provided by medical personnel assigned, attached, or in sustainment units. The senior medical person designated by the commander manages the training program.

RESPONSIBILITIES

11-3.   In sustainment operations, roles differ slightly from other operations.

COMMANDER

11-4.   The commander ensures that his sustainment operations meet the tactical plan. He will--

- Assure sustainment operations sustain his company's fighting potential.
- Identify special requirements for the mission.
- Integrate and synchronize sustainment activities into the tactical plan.
- Provide guidance to the operators.

EXECUTIVE OFFICER

11-5.   The XO coordinates and supervises the company's logistical effort. During planning, he receives status reports from the platoon leaders, platoon sergeants, and first sergeant. He then reviews the tactical plan with the company commander to determine company sustainment requirements, and coordinates these needs with the battalion S-4. During execution, as determined by the company commander, the XO locates at the second most important place on the battlefield. At times, this is where he can best supervise sustainment operations. The XO also performs the following functions.

- Determines the location of the company's resupply point based on data developed during operational planning and the war-gaming process.
- Selects resupply method according to mission, enemy, terrain, troops, time, civilians (METT-TC) (Tailgate, Service Station, In Position).
- Maintains logistics status (LOGSTAT).
- Receives LOGSTAT from platoons.
- Completes company rollup and forwards to the combat trains command post (CTCP).
- Ensures that the company executes sustainment according to the battalion plan and SOP (along with the first sergeant).
- Ensures his unit sustainment requirements are met.

FIRST SERGEANT

11-6.   In addition to his tactical responsibilities, the first sergeant is a key player in sustaining the company. He is also key in the execution of the company's plan and may supervise the company trains based upon the commander's intent and the factors of METT-TC. He may assist the XO with LOGSTAT management and in preparing paragraph 4 of the operation order (OPORD). He normally supervises the evacuation of casualties, enemy prisoner of war (EPW), and damaged equipment in addition to supervising company resupply activities and monitoring company maintenance activities. The first sergeant orients new replacements and assigns them to squads and platoons in accordance with (IAW) the company commander's guidance. He assures proper tracking of casualties between battalion, platoon leadership, and the senior trauma specialist; and oversees the noncommissioned officer (NCO) chain performing sustainment functions and tasks IAW the company SOP. The first sergeant may also perform the following functions:

- Conduct sustainment rehearsals at the company level and integration with maneuver rehearsals.
- Perform command and control (C2) over company medic and oversee the evacuation plan from platoon to company CCP.
- Maintain the company battle roster.
- Maintains personnel status (PERSTAT)
- Receives PERSTAT from the platoons

SUPPLY SERGEANT

11-7.   The supply sergeant is the company representative for resupply to the company and based upon METT-TC may locate in either the combat trains or battalion field trains. He assists the FSC in assembling the logistics package (LOGPAC) and moves with the LOGPAC forward to the company. He coordinates the company's sustainment requirements with the FSC distribution platoon leader and the Infantry battalion S-4. The supply sergeant may control the casualty evacuation (CASEVAC) vehicle when it is unable to remain forward with the company. He monitors the tactical situation and adjusts the sustainment plan as appropriate to meet the tactical plan and the company commander's guidance. He may assist the commander by establishing caches. He forecasts the company's consumption of food; water; ammunition; petroleum, oils, and lubricants (POL); and batteries; based on the operation. The supply sergeant also performs the following sustainment functions.

- Coordinate with the battalion S-4 for resupply of Classes I, III, and V.
- Maintain individual supply and clothing records.
- Requisition Class II resupply as needed.
- Request Class IV and Class VII equipment and supplies.
- Coordinate for maintenance support from the Forward Support Company maintenance section to include turn in and pick up maintenance documents, routine Class IX supplies, and recoverable materials.
- Pick up replacement and return to duty personnel and, if necessary, deliver them to the first sergeant.
- Coordinate for receipt and evacuation of human remains and personal effects.
- Transport, guard, and transfer EPW as required.
- Accompany the LOGPAC to the logistics release point.
- Guide the LOGPAC to the company resupply point.
- Accompany the LOGPAC along with EPW and damaged vehicles (if applicable) back to the brigade support area (BSA).
- Coordinate with the battalion S-1 section to turn in and pick up mail and personnel action documents.
- Collect hazardous material and transport it to collection points as part of LOGPAC procedures.
- Maintain and provide supplies for company field sanitation activities.

PLATOON SERGEANT

11-8.   Each PSG in the company performs the following sustainment functions.

- Ensure Soldiers perform proper maintenance on all assigned equipment.
- Compile and submit all personnel and logistics status reports for the platoon as directed or in accordance with SOP.
- Collect DA Form 2404 (*Equipment Inspection and Maintenance Worksheet*) or DA Form 5988E (*Equipment Inspection and Maintenance Worksheet [EGA]*).
- Obtain supplies and equipment (all classes except Class VIII) and mail from the supply sergeant and ensures proper distribution within the platoon.

COMBAT MEDIC

A combat medic or senior company medic is attached to the weapons company to provide emergency medical treatment for sick, injured, or wounded company personnel. For a detailed list of combat medic responsibilities, see Chapter 1 of this manual.

Section II. TRAINS, SUPPLY, AND TRANSPORTATION

The logistical focal point is described as the trains. Sustainment personnel and equipment organic or attached to a force that provides support such as supply, evacuation, and maintenance services comprise the unit trains.

TRAINS

11-9.   The company trains are the focal point for company sustainment operations. It is the most forward sustainment element, and provides essential medical treatment and critical resupply support. The size and composition of the company trains vary depending upon the tactical situation. The trains may consist of nothing more than preplanned locations on the ground (a control measure such as a checkpoint) during fast-paced offensive operations, or the trains may contain two to five tactical vehicles during resupply operations. The company trains are established to conduct evacuation (of wounded in action (WIA), weapons, and equipment) and resupply as required. The company trains are located in a covered and concealed position, close enough to the company to provide responsive support, but out of enemy direct fire. The first sergeant or XO will position the trains and supervise sustainment operations. Support to the company trains comes from the battalion's supporting FSC. In a non-contiguous area of operations (AO) the BSA, combat trains and company trains may be located within a forward operating base (FOB) for added security. The combat trains may be located either in a FOB with the BSA or with the battalion itself. Figure 11-1 shows a typical trains layout.

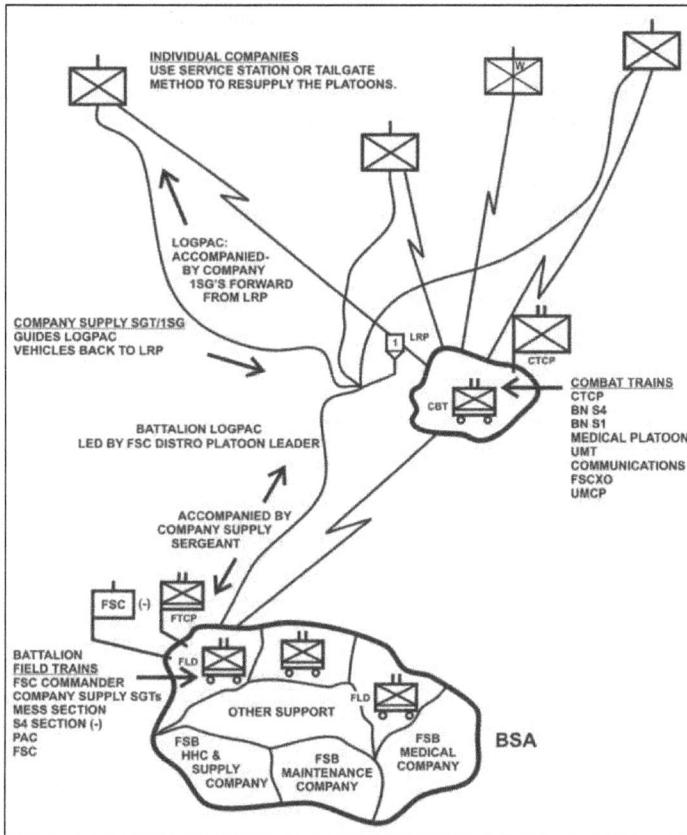

Figure 11-1. Trains layout.

SECURITY

11-10.   Security of sustainment elements is critical to the success of the Infantry company and battalion missions. For this reason, the company trains must develop plans for continuous security operations. Generally, company trains are located between 500 and 1,000 meters away from the company's combat operations. By placing at least one terrain feature between it and the enemy, the company trains will be out of engagement by the enemy's direct fire weapons. This location gives the company virtually immediate access to essential sustainment functions while allowing the trains to remain in a covered and concealed position behind the company combat elements. Where feasible, they may plan and execute a perimeter defense. The trains, however, may lack the personnel to conduct a major security effort. In such situations, they must plan and implement passive security measures to provide protection from enemy forces.

FORWARD SUPPORT COMPANY

11-11.   The FSC is a multifunctional sustainment unit organized to provide habitual and direct support to the Infantry battalion, Figure 11-2, and subsequently to the Infantry companies and weapons company. The FSC directly supports the Infantry battalion and a close SOP supported relationship exists between the units. Both the BSB and Infantry battalion commanders ensure the FSC is integrated tightly into the Infantry battalion's operations in garrison, training, and in combat. In the modular force, the FSC is responsible for conducting the majority of sustainment operations that were conducted previously by the Infantry battalion HHC. These responsibilities include—

- Field level vehicle and equipment maintenance and recovery.
- Resupply operations for all classes of supply (except medical) and water.
- Transportation for all classes of supply.
- Supplemental transportation of personnel with no organic wheel movement capability. The FSC can move one Infantry company at any one time.
- LOGPAC operations.

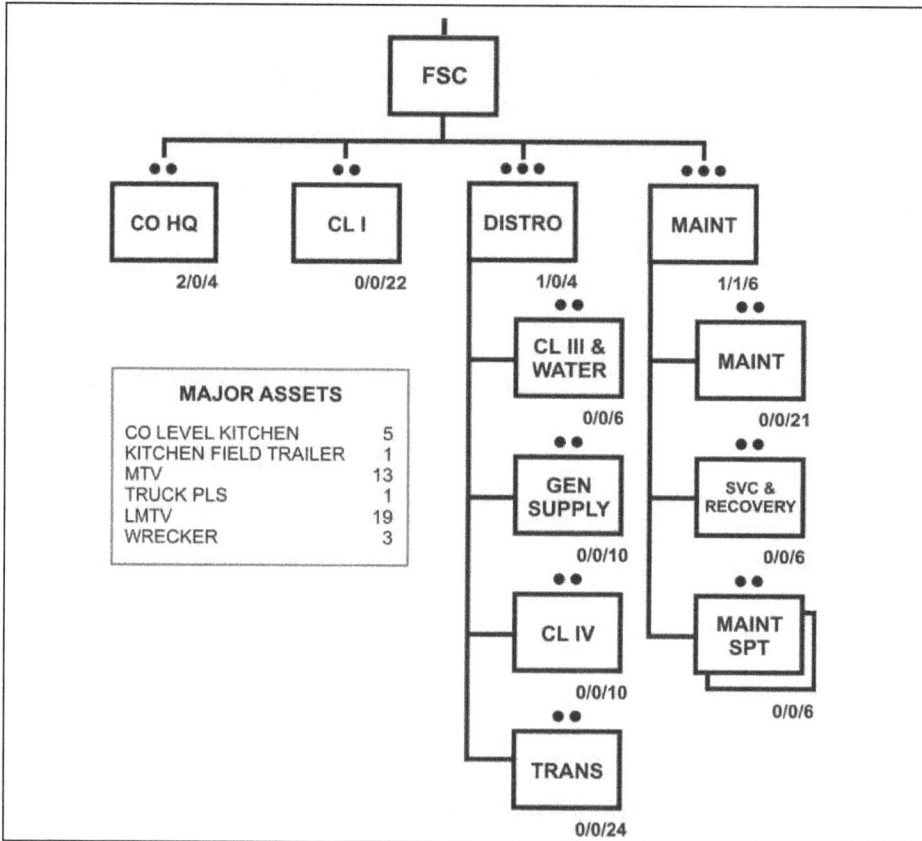

Figure 11-2. Forward support company.

11-12.   The FSC commander is the senior logistics commander at battalion level. He is not the planner; however, he assists the battalion S-1 and S-4 with the battalion's logistics planning. The FSC commander is responsible for executing the logistics plan IAW the battalion commander's guidance as developed by the battalion S-1 and S-4. The FSC commander responds directly to the guidance and directives given by the Infantry battalion XO who serves as the battalion logistics integrator and assists the battalion S-1 and S-4 in logistics synchronization and troubleshooting. Many functions described in this section are a coordinated effort between the FSC commander and the battalion S-1 and S-4. The FSC commander provides information, input, or feedback to the battalion S-1 and S-4 for their use in planning and coordination. He also provides the battalion commander a logistics common operational picture. The FSC regularly interfaces with the BSB in order to provide logistics support to the battalion. He ensures requests are filled correctly by the support operations officer and the distribution company in the BSB.

11-13.   The FSC XO is the principle assistant to the FSC company commander. As second in command, he must understand both operations that provide support to the Infantry battalion, and the other functions of the FSC. He often serves as the FSC liaison officer at the CTCP.

11-14.   The first sergeant is the commander's primary logistics and tactical advisor and the company's primary internal logistics operator. He often assists in the operation of the battalion field trains command post and FSC headquarters (HQ).

11-15.   The distribution platoon provides supply and transportation support to the Infantry battalion. The distribution platoon provides Class I (to include food service support), II, III (P, B), IV, V, VI, and VII, to the battalion. The distribution section has the ability to conduct simultaneous Class III and V retail support to the maneuver companies, the Infantry battalion HHC, and the FSC itself. The distribution platoon leader of the FSC takes over the responsibilities previously held by the support platoon leader in the Infantry battalion. The key activity of the distribution platoon is the conduct of LOGPAC operations to the battalion, and acquiring replenishment sustainment stocks from sustainment brigade units through combat replenishment operations and sustainment replenishment operations.

11-16.   The FSC's maintenance platoon provides field maintenance to itself and the Infantry battalion. The platoon consists of a headquarters section and maintenance control section, recovery and service section, and two field maintenance support teams. The maintenance platoon provides C2 and reinforcing maintenance to the field maintenance support teams. The field maintenance support teams provide field maintenance and battle damage assessment and repair (BDAR) primarily to the weapons company and the Infantry battalion HHC. As the battalion commander task organizes the force, all or part of a field maintenance support team goes with the company teams in order to maintain habitual support. The maintenance platoon maintains a limited quantity of combat spares (prescribed load list (PLL), shop, and bench stock) in the maintenance control section. The maintenance platoon's supply section can provide Class IX support (combat spares) to each maneuver company and the HHC. It maintains combat spares (PLL, shop, and bench stock) for the unit it supports and also provides exchange of reparable items.

BATTALION TRAINS

11-17.   The weapons company receives most of its' support from the FSC located in the battalion trains. The battalion uses consolidated unit trains only when occupying a battalion assembly area or when the terrain restricts movement so that the battalion must depend on aerial resupply and evacuation for support. In this case, the unit trains and all sustainment assets are placed in one central location. However, the Infantry battalion normally operates in echeloned trains where the trains are split into multiple locations. Echeloned trains for the battalion normally consist of two types: the battalion combat trains and the field trains.

Combat Trains

11-18.   Generally, combat trains are located between 1 and 4 kilometers away from the company's combat operations. This allows the combat trains to be outside the range of enemy mortars. The combat trains should not be considered a permanent or stationary support area. The battalion combat trains usually consist of the S-1, the HHC's medical platoon, the unit ministry team, communications personnel, forward elements of the FSC, and emergency resupply trucks (e.g. CL III and V). They are supervised by the CTCP, which is headed by the battalion S-4. The trains are positioned based upon the factors of METT-TC. The battalion's combat trains control all resupply operations for the Infantry battalion. At times, the battalion may move company supply sections forward, and an Infantry company may store its sustainment load with its company supply section in the combat trains. The company sustainment load normally consists of rucksacks, duffel bags containing extra clothing and personal items, chemical protective over garments, and sleeping bags. As the alternate main command post, and in the event that they must assume responsibilities as the main command post, the combat trains command post must maintain situational understanding (SU) of current and future battalion operations.

Field Trains

11-19.   The fields trains are positioned based on METT-TC considerations and often will be located in the BSA. The field trains normally consist of the FSC, Infantry battalion PAC, personnel transitioning to and from the battalion and the HHC, and Infantry company and weapons company supply sections. Usually, the Infantry and weapons companies will store its sustainment loads with its company supply section in the field trains. The units in the field trains operate as the primary direct coordination element between the Infantry companies and the BSA. The FSC fills orders with on-hand stocked items. Requests for those items not on-hand in the FSC are forwarded.

SUPPLY

11-20.   The weapons company normally deploys with 72 hours of supplies. The commander uses the unit basic load as the frame of reference for determining 72 hours worth of supplies. The company commander considers his situation to decide on the best means of resupplying his company. Resupply requests are classified as either routine or emergency. Cues and procedures for each method are specified in the company SOP and are rehearsed during company training exercises. The resupply method is typically either tailgate or service station depending on METT-TC. Infantry companies are supported by the Infantry battalion and its' direct support FSC, which in turn is supported by the BSB. Supplies are divided into 10 major categories, which are referred to as classes. For a complete description of each type of supply and how they relate to the company see FM 3-21.10. The 10 classes are:

> Class I – Subsistence Items and Water
> Class II – Consumable supplies
> Class III – Petroleum, oils and lubricants
> Class IV – Construction and Barrier Materials
> Class V – Ammunition
> Class VI – Personal Demand Items
> Class VII – Major End Items
> Class VIII – Medical Materiel
> Class IX – Repair Parts and Components
> Class X – Material to Support Civil Programs

ROUTINE RESUPPLY

11-21.   Routine resupply operations cover items in Classes I, III, V, and IX, as well as mail and any other items requested by the company. Resupply operations normally occur once a day. Whenever possible, routine resupply should be conducted daily, ideally during periods of limited visibility. Resupply operations mimic those of the Infantry rifle company. Detailed descriptions of logistic package operations (LOGPAC), and resupply methods and procedures can be found in FM 3-21.10. The three methods of resupply are:

- Service Station resupply
- Tailgate resupply
- In-position resupply

EMERGENCY RESUPPLY

11-22.   Occasionally (normally during combat operations), the company may have such an urgent need for resupply that it cannot wait for a routine LOGPAC. Emergency resupply may involve Classes III, V, and VIII, as well as chemical, biological, radiological or nuclear (CBRN) supplies and, on rare occasions, Class I. Emergency resupply can be conducted using either the service station or tailgate method, but more often the in-position method. The fastest appropriate means is normally used although procedures might have to be adjusted when the company is in contact with the enemy. In the service station method, individual squads may pull back during a lull in combat to conduct resupply and then return to the fight. With tailgate resupply, the company brings limited supplies forward to the closest concealed position behind each element.

PRESTOCK OPERATIONS

11-23.   Prestock resupply, which includes pre-positioning and caching, is most often required in defensive operations. Normally only Class IV and V items are pre-positioned. Prestock operations must be carefully planned and executed at every level. All leaders must know the exact locations of prestock sites, which they verify during reconnaissance or rehearsals. The company must take steps to ensure survivability of the prestock supplies. These measures include digging in prestock positions and selecting covered and concealed positions. The company commander must also have a plan to remove or destroy pre-positioned supplies to prevent the enemy from capturing them.

Caches

11-24.   A cache is a pre-positioned and concealed supply point. It can be used in any operation. Caches are an excellent tool for reducing the Soldier's load and can be set up for a specific mission or as a contingency measure. However, concealing the bulky and sensitive supplies, such as fuel and missiles, for weapons company vehicles and heavy weapons systems is difficult to do. Leaders must weight the risks to determine if a cache is warranted. A security risk always exists when returning to a cache. An above ground cache is easier to get to but is more likely to be discovered by the enemy, civilians, or animals.

SECURITY

11-25.   While these supply techniques are used in both offensive and defensive operations, the transfer of supplies to the company is usually conducted from a defensive posture. As such, the security considerations for a resupply operation are like those for a perimeter defense.

SUPPLY CONSIDERATIONS

11-26.   The techniques just described are the normal methods for resupply within the company. However, a basic understanding of nonstandard techniques, different modes of delivery, and specific supply issues is also required to successfully execute the sustainment function (FM 3-21.10). These techniques include--

- Foraging and scavenging.
- Aerial resupply.
- Cross-leveling.
- Backhauling.
- Managing consumption of water.

TRANSPORTATION

11-27.   Movement of supplies, equipment, and personnel with the limited vehicle assets available requires careful planning and execution. The weapons company has limited organic transportation for resupply operations. The 2 ½ ton cargo truck provided for company resupply will most often be used to carry class I and small amounts of Class III, V, IX or other class supplies. Vehicle assets from battalion or the forward supply company are provided to supplement company assets for resupply operations.

11-28.   When extra vehicles are provided to the company, they are employed to capitalize on their capability to execute the mission requirement, and must be returned for follow-on company or parent-unit missions. Transportation assets are scarce, often resulting in trade-offs. For example, upload increased quantities of ammunition and less water, or carry unit rucksacks and be unavailable for resupply. The company commander must ensure that the asset is being employed to accomplish the most important mission. Time is critical and the company must reduce on-station time so that all company requirements can be met. Since most vehicles do not have radios, leaders must ensure that drivers know where they are going and how to get there. Land navigation training, marked routes, and strip maps referenced to landmarks are all ways to keep drivers from getting lost.

11-29.   Because of the limited ground transportation, company personnel must know how to conduct aerial resupply (FM 90-4). An understanding of pickup zones (PZ)/landing zones (LZ) selection, sling loading, bundle drops, and allowable cargo loads might be critical to company sustainment.

Section III. MAINTENANCE

The maintenance of weapons and equipment is continuous. Every Soldier must know how to maintain his weapon and equipment in accordance with the related technical manual. The commander, XO, and first sergeant must understand maintenance for every piece of equipment in the company.

UNIT MAINTENANCE

11-30.   Proper maintenance is the key to keeping vehicles, equipment, and other materials in serviceable condition. This continuous process starts when the operator of each piece of equipment or vehicle takes preventive measures and continues through repair and recovery of the equipment. Proper maintenance also includes inspecting, testing, servicing, repairing, requisitioning, recovering, and evacuating equipment.

MAINTENANCE STRUCTURE

11-31.   The Infantry brigade combat team (IBCT) uses the two level maintenance structure for repair and recovery of equipment. The two levels are the "Field Level Maintenance" designated as "On System Maintenance" and "Sustainment Level Maintenance" designated as "Off System Maintenance." Field level maintenance is focused at the IBCT level with one FSC in support of each battalion. Organic to the FSC is a maintenance platoon designated as a combat repair team (CRT) that is responsible for repair and recovery of battalion equipment.

VEHICLE MAINTENANCE

11-32.   Infantry weapons companies are uniquely different than rifle companies in that they are highly mobile units. All weapons company personnel operate from some type of vehicle with the majority being high mobility multipurpose wheeled vehicles (HMMWV). It is imperative that proper vehicle maintenance is maintained in order to keep the unit mobile and ready to perform its' mission. Operators should carefully follow unit standing operating procedures for maintaining vehicles. Limited repair may be accomplished by the operator depending on the extent of the damage or malfunction. If necessary, send the vehicle rearward for repair. A recovery team from the FSC maintenance platoon performs vehicle recovery. The weapons company does not have a company level maintenance area or personnel outside operator maintenance. Repair of evacuated vehicles will be accomplished by the FSC CRT either at the battalion unit maintenance collection point (UMCP) located near the battalion combat trains, or at the battalion field trains located in the brigade support area.

11-33.   Vehicle maintenance is critical to mission accomplishment. Poorly maintained vehicles will fail. As they do, the operating tempo for functional vehicles increases. Potential adverse effects can result in:

*   Reduced weapon carrying capacity and therefore reduced combat power.
*   Increased probability of platoons and sections having vehicle assigned from other units during missions.
*   Increased maintenance problems for overused vehicles.

Commanders are responsible for operator and crew level maintenance on vehicles and equipment. The FSC's organic maintenance platoon and its two field maintenance support teams also provide field level maintenance for vehicles and equipment. Normally the field maintenance support teams are tasked to provide maintenance support to the Infantry battalion headquarters and weapons companies. If the Infantry battalion task organizes, the field maintenance support teams provide prioritized support as specified by the battalion. The BSB's field maintenance company provides very limited backup support to FSCs, since it primarily supports to non-maneuver units (brigade combat team (BCT) HQ, BSB, and brigade special troops battalion (BSTB)). It also serves as the maintenance point for low-density equipment (e.g., tube-launched, optically-tracked, wire-guided (TOW) missile systems). When required, the BSB dispatches field maintenance teams to perform on-site diagnoses, make minor adjustments, and conduct repairs. Equipment that cannot be repaired by the BSB usually is evacuated to sustainment brigade units.

WEAPONS AND OTHER EQUIPMENT

11-34. Maintenance on other equipment such as weapons and communications equipment has limited field level maintenance available. Maintenance beyond the skill level of assigned personnel will need evacuation to the FSC or the BSB for repair.

UNIT MAINTENANCE COLLECTION POINT

11-35. The UMCP is normally located near the battalion combat trains or collocated with the combat trains for security, and should be on a main axis or supply route. The UMCP is manned by elements of the FSC. The UMCP provides vehicle and equipment evacuation, and maintenance support to the field maintenance support teams. Field maintenance support teams evacuate vehicles and equipment to the UMCP that cannot be repaired within 2 hours. Normally, vehicles or equipment evacuated to the UMCP that cannot be towed or repaired within 4-6 hours, are further evacuated to the field trains, BSB, or higher-level support unit.

11-36. UMCP does not have to be located in the battalion combat trains; however, if not in the same location, the UMCP is normally in the general vicinity. The advantages to collocating the UMCP at the combat trains is for increased security, and coordination of class IX resupply. The trains must be mobile enough to support frequent changes in location, time and terrain permitting, under the following conditions when—

- Heavy use or traffic in the area may cause detection.
- Area becomes worn by heavy use such as in wet and muddy conditions.
- Security is compromised.

MAINTENANCE CONSIDERATIONS

11-37. The maintenance of weapons and equipment is continuous. Every Soldier must know how to maintain his weapon and equipment IAW the related technical manual. Proper operator level maintenance is key to keeping vehicles, equipment, and other materials in serviceable condition. It is a continuous process that starts with preventive measures taken by each operator of each piece of equipment or vehicle and continues through repair and recovery of the equipment. It includes the functions of inspecting, testing, servicing, repairing, requisitioning, recovering, and evacuating equipment. See FM 4-30.3 for more information on maintenance operations and procedures.

11-38. Maintenance functions begin with preventive maintenance checks and services, a daily responsibility for each piece of equipment to include inspection and completion of maintenance forms when required. The DA Form 5988-E is the primary means through which the company obtains maintenance support or repair parts. The forms follow a path from operator/crew level to the BSA and back. The company XO or first sergeant supervises the "flow" of these critical maintenance documents and parts based on the unit's SOP. These instructions must be integrated into the SOPs for patrol bases, assembly areas, defenses, and reorganization to ensure that maintenance is done without jeopardizing unit security.

11-39. Inoperative equipment is fixed as far forward as possible. When a piece of equipment is damaged, it should be inspected to see if it could be repaired on the spot. Company armorers keep a small-arms repair kit in the company vehicle. If equipment cannot be repaired forward, it is evacuated immediately to the UMCP and returned with a LOGPAC. Even if the item cannot be evacuated at once, the sustainment system is alerted to prepare for repair or replacement. If a replacement is available (from an evacuated Soldier or inoperative equipment), it is sent forward. If not, the leader must work around it by prioritizing the use of remaining equipment.

11-40. In addition to operator maintenance, selected Soldiers are trained to perform limited maintenance on damaged weapons and BDAR. (see FM 4-30.31) The purpose of BDAR is to return disabled combat equipment to the tactical commander as quickly as possible. It is characterized by rapid damage assessment and repair, and the bypassing or the temporary fixing of components to support a combat mission or enable self-recovery. The CTCP implements the commander's guidance on whether or not to use BDAR in lieu of normal maintenance procedures. Such enabling repairs are usually temporary. At the completion of immediate combat operations, mechanics from the FSC will make repairs that will return the equipment to fully mission-capable status. Since it may not be possible to train BDAR techniques in peacetime using actual equipment, the best substitute is to train system-oriented crews and mechanics to understand the principles associated with weapon systems. BDAR actions include--

- Using shortcuts to install or remove parts.
- Modifying and installing components designed for other vehicles or equipment.
- Using parts serving a noncritical function on a like vehicle.
- Using substitute fuels, fluids, or other POL.
- Using readily available materials to execute a temporary repair.

VEHICLE RECOVERY

11-41. Many recovery operations consist of self-recovery methods when the vehicle becomes stuck, mechanical disabled, or disabled due to enemy action. Establish security before the vehicle is recovered. Vehicle recovery is easiest when the tires still have traction and when crewmembers can help the vehicle move through the original tire tracks. When the vehicle is stuck in snow, sand, or mud, the crew can lower tire pressure to increase traction. Using a second vehicle to help winch or pull a stuck vehicle is normally the quickest recovery method. The company should always carry tow straps or chains. They should have hooks or clevises attached to both ends for anchoring to the vehicles. If possible, the company carries at least one tow bar for each vehicle section to assist in long-range recovery or to tow a vehicle at high speed. When a vehicle is stuck in mud or sand, the unit uses pioneer tools to emplace dry or solid matter under the tires for traction. Sandbags or other materials can be dug into and under the wheels to assist traction. Vehicles should carry empty sandbags for this purpose. When using the vehicle winch, crews should follow these basic dos and don'ts.

- Do--
  -- Use the stuck vehicle's wheel power to help the winch.
  -- Carefully prepare the winching operation.
  -- Position personnel where they will not be injured should the cable snap or unhook.
  -- Ensure the anchor points are solid.
  -- Use artificial surfaces for traction when the vehicle is stuck in water or soft sand.
- Do not--
  -- Overtake the cable.
  -- Exceed the maximum angle of pull.

11-42. The commander should make contingency plans for vehicles that cannot be repaired or recovered. The company will make every attempt to recover the vehicle and return it where it can be repaired, if needed. However, if the company cannot recover the vehicle, then they may have to destroy it in place to prevent the enemy from capturing it.

DESTRUCTION

11-43. When a vehicle or piece of equipment cannot be recovered or is damaged beyond repair, the platoon reports the situation to the company commander. The commander gives permission for destruction of the materiel if that is the only way to prevent enemy capture. Operators remove all salvageable equipment and parts and take all classified materials or paperwork that could be of intelligence value to the enemy. The platoon then destroys the vehicle or equipment IAW the company SOP.

Section IV. ARMY HEALTH SYSTEM SUPPORT

Effective timely medical care is an essential factor in sustaining the company's combat power during continuous operations. The company commander must ensure that the company's leaders and its medical personnel are aware of the potential health threats and implements field sanitation and preventive medicine measures to keep Soldiers healthy. They must also be prepared to care for wounded personnel or non-battle injuries through self-aid, buddy-aid, enhanced first-aid, CLS or emergency medical treatment and preparing casualties for evacuation. AHS provides for both the conservation of Soldier's health through FHP, and for treating wounded, sick or injured Soldiers through HSS.

FORCE HEALTH PROTECTION

11-44. FHP covers those measures to promote, improve, or conserve the mental or physical well-being of Soldiers. These measures help enable the prevention of injuries and illnesses as well as assisting in protecting Soldiers from health hazards and helping to ensure Soldiers are healthy, fit and ready for combat.

PREVENTIVE MEDICINE

11-45. History continues to show that more Soldiers are lost in combat due to illness caused by disease and nonbattle injury (DNBI) than to combat wounds. Therefore, maintaining the health and fighting fitness of Soldiers is a vital responsibility of all leaders. Commanders reduce the health threat by emphasizing preventive measures. All leaders must be active participants in the areas of hygiene, sanitation, counseling, and in the treatment of stress and combat and operational stress reaction (COSR). The IBCT preventive medicine (PVNTMED) functional assets include—

- Preventive medicine.
- Combat and operational stress control.
- Preventive dentistry and good oral hygiene.

11-46. Rules of hygiene should be established in the tactical standing operating procedure (TSOP) and observed daily to prevent the spread of disease. Immunizations must be current. Soldiers should wash and change undergarments daily. Proper clothing and inspections can assist in the prevention of cold and hot weather injuries. Comprehensive field sanitation will prevent the spread of debilitating diseases. Use only approved or tested water sources. Utensils used for eating must be properly cleaned before reuse. In static situations, Soldiers use slit trenches or latrines; at other times they use cat holes. All must be covered after use to prevent the spread of disease.

11-47. Rest is extremely important and the effects of sleep degradation are disastrous to unit missions and personnel. Sleep plans must be practiced and established in the TSOP. When possible, Soldiers should sleep outside vehicles to allow them to fully stretch out and get the full benefit of at least four hours of continuous sleep.

11-48. The combat operational environment is full of risks associated with vehicles, weapons, stress, and fatigue that can prove dangerous in matters unrelated to combat. The TSOP incorporates safety concerns in establishing procedures for assembly areas and other locations of troop concentrations. Equipment and weapons operating procedures emphasize safety, but it is up to leaders to continually enforce proper equipment-operating procedures and safety TSOP. Continuous focus on safety can prevent accidents.

COMBAT AND OPERATIONAL STRESS CONTROL

11-49.   Many stressors in a combat situation are due to deliberate enemy actions aimed at killing, wounding, or demoralizing our Soldiers and our allies. Other stressors are due to the natural environment, such as intense heat and cold, humidity, or poor air quality. Still others are due to leaders' own calculated or miscalculated choices (such as, decisions about unit strength, maneuver, and time of attack, and plans for medical and logistical support). Sound leadership works to keep these operational stressors within tolerable limits and prepares troops mentally and physically to endure them. In some cases, excessive stress can affect both leaders' and Soldiers' decision-making and judgment, resulting in missed opportunities, or worse, in high casualties and/or failure to complete the mission. Finally, some of the most potent stressors are interpersonal in nature and can be due to conflict in the unit or on the home front. In the extreme, reactions to such stressors may involve harm to self or to others. These stressors must be identified and when possible, corrected or controlled. For behavioral health/combat operational stress control (COSC) support, contact the supporting medical company through the medical support section. For information on control of combat stressors and for details about specific leader and individual actions to control stress, see FM 4-02.51, FM 22-51, and FM 6-22.5.

11-50.   Combat and operational stress control focuses on FHP aspects of treatment and prevention of COSR including the rapid reversal of COSR. These PVNTMED capabilities are essential to enhancing Soldier survivability across full spectrum operations. By making continual health hazard assessments a priority, disease and injury can be minimized. All BCTs have a mental health section consisting of a behavioral science officer and a mental health specialist. The BCT chaplain assists with behavioral health and COSC services by helping unit commanders identify Soldiers who are stressed. "

UNIT FORCE HEALTH PROTECTION PROGRAM

11-51.   The weapons company commander and all leaders, in conjunction with the company combat medic and field sanitation team, emphasize and enforce high standards of health and hygiene at all times. A proactive FHP program implemented at the Infantry weapons company level should include personal health and hygiene, preventive medicine, preventive dentistry, combat and operational stress control, food safety, and awareness of potential health threats. Company leaders and members must be informed on preventive medicine measures to counter health threats and to maintain their health and overall fitness to perform their mission. Health and hygiene and FHP activities may require —--

- Developing a FHP SOP.
- Daily shaving to ensure proper fit of the protective mask.
- Regular bathing and changing of clothes.
- These include cold injuries such as frostbite, trench foot, and immersion foot, and heat injuries like heat exhaustion and heat stroke. Soldiers must understand the effects of conditions such as sunburn and wind-chill.
- Prevention of diseases. Insect-borne diseases such as malaria and Lyme disease, and diarrhea diseases can be prevented with effective field sanitation measures, including unit waste control, water purification, rodent control, and use of insect repellents.
- Combat and operational stress control (COSC) to include training for preventing and/or identifying and providing initials care for a Soldier with a combat and operational stress reaction.
- Adherence to and strict implementation of the unit sleep plan.
- Requesting assistance from supporting mental health section with COSC classes for stress reduction techniques and the prevention of combat and operational stress reactions (COSR).
- Conducting sanitation inspections of troop living area, food service areas, waste disposal and potable water distribution point and equipment.

HEALTH SERVICE SUPPORT

11-52.   A major function HSS is the care of sick, wounded, or injured Soldiers. It encompasses the treatment and evacuation of casualties. It also covers the training of nonmedical personnel in combat lifesaver in order to care for injured personnel until treatment by medical personnel is available.

CASUALTIES

11-53.   First response is defined as the initial, essential stabilizing care rendered to wounded, injured, or ill Soldiers at the point of initial injury or illness. The first responder is the first individual to reach a casualty and provide first aid, enhanced first aid, or emergency medical treatment. First aid can be performed by the casualty (self-aid) or another individual (buddy aid), while enhanced first aid is provided by the CLS. The individual who has medical military occupational specialty (MOS) training is the combat medic. He provides emergency medical treatment for life-threatening trauma, stabilizes and prioritizes (triages) wounded for evacuation to the battalion aid station (BAS). At the BAS, wounded Soldiers receive advanced trauma medicine by the medical treatment teams composed of the surgeon, physician's assistant, and health care specialists.

Casualty Response

11-54.   Casualty response for the weapons company is similar to that of the rifle company with few exceptions. For additional details on casualty response, see FM 3-21.10. The tiered levels of responsibility to a casualty remain as follows:

- Combat Lifesaver--The nonmedical Soldier trained to provide enhanced first aid/lifesaving procedures beyond the level of self-aid or buddy aid.
- Senior Combat Medic (Company Senior Medic)--The company's primary medical treatment practitioner and the supervisor of all battlefield medical operations.
- Combat Medic--The platoon medic is often called "doc" or "medic."
- Platoon Sergeant - Typically responsible for ensuring that wounded or injured personnel receive immediate first aid and that the commander is informed of casualties.
- First Sergeant - Oversees the operation of the company CCP and supervises/coordinates casualty operations.
- Commander - Bears overall responsibility for medical services.

Evacuation

11-55.   The two areas of medical support are treatment and evacuation. Casualty transport, commonly called CASEVAC, is the movement of casualties by nonmedical assets without en route medic care. Medical evacuation (MEDEVAC) is the movement of casualties using medical assets while providing en route medical care. Ideally, casualties are transferred to a CCP by CASEVAC and from the CCP normally by the supporting ground ambulance from the medical platoon in DS of the weapons company or supporting air ambulance asset. Effective evacuation of casualties has a positive impact on the morale of a unit. Ideally, casualties are cared for at the point of injury (or under nearby cover and concealment) by self- or buddy aid, receive enhanced first aid from the combat lifesaver, and emergency medical treatment from the combat medic (company or platoon medic) prior to or during CASEVAC operations.

11-56.   Before casualties are evacuated to the CCP or beyond, leaders should remove all key operational or sensitive items and equipment, including communications security (COMSEC) devices or signal operating instructions (SOI), maps, position location devices. Every unit should establish an SOP for handling the weapons and ammunition of its WIAs. Protective masks must stay with the individual.

Casualty Reporting

11-57.   Each individual Soldier should carry a blank DA Form 1156 (*Casualty Feeder Card*) *for* casualty reporting purposes. The 2007 version of DA Form 1156 is also the witness card. Persons having firsthand knowledge of a reportable casualty should prepare the casualty feeder card. Squad leaders and platoon sergeants are encouraged to carry extra copies of DA Form 1156. Soldiers will report casualties they witness or find, to include American civilians, personnel of other Services, Allied forces, and Soldiers from other units, using DA Form 1156. If DA Form 1156 is not available, casualty information will be written on blank paper. This information will be forwarded to the company commander/first sergeant. The company commander/first sergeant or a designated Soldier will collect the casualty feeder cards and verify as much information as possible and update the battle roster and casualty log. The reports will then be forwarded to the BN S-l.

SOLDIERS WOUNDED IN ACTION

11-58.   During the fight, casualties should remain under cover where they received initial treatment (self- or buddy aid). As soon as the situation allows, casualties are moved to the platoon CCP. From the platoon area, casualties are normally evacuated to the company CCP and then back to the BAS. The unit SOP addresses specifics for evacuation as well as the marking of casualties in limited visibility operations. Once the casualties are collected, evaluated, and treated, they are prioritized for evacuation back to the company CCP. Once they arrive at the company CCP, the above process is repeated while awaiting their evacuation back to the BAS. When possible, the HHC medical platoon ambulances provide evacuation and en route care from the Soldier's point of injury or the company's CCP to the BAS.

Evacuation of Soldiers Wounded in Action

11-59.   As a highly mobile unit, the weapons company has additional resources for casualty evacuation as the situation permits. Depending on the METT-TC conditions, the weapons company may have the opportunity to perform quicker CASEVAC procedures using platoon or company vehicles to the platoon and/or the company CCP. This allows for more options for casualty evacuation especially if the attached ambulance is unavailable. Casualties may also be evacuated directly from the platoon CCP via air ambulance or using nonstandard air platforms for CASEVAC. However, flights may be restricted due to the threat of enemy ground to air small arms, shoulder fired or other air defense weapons. In these cases, casualties often must be moved to the company CCP before further evacuation making the use of organic vehicles a great asset. If the capacity of the battalion's organic ambulances is exceeded, and platoon vehicles are not available due to mission requirements, unit leaders may use supply or other vehicles to backhaul casualties to the CCP or BAS. Field Manual 3-21.10, unit SOPs and OPORDs address casualty treatment and evacuation in further detail. They cover the duties and responsibilities of key personnel, the evacuation of chemically contaminated casualties (on separate routes from noncontaminated casualties), and the priority for operating key weapons and positions. They specify preferred and alternate methods of evacuation and make provisions for retrieving and safeguarding the weapons, ammunition, and equipment of casualties. For procedures in the use of the casualty feeder card, DA Form 1156, see FM 1-0, Human resources Support and FMI 1-0.01, S1 Operations.

Section V. OTHER OPERATIONS

To maintain effective, consistent combat power, the company must have specific plans and procedures that allow each element to integrate replacement personnel and equipment quickly. Unit standing operating procedure (SOP) defines how Soldiers and equipment are prepared for combat, including areas such as uploading, load plans, precombat inspections (PCI), and in-briefings.

REORGANIZATION

11-60.   Reorganization includes all measures taken by the commander to maintain the combat effectiveness of his unit or return it to a specified level of combat capability. Any reorganization actions not completed during an operation are accomplished during consolidation. These action include:

- Redistributing or cross-leveling supplies, ammunition, and equipment as necessary.
- Matching operational weapons systems with crews.
- Forming composite units by joining two or more attrited units to form a single, mission capable unit.
- Replacing key personnel lost before or during the battle.
- Reporting unit location and status to keep the next higher commander informed.
- Recovering, treating, and evacuating causalities, prisoners of war, and damaged equipment.
- Resupply of basic loads of ammunition, fuel, and repair parts as time permits.
- Integrating replacement Soldiers and systems into the unit.
- Revising communication plans as required.
- Reestablishing unit cohesion.
- Conducting essential training including training replacements.

ENEMY PRISONERS OF WAR, DETAINEES, AND OTHER RETAINED PERSONS

11-61.   All persons captured, detained, or retained by US Armed Forces during the course of military operations are considered "*detained*" persons until their status is determined by higher military and civilian authorities. The BCT has a military police platoon organic to the BSTB to take control of and evacuate detainees. However, as a practical matter, Infantry squads, platoons, companies and battalions capture and must provide the initial processing and holding for detainees. For further details on the handling of prisoners, detainees and other personnel see FM 3-21.10.

This page intentionally left blank.

Chapter 12

Urban Operations

The weapons company takes part in urban operations as part of the battalion. Weapons companies, platoons, and squads will seldom conduct urban operations (UO) independently and will most likely conduct assigned missions as part of a battalion operation. The weapons company may have one or more of its platoons detached to other companies within the battalion and have one or more Infantry platoons attached. It may act as a battalion reserve during operations and maneuvers as required to reinforce other battalion units. If the urban area is small, the weapons company may be assigned the task of isolating the objective by covering by fire avenues of approach or exit. UO places a high demand on effective leadership at the company, platoon, section, and squad levels. For more detailed information, refer to FM 3-21.10: The Infantry Rifle Company, and FM 3-21.20: The Infantry Battalion.

Section I. TACTICAL CONSIDERATIONS

Urban areas consist mainly of manmade features such as buildings, streets, and subterranean systems. These features of urban terrain create a variety of tactical problems and possibilities. To ensure the company can operate effectively in the urban environment, the unit's observation and direct fire plans must address the ground level fight in streets and on the ground floors of buildings, the above ground fight in multistoried buildings, and the subterranean fight. See FM 3-06, Urban Operations, and FM 3-06.11, Combined Arms Operations in Urban Terrain, for more information on the types of urban environments. The following considerations apply:

- Built up areas complicate, confuse, and degrade command and control.
- Streets are usually avenues of approach but they canalize forces and make obstacles more effective.
- Buildings offer cover and concealment and severely restrict movement of military elements, especially vehicles.
- Buildings severely restrict fire distribution and control, especially fields of fire. Every street corner and successive cross street becomes a potential enemy field of fire, requiring careful overwatch.
- Thick walled buildings provide ready-made fortified positions.
- Subterranean systems include subways, sewers, cellars, and utility systems

COMMAND AND CONTROL

12-1. The following considerations pertain to command and control in urban operations.

COMMUNICATIONS

12-2. The single-channel ground and airborne radio system (SINCGARS) is the first choice for communication in urban operations. However, during these operations, low-level task organization can take place that require elements to establish additional communications links. These links, and some Force

XXI Battle Command, Brigade and Below (FBCB2) traffic, can be impaired or disrupted by buildings and other urban terrain features.

FIRE CONTROL

12-3. Urban operations require extensive direct fire planning and restrictive fire control measures. Extensive use of restrictive fire lines (RFL) and other graphic control measures are essential.

PROXIMITY AND VISIBILITY

12-4. During urban operations, friendly elements often must operate in confined and restrictive areas. Because of these conditions, friendly elements may not be able to see other nearby friendly forces. These factors significantly increase the danger of fratricide. Therefore, increased communications and use of graphic control measures are critical. Phase lines, routes, and checkpoints will be most commonly used by a weapons company element.

PERSONNEL FACTORS

12-5. Urban operations impose significant, and often extreme, physical and psychological demands on Soldiers and leaders. Increased use of supplies by Infantry (such as: water, ammunition, marking materiel, etc.), and the increased chance of casualties from urban operations add to these demands.

ROE/ROI AND CIVILIANS

12-6. The rules of engagement (ROE) and/or rules of interaction (ROI) may restrict the use of certain weapons systems and tactics, techniques, and procedures (TTP). This is because noncombatants are integral parts of the urban environment and as such, create special operational challenges. If allowed by his commander and the ROE, the weapons company commander can use his organic weapons to--

- Destroy enemy units and positions with machine gun fire.
- Provide accurate and destructive fires with close combat missiles.
- Suppress enemy fire positions with machine gun fire.
- Find and suppress enemy forces by conducting reconnaissance by fire missions

THE SLOW PACE OF URBAN OPERATIONS

12-7. Urban operations are usually slow and deliberate, and mounted weapon systems must maintain the same pace as the dismounted Infantry. This can be accomplished by using graphical control measures such as phase lines and maintaining close coordination and communication with the accompanying Infantry. Staying within visual contact, supporting distance, and maintaining situational understanding of the Infantry fight also enables the weapons leader to keep pace with the Infantry and provide fire support.

MANEUVER

12-8. The following factors relate to weapons company unit's maneuver in the urban environment:

PREPARATION

12-9. Urban operations require extensive intelligence activities, efficient communication, and effective rehearsals. This places a requirement at the company and platoon levels to conduct a thorough intelligence preparation of the battlefield (IPB). The IPB can be enhanced through the use of--

- Unmanned aircraft systems (UAS).
- Reconnaissance patrols.

- Sniper teams and Weapons units to observe the area.
- Intelligence from units with experience of the area.
- Satellite photographs.
- Information from friendly civilians and/or informants.

PLANNING AND EXECUTION

12-10. Because of the control required and the decentralized nature of combat during urban operations, detailed centralized planning and decentralized execution is required. Realistic and detailed rehearsals are essential so that Soldiers at all levels understand the plan and the missions of other units.

COOPERATION

12-11. Urban operations can be successful only when Infantry, direct fire support vehicles, and other units (such as indirect fire and engineers) closely cooperate together at the lowest possible level. This can be accomplished by having a simple and well-rehearsed plan and close coordination during its execution.

TASK ORGANIZATION

12-12. Task organization usually is done no lower than platoon level.

MUTUAL SUPPORT

12-13. Weapons company units provide firepower to support the Infantry and other weapons company units while the Infantry provides, by their proximity, close-in security for the weapons company units.

ENEMY ORGANIZATIONS AND CAPABILITIES

12-14. In addition to conventional forces, the enemy in urban areas may include--

- Unconventional forces.
- Paramilitary forces.
- Militia and special police organizations
- Organized criminal organizations.

12-15. Trends indicate that potential opponents in urban operations increasingly find and use sophisticated technology and unorthodox operational approaches to counter the responses of U.S. forces and its allies. To offset their inherent weaknesses, enemy forces seek the advantage in urban and complex terrain by remaining dispersed and decentralized. These forces can employ the full range of military ordinance and organizations: from small arms, mortars, machine guns, antiarmor weapons, improvised explosive devices (IED), and mines, to very capable mechanized and armored forces equipped with current-generation equipment. The enemy uses these various approaches to counter the technological and numerical advantages of U.S. and allied systems and forces. In addition, enemy forces seek to exploit constraints placed on U.S. forces because of cultural bias, media presence, ROE/ROI, and distance from the crisis location. The urban environment itself also presents many passive dangers, such as disease from unsanitary conditions and psychological stresses.

FUNDAMENTALS OF ENEMY OPERATIONS

12-16.   While the nature of active enemies vary widely among specific urban areas, many principles and techniques are common to all such elements. Several methods that can be used against U.S. forces in the urban environment include--

- Trying to use the populace to provide camouflage, concealment, and deception for their operations. The populace of a given urban area represents a form of key terrain; the side that manages it best has a distinct advantage.
- Using the civilian populace to actively support their forces by providing: intelligence, logistical support and transportation.
- Attempting to make the civilian populace a burden on our logistical and force protection resources.
- Using the presence of the media to turn the sentiments of the civilian populace and other countries against U.S. forces.
- Identifying and occupying key facilities, such as telecommunication sites, water treatment plants, and power generation and transmission sites.
- Using the physical environment of an urban area to advantage. These include--
- Height advantage given by rooftops and tall buildings provide vantage points and ambush positions. Top attack positions allow the enemy to strike vehicles at their most vulnerable points and to use enfilading fire against exposed, dismounted Soldiers.
- Basements and other subterranean areas provide covered and concealed positions that allow movement and access throughout the area of operations.

FIRE SUPPORT

12-17.   The urban environment affects how and when the weapons company employs indirect fires. The following can impact the planning and execution of indirect fire support:

- The urban environment creates special requirements for centrally controlled fires and more restrictive fire control measures.
- Urban operations require the careful use of variable-timed ammunition to prevent premature arming.
- Indirect fire may cause unwanted rubble.
- The close proximity of friendly troops to enemy forces and other indirect fire targets necessitates careful coordination.
- White phosphorous (WP) ammunition can create unwanted fires or smoke.
- Artillery can be used in direct fire mode against point targets.
- Fuse delay should be considered to ensure rounds penetrate buildings or fortifications as required.
- Mortars are the most responsive indirect fires available to the platoon in the urban environment. They are well suited for combat in built-up areas because of their high rate of fire, steep angle of fall, and short minimum range.

SUSTAINMENT

12-18.   Guidelines for providing effective sustainment to units fighting in an urban environment include the following:

- Protect supplies and sustainment elements from the effects of enemy fires by preventing and/or avoiding detection, and by using effective cover and concealment.
- Provide security for sustainment units when they are moving within the combat area.

- Plan for a higher consumption rate of supplies, especially ammunition.
- Disperse and decentralize sustainment elements.
- Position support units as far forward as the tactical situation permits.
- Plan the locations of casualty collection points and evacuation sites.
- Plan for and use host country support and civil resources when authorized and practical.

PLANNING CONSIDERATIONS

12-19. During urban operations inside a built up area, the weapons company will often be task organized with one or more Infantry platoons attached and one or more weapons platoons detached to Infantry companies. Although the weapons company vehicles are mobile, the Infantry platoons are not and the company team's speed is thus reduced. This is not a major drawback since by their very nature urban operations require increased security and the terrain may be difficult to traverse. If the weapons company has a mission to isolate a small urban area, then its tactics and maneuver are the same as in the offense and defense.

EMPLOYMENT CONSIDERATIONS

12-20. Because of the decentralized nature of urban combat and the need for a high number of troops to conduct operations in dense, complex terrain, Infantrymen represent the bulk of forces. At the tactical level, Infantry forces have disadvantages that can be overcome by mechanized Infantry, weapons company, or armor units. Conversely, vehicles face problems in the confines of urban areas that place them at a severe disadvantage when operating alone and unsupported by Infantry. Only by working together in combined arms teams can these forces accomplish their missions with minimal casualties while avoiding unnecessary collateral damage.

Strengths and Weaknesses of Infantry and Weapons Company Units.

Strengths

12-21. The Infantry provides the following strengths in an urban environment:

- Infantry small-arms fire within a building can eliminate resistance without seriously damaging the structure.
- Infantry can physically clear and occupy buildings.
- Infantrymen can move stealthily into position without alerting the enemy. Infantrymen can move over, around, or through most urban terrain regardless of the amount of damage to buildings.
- Infantrymen have excellent all-round vision and can engage targets with small arms fire under almost all conditions.

12-22. Weapons company units in an urban environment provide the following strengths.

- The precision direct fires of missile systems and the destructive effects of the heavy machine guns provide excellent support to Infantry in an urban environment.
- The thermal sights on close combat missile systems can detect enemy activity through darkness and most smoke.
- The ability to conduct mounted patrols that can monitor large areas of a city while making their presence known to the entire populace, both friendly and unfriendly.
- The mobile firepower of weapons company vehicles can add security to resupply convoys.
- The armored weapons company vehicles can resupply Infantry units and evacuate casualties.

Limitations

12-23.   Infantry forces have the following limitations in an urban environment.

- They lack heavy supporting firepower, protection, and long-range mobility.
- Exposed Infantry forces are subject to taking a high number of casualties.
- Infantry forces are more subject to fratricide-related casualties from friendly direct and indirect fire.

12-24.   Weapons company forces have the following limitations in an urban environment.

- Weapons squads can be blinded easily by various obscurants in the urban environment.
- If isolated or unsupported by Infantry, Weapons company vehicles are vulnerable to enemy close in attack. They are also vulnerable to heavy machine guns and light or medium anti armor weapons.
- Weapons company vehicle gunners cannot easily identify enemy targets from friendly units in the confusing urban environment.
- Improvised barricades, narrow streets and alleyways, or large amounts of rubble can block vehicles.
- Leaders and gunners usually require accurate target identification from forward Infantry units.
- The minimum arming distance for close combat missile systems may reduce their effectiveness in close terrain. Hanging wires and other debris may also limit their effectiveness.
- Restrictive terrain may limit the crews ability to clear the backblast area for Improved Target Acquisition System (ITAS) firing.
- Close combat missile systems may also be limited by the brief target exposure time for moving vehicles.
- Heavy weapons may cause unwanted collateral damage and can destabilize certain structures.

Section II. EMPLOYMENT

Urban combat is often so decentralized and avenues of approach for vehicles so canalized that the situation requires fewer weapons company vehicles employed over broader areas. The decision to disperse rather than concentrate weapons company vehicles in a specific area should be made only after a careful consideration of the factors of mission, enemy, terrain, troops, time, civilians (METT-TC) and the anticipated operations in the near future. Decentralized weapons company support greatly increases a small Infantry unit's combat power; however, dispersed weapons company elements in UO cannot be easily extricated and quickly massed to achieve an overwhelming effect on the enemy. Weapons company units can support Infantry during UO by--

- Isolating objectives with direct fire to prevent enemy withdrawal, reinforcement, or counterattack.
- Assisting Infantry entering into buildings when enemy fire, debris, or obstacles block doorways.
- Securing portions of an objective by covering armored or mechanized avenues of approach.
- Providing suppressing fire support during Infantry movement
- Attacking appropriate targets designated by Infantry units.
- Establishing roadblocks or checkpoints.

TASK ORGANIZATION

12-25.   The following basic methods may be used for task-organizing the weapons company for UO.

WEAPONS COMPANY RETAINED UNDER INFANTRY BATTALION CONTROL

12-26.   With this task organization, likely missions for the weapons company unit are to support by fire or to overwatch movement of the Infantry. This task organization poses the most difficulty in maneuvering the weapons company unit with the dismounted Infantry. Moreover, it exposes the weapons company vehicles to close-in attack. However, it provides greater flexibility to the battalion commander in supporting the Infantry during the fight. This task organization provides the battalion commander the ability to quickly shift and mass the preponderance of his firepower to destroy the enemy or to counter his maneuver. This can be enhanced by combining the weapons company with an aerial platform, such as an Army aviation unit or UAS.

WEAPONS COMPANY PLATOON(S) ATTACHED TO INFANTRY COMPANIES

12-27.   Weapons company platoons are attached to Infantry companies. With this method, the maneuver Infantry companies have a weapons company platoon to support the UO fight and to deploy at the critical place and time. This task organization allows for the close support to the Infantry and direct control by the Infantry company commander. This is in line with the decentralized combat that characterizes urban warfare.

INDIVIDUAL WEAPONS SECTION AND SQUADS UNDER INFANTRY PLATOON CONTROL

12-28.   In this technique, a weapons company section or squad may be attached to an Infantry or reconnaissance platoon, usually by the Infantry company commander. The purpose of this type of task organization is to provide selected platoons with increased direct fire in an urban area. However, a weapons section can provide its own mutual support while a single squad cannot. Leaders must also ensure that the platoon secures the weapons section or squad at all times. The Infantry platoon leader however, may have difficulty effectively controlling this organization because of the increased span of control and insufficient knowledge of the personnel and capabilities of the weapons company unit.

GUIDELINES

12-29.   The task organization must be tailored to accomplish the mission. Regardless of the technique selected, the following guidelines apply:

- Weapons company sections may operate in support of Infantry.
- If using weapons company vehicles to support Infantry squads and fire teams moving from building to building as part of the maneuver plan, the leader of the forward Infantry element must control the movement of these vehicles.
- When controlling a weapons platoon or section, an Infantry company commander (or weapons platoon or section leader) should move forward to a position where he can personally maneuver it effectively in support of the Infantry.
- A task organization should not exceed the leader's span of control (two to five subordinate units).
- Weapons company sections or squads need Infantry support when the two elements are working together. Do not leave vehicles alone. These sections or squads are ill prepared to provide their own security during UO. Individual vehicles are extremely vulnerable to dismounted attack when operating in a complex urban environment.
- Weapons unit leaders may have to dismount to reconnoiter the next positions or to communicate directly with the Infantry leader.
- Weapons unit vehicles often move by alternating or successive bounds with vehicles on each side of the street.

TACTICAL CONSIDERATIONS

12-30.   The following are some considerations for the employment of the weapons company as part of the Infantry battalion operations in urban terrain. Thorough planning will increase response and reduce uncertainty (for example, numbering buildings and apertures allow the weapons units to respond quickly to the Infantry leaders requests for direct fire).

DIRECT-FIRE SUPPORT

12-31.   Weapons company weapon units are powerful systems for supporting assault forces to isolate the objective area and secure a foothold. As the Infantry force moves to clear the built-up area, the weapons company unit remains in its initial support-by fire position. When possible, the weapons company unit should move to a subsequent position where its direct fires can prevent enemy armor or mechanized reinforcement from attacking the objective and can engage those enemy forces withdrawing from the objective. Because of the non-contiguous nature of UO, enemy forces may move to the rear or flanks of the now-isolated weapons company vehicles and destroy them. If a small element of Infantry cannot be spared to support the weapons company unit, then vehicles should move to positions of cover and concealment and mutual support. Weapons company Soldiers should be alert, especially for enemy Infantry approaching from above, from the rear, or from the flanks.

MUTUAL SUPPORT

12-32.   Infantry and weapons company forces work together to bring the maximum combat power available to bear on the enemy. Infantry forces provide the eyes and ears, locating and identifying targets for the weapons company units to engage. Infantry and weapons company forces move along covered and concealed routes to assault enemy elements. Infantry forces provide protection from enemy Infantry while weapons company forces provide supporting direct fires against enemy positions and vehicles. Weapons company units try to direct fires onto the other side of the avenue of approach (example: The right hand vehicle(s) fire on targets on the left-hand side of the avenue of approach).

MOVEMENT

12-33.   Infantry elements normally lead the movement through built-up areas. The weapons company unit follows closely behind and provides close direct fire support. If the Infantry discovers an enemy fortification or vehicle, the weapons company unit responds immediately with direct fire to destroy, fix, or suppress the enemy, allowing the Infantry unit to develop the situation. After allowing sufficient time to develop the situation or conduct short-range reconnaissance, the Infantry leader directs the weapons company unit to move to support by fire position, if necessary, and identifies specific targets to engage.

COORDINATION

12-34.   Coordination between weapons company and Infantry leaders must be close and continuous. The weapons company vehicle commander (platoon, section, or squad leader) may need to dismount the vehicle and move, accompanied by the Infantry leader, to a position where he can see the route or target better. All involved must understand the signals for initiating, shifting, lifting, or ceasing direct fires. The greatest barrier to close coordination and command and control in UO is the intense noise and complexity of situations. Verbal commands must be backed up by simple, nonverbal signals.

COMMUNICATIONS

12-35.   Weapons company leaders must maintain communications with the Infantry commander. Individual weapons company squads and Infantrymen communicate with one another using one or more of the following techniques.

Visual Signals

12-36.   Visual signals, either prescribed by a SOP or coordinated during linkup, can facilitate some simple communications.

FM Radios

12-37.   Frequency modulation (FM) radios provide a reliable means of communications between Infantry and close supporting weapons company units. These radios allow the Infantry to use terrain more effectively to provide close-in protection for the weapons company unit. Infantrymen can observe enemy elements while limiting exposure to enemy fires directed against the weapons company unit. This is a fast and reliable method of communications that does not require additional assets. However, some urban environments can severely degrade FM radio communications over long distances or between forces that are inside and outside buildings. All leaders (weapons company and Infantry) must take this possibility into careful consideration during their thorough analyses of the factors of METT-TC. The Infantry company commander relies on the radio to help control the battle. It is essential that platoon leaders and radiotelephone operators be well trained in sending reports. Timely, accurate, brief, and complete reporting from the subordinate elements to the commander is critical for mission success.

Smoke

12-38.   The use of smoke must be carefully coordinated. Although weapons company weapon system sights can see through most obscurants, controlling weapons company and Infantry forces becomes significantly more difficult when these forces are enveloped in dense smoke clouds. Smoke generated from adjacent units can also affect control.

Other Considerations

12-39.   The following considerations also apply during UO.

- Identify available terrain during planning that will support weapons company vehicle cross-country movement. While the rate of march may be slower, security may be significantly enhanced.
- Involve weapons company leaders in the mission analysis. Their expertise will hasten the understanding of what weapons company units can and cannot do and will aid the Infantry commander in making the best employment decision.
- Urban operations are resource intensive. Weapons company vehicles can carry ammunition, water, and other supplies to support the urban fight.
- The Infantry battalion and company commanders can use the FBCB2 mounted on the weapons company vehicles to track the progress of the forward platoons. Since the vehicles should be relatively close behind the Infantry, their position should be relatively close to the friendly forward elements.
- Commanders must specifically allocate time in the planning process for precombat inspections (PCIs) and precombat checks (PCCs) of the weapons company unit.
- Conduct a rehearsal at the level where the weapons company units are task-organized. Try to replicate conditions for mission execution during rehearsals (for example, day, limited visibility, civilians on the battlefield, host nation support, and ROE). Include the following:
  -- Graphic and fire control measures.
  -- Direct fire plans.
  -- Communications.
  -- Breach drills.
  -- Techniques for employing weapons company vehicles and the Infantry.

- To minimize casualties when moving outside or between buildings:
  - -- Cover all possible threat locations with either observation or direct fire.
  - -- Use smoke to set a screen to block enemy observation of friendly movement for those areas not possible to cover with observation or direct fire.
  - -- Move weapons company units forward to support Infantry movement. Position the weapons company units before the Infantry continues moving.
  - -- Preplan positions if possible, but devise a marking system and communication signals to designate "situation-dependent" positions to help maintain momentum.
  - -- Weapons company vehicles must move at the Infantry's rate of movement.
- Use simple, clearly understood graphic control measures. The following are particularly useful during UO:
  - -- Phase lines.
  - -- Number and lettering systems for buildings.
  - -- Tentative support-by-fire positions.
  - -- No-fire areas.

Section III. OFFENSIVE URBAN OPERATIONS

The weapons company plans and executes offensive operations in the urban environment based on the factors of METT-TC and established doctrine. This section focuses on the unique problems and challenges these operations pose.

PHASES

12-40. Urban offensive operations can be broken down into phases. In combat these are by no means clear and clean cut.

RECONNOITER THE OBJECTIVE

12-41. The reconnaissance phase of urban operations must provide the weapons company commander and other friendly elements with adequate intelligence to stage a deliberate attack. Communications with friendly elements in or near the urban area is essential to gain up-to-date information on the objective. Current information of the area can be provided by UAS over flights, satellite photography, and observation by sniper teams. Commanders do not want to arouse the enemy's suspicions by concentrating too much reconnaissance in one area and should include other areas for reconnaissance that are not part of the attack. The weapons company may support the reconnaissance effort by conducting mounted patrols, providing overwatch and reaction forces to support dismounted patrols, or by observing the objective with its day and night optics

MOVE TO THE OBJECTIVE

12-42. Once the unit reconnoiters the objective, forces move to the objective by the most expedient, covered, and concealed route to prevent detection by the enemy. The weapons company can provide overwatch during movement or move with the battalion units to provide additional security and firepower.

ISOLATE THE OBJECTIVE

12-43. Isolating the objective involves seizing terrain that dominates the area so that the enemy cannot supply or reinforce its defensive forces. This is critical for successful mission accomplishment. The weapons company can be given this mission because of its mobility, and therefore the ability to quickly reinforce threatened areas, and its long-range firepower. The commander may position the weapons company unit outside the built-up area, where they can cover high-speed avenues of approach. Before providing support for the attack, weapons units maneuver into support by fire or attack-by-fire positions. Infantry may be required to clear these positions before their occupation. Once isolated, the battalion should gain a foothold as quickly as possible.

GAIN A FOOTHOLD

12-44.   Gaining a foothold involves seizing an intermediate objective that provides attacking forces with cover from enemy fire as well as a place at which they can enter the built-up area. When a weapons company unit operates with the company, it provides direct fire support as the Infantry gains the foothold. As the Infantry attacks to gain the foothold, it should be supported by direct and indirect suppressive fires, and by obscuring or screening smoke operations. The weapons company unit can provide overwatch or serve as a base of fire for the Infantry until the area is secured.

CLEAR THE URBAN AREA

12-45.   When determining the extent to which the urban area must be cleared, the commander of the attacking force must consider METT-TC factors. He may decide to clear only those parts of the area necessary to the success of his mission. To do this, however, at least one of the following factors must apply:

- An objective can be seized quickly.
- Enemy resistance is light or fragmented.
- Buildings in the area are of light construction with large open areas between them. In this situation, the commander would clear only those buildings along the approach to his objective, or those buildings necessary to ensure the unit's security.

12-46.   On the other hand, the attacking unit might have a mission to systematically clear an area of all enemy forces. Through detailed analysis, the commander can anticipate if the unit will be opposed by a strong, organized resistance, or if it will be operating in areas where buildings are close together. This mission requires a street-by-street, room-by-room operation.

12-47.   The weapons company can support the Infantry during the clearing phase by providing direct fire support, rapidly moving its elements to reinforce units, or to block access to the objective area. Its effectiveness however may be limited by the lack of maneuver space, obstructions, and ROE restrictions.

CONSOLIDATE AND REORGANIZE

12-48.   Once the objective is secure, the unit must prepare for counterattack, or continue the mission in accordance with (IAW) the operation order (OPORD)/SOP. If the unit must prepare for a counterattack, it must consolidate and reorganize equipment, supplies, and personnel quickly. The weapons company moves its units to reinforce critical areas, provide observation, or provide security for elements bringing supplies forward.

TASK ORGANIZATION

12-49.   Based on a METT-TC analysis, the battalion commander determines his decisive and shaping attacks. He may also task organize his companies so that each has Infantry and direct fire support units. In urban operations, company commanders can in turn task organize their platoons so that they include Infantry and direct fire support. The weapons company may have one or more platoons detached and have an Infantry platoon attached. The weapons company may be assigned any mission to include a shaping attack or acting as the reserve.

Section IV. DEFENSIVE URBAN OPERATIONS

As in the offense, defensive operations in the urban environment require thorough planning and precise execution based on METT-TC and established doctrine. This section examines urban considerations that affect the weapons company in the defense.

ENEMY FORCES OUTSIDE URBAN AREA

12-50.   While positioned in an urban area as part of a larger force, the commander may task the weapons company to defend against an enemy approaching from outside of the built-up area. In general, procedures and considerations are the same as those for defensive operations in open terrain. For example, the commander designates battle positions (BP) that take advantage of all available weapons systems. Objectives are similar as well and may include preventing the:

- Isolation of the defensive position.
- Reconnaissance of the defensive position
- Gaining a foothold in the urban area.

12-51.   These operations can transition into an in-depth defense of the urban area if the attacker continues to commit forces to the battle, and the defending force fails to divert or destroy them.

ENEMY FORCES WITHIN URBAN AREA

12-52.   When facing enemy forces within the urban area, the battalion commander may order the weapons company to take part in defensive operations. These defensive operations include defense within an area of operations (AO), defend a strongpoint, and/or defend a BP. Procedures and considerations for these defensive operations are generally similar to those used in more conventional open terrain situations.

12-53.   See FM 3-06.11 for detailed information on these operations. The commander should designate engagement areas that take advantage of integrated obstacles and urban terrain features, and that can be covered by direct and indirect fires.

ROLE OF WEAPONS COMPANY

12-54.   In defensive urban operations, the weapons company provides the commander with a mobile force that can respond quickly to the enemy's scheme of maneuver. The company's vehicles should be located to cover likely enemy avenues of approach in positions that allow the vehicles to take advantage of their long-range fires. Effective positioning enables the commander to employ the company in a number of ways, such as--

- On the edge of the city in mutually supporting positions.
- On key terrain on the flanks of towns and villages.
- In positions from which they can cover barricades and obstacles by fire.
- As part of the reserve.

12-55.   While weapons platoons are usually employed as a two-section platoon, the commander has the option to task organize them with Infantry platoons and squads. This provides local security for the vehicles.

FIGHTING AND FIRING POSITIONS

12-56. Vehicle positions provide the optimal cover, concealment, observation, and fields of fire. At the same time, they must not restrict the vehicles' ability to move when necessary. The following considerations apply--

- If fields of fire are restricted to the street area, weapons platoon vehicles should operate in hull-down positions, which provide cover and enable fire directly down the streets. Examples of using hull-down positions are piles of rubble, walls, reverse slope of high ground, and burned out vehicles. In hull-down positions, the vehicles are protected while retaining their ability to rapidly move to alternate positions.
- Before moving into position to engage the enemy, a weapons company vehicle can occupy a hide position for cover and concealment. Hide positions exist in various locations, such as inside buildings or underground garages, adjacent to buildings using the buildings to mask enemy observation, or in culverts.
- Before pulling into a building to use it as a vehicle hide position, make sure the floor will support the vehicle weight. Make sure the selected structure has not been damaged to the point that it could collapse onto the vehicle.
- Primary, supplementary, and alternate battle positions are identified and routes between are reconnoitered. Units are positioned in depth.
- Battle positions may have room for only a single vehicle.
- The hide position prevents the crew from seeing the advancing enemy. Therefore, an observer from the weapons unit or a nearby Infantry unit must alert the crew from an observation post in an adjacent building. When the observer acquires a target, he signals the weapons company vehicles to move to the firing position and, at the proper time, to fire.
- After firing, the vehicle moves to an alternate position to avoid compromising its location.

EMPLOYMENT OF INFANTRY SQUADS

12-57. In a company defense, the limited number of available Infantrymen may require that squad positions be interspersed between the weapons company positions for mutual support. The weapons crew's observation is primarily focused on the enemy and possible enemy locations. Both the Infantry Soldier and the vehicle crew are responsible for being alert and maintaining safe positions in relation to each other.

EMPLOYMENT OF RESERVE FORCE

12-58. The commander's defensive scheme of maneuver in urban operations may include employment of a reserve force. It must maintain situational awareness by monitoring appropriate digital messages and radio frequencies. This force may function to--

- Regain key positions through counterattack.
- Block enemy penetrations.
- Protect the flanks of the friendly force.
- Provide a base of fire for disengaging elements.

12-59. The following are some characteristics of the reserve force during combat in built-up areas:

- It usually consists of a combined arms force.
- It must be as mobile as possible.
- It must maintain an appropriate readiness status.

This page intentionally left blank.

Glossary

A

AA	avenue of approach
AHS	Army Health System
ANCD	automated net control device
AO	area of operations
ARNG	Army National Guard
ARNGUS	Army National Guard of the United States
ATGM	antitank guided missile

B

BAS	battalion aid station
BCT	brigade combat team
BDA	battle damage
BDAR	battle damage assessment and repair
BHL	battle handover line
BII	basic issue item
BMP	Infantry fighting vehicle (Russian: *boevaia mashina pekhoty*)
BP	battle position
BRDM	armored reconnaissance vehicle (Russian: *boevaia razvedyvatel'naia dozornaia mashina*)
BSA	brigade support area
BSB	brigade support battalion
BSTB	brigade special troops battalion

C

C2	command and control
CAS	close air support
CASEVAC	casualty evacuation
CBRN	chemical, biological, radiological, and nuclear
CCP	casualty collection point
CF	conventional forces
CFZ	critical friendly zone
CLS	combat lifesaver
CLU	command launch unit
CO	commanding officer
COA	course of action
COMSEC	communications security
COSC	combat and operational stress control
COSR	combat and operational stress reaction
CP	command post
CRT	combat repair team

CTCP combat trains command post

D

DA	Department of the Army
DFCM	direct fire control measures
DLIC	detachment left in contact
DNBI	disease and nonbattle injury
DoD	Department of Defense
DS	direct support
DZ	drop zone

E

EA	engagement area
EOF	escalation of force
EPW	enemy prisoner of war

F

FBCB2	Force XXI Battle Command, Brigade and Below
FDC	fire direction center
FEBA	forward edge of the battle area
FHP	Force Health Protection
FIST	fire support team
FLOT	forward line of own troops
FM	field manual; frequency modulation
FO	forward observer
FOB	forward operating base
FPF	final protective fire
FRAGO	fragmentary order
FSC	forward support company
FSCM	fire support coordination measure
FSO	fire support officer

G

GPS	global positioning system

H

HC	hexacholoroethane
HHC	headquarters and headquarters company
HMMWV	high mobility, multipurpose wheeled vehicle
HQ	headquarters
HSS	Health Service Support

I

IAW	in accordance with
IBCT	Infantry brigade combat team
ID	identification

IED	improvised explosive device	PLL	prescribed load list
IPB	intelligence preparation of the battlefield	PLT	platoon
		POL	petroleum, oil, and lubricants
IR	infrared	PSYOP	psychological operations
ISR	intelligence, surveillance, and reconnaissance	PVNTMED	preventive medicine
		PZ	pickup zone
ITAS	Improved Target Acquisition System		

Q

QRF	quick reaction force

J

JAAT	joint air attack team

R

RED	risk estimate distance
RFL	restrictive fire line

L

LD	line of departure
LDR	leader
LOGPAC	logistics package
LOGSTAT	logistics status
LOS	line of sight
LZ	landing zone

ROE	rules of engagement
ROI	rules of interaction
RP	release point
RPG	rocket-propelled grenade

S

S-1	personnel staff officer
S-2	intelligence staff officer
S-3	operations staff officer
S-4	logistics staff officer
SAD	state active duty
SBF	support by fire
SHORAD	short-range air defense
SINCGARS	single-channel ground and airborne radio system
SITREP	situation report
SOF	special operations forces
SOI	signal operating instructions
SOP	standing operating procedure
SOSRA	suppress, obscure, secure, reduce and assault
SU	situational understanding

M

MBA	main battle area
MEDEVAC	medical evacuation
METT-TC	mission, enemy, terrain, troops, time, civilians
MOPP	mission-oriented protective posture
MOS	military occupational specialty
MRE	meal, ready to eat
MSD	minimum safe distance
MSL	minimum safe line
MTC	movement to contact

N

NAI	named area of interest
NBC	nuclear, biological, chemical (in legacy terms only, see CBRN)
NCO	noncommissioned officer
No	number
NVD	night vision device

T

TAS	target acquisition system
TCP	traffic control point
TLP	troop leading procedure
TOW	tube-launched, optically-tracked, wire-guided
TRP	target reference point
TSE	tactical site exploitation
TSOP	tactical standing operating procedure
TTP	tactics, techniques, and procedures

O

OE	operational environment
OP	observation post
OPLAN	operation plan
OPORD	operation order
OPSEC	operations security

U

UA	unmanned aircraft
UAS	unmanned aircraft system
UMCP	unit maintenance collection point

P

PCC	precombat check
PCI	precombat inspection
PERSTAT	personnel status
PL	platoon leader; phase line

UO	urban operations
US	United States
USAIS	United States Army Infantry School
USAR	United States Army Reserve
USSOCOM	United States Special Operations Command

W

| WCS | weapons control status |

WFF	warfighting function
WIA	wounded in action
WMD	weapons of mass destruction
WP	white phosphorus

X

| XO | executive officer |

This page intentionally left blank.

References

SOURCES USED

These are the sources quoted or paraphrased in this publication.

DEPARTMENT OF DEFENSE PRODUCTS

DoD Directive 2311.01E	*DoD Law of War Program.* 9 May 2006.
DoD Directive 5240.01	*DoD Intelligence Activities.* 27 August 2007.

FIELD MANUALS

FM 3-05	*Army Special Operations Forces.* 20 September 2006.
FM 3-05.70	*Survival.* 17 May 2002.
FM 3-07.31	*Multi-service Tactics, Techniques, and Procedures for Conducting Peace Operations.* 26 October 2003.
FM 3-11	*Multiservice Tactics, Techniques, and Procedures for Nuclear, Biological, and Chemical Defense Operations.* 10 March 2003.
FM 3-21.91	*Tactical Employment of Antiarmor Platoons and Companies.* 26 November 2002.
FM 3-22.27	*MK 19, 40-Mm Grenade Machine Gun, Mod 3.* 28 November 2003.
FM 3-22.32	*Improved Target Acquisition System M41.* 8 July 2005.
FM 3-22.34	*TOW Weapon System.* 28 November 2003.
FM 3-22.37	*Javelin—Close Combat Missile System, Medium.* 20 March 2008.
FM 3-22.65	*Browning Machine Gun, Caliber .50 HB, M2.* 3 March 2005.
FM 3-34.170	*Engineer Reconnaissance.* 25 March 2008.
FM 3-34.214	*Explosives and Demolitions.* 11 July 2007.
FM 3-90	*Tactics.* 4 July 2001.
FM 3-90.5	*The Combined Arms Battalion.* 7 April 2008.
FM 5-7-30	*Brigade Engineer and Engineer Company Combat Operations (Airborne, Air Assault, Light).* 28 December 1994.
FM 7-85	*Ranger Unit Operations.* 9 June 1987.
FM 7-98	*Operations in a Low-Intensity Conflict.* 19 October 1992.
FM 17-95	*Cavalry Operations.* 24 December 1996.

DEPARTMENT OF ARMY FORMS

DA forms are available on the APD website (www.apd.army.mil)

DA Form 1156	*Casualty Feeder Card.*
DA Form 2028	*Recommended Changes to Publications and Blank Forms.*
DA Form 2404	*Equipment Inspection and Maintenance Worksheet.*
DA Form 5988E	*Equipment Inspection and Maintenance Worksheet (EGA).*

JOINT PUBLICATIONS

JP 1	*Doctrine for the Armed Forces of the United States.* 14 May 2007.

OTHER

Technical Memo 5-87   *Modern Experience in City Combat*, US Army Human Engineering
Laboratory, March 1987

DOCUMENTS NEEDED

These documents must be available to the intended users of this publication.

JOINT PUBLICATIONS

JP 3-07.2   *Antiterrorism*. 14 April 2006.

JP 3-07.3   *Peace Operations*. 17 October 2007.

FIELD MANUALS

FM 1-02   *Operational Terms and Graphics*. 21 September 2004.

FM 3-0   *Operations*. 27 February 2008.

FM 3-07   *Stability Operations and Support Operations*. 20 February 2003.

FM 3-11.3   *Multiservice Tactics, Techniques, and Procrdures for Chemical, Biological, Radiological, and Nuclear Contamination Avoidance*. 2 February 2006.

FM 3-21.8   *The Infantry Platoon and Squad*. 28 March 2007.

FM 3-21.10   *The Infantry Rifle Company*. 27 July 2006.

FM 3-21.11   *The SBCT Infantry Rifle Company*. 23 January 2003.

FM 3-21.20   *The Infantry Battalion*. 13 December 2006.

FM 23-10   *Sniper Training*. 17 August 1994.

FM 27-10   *The Law of Land Warfare*. 18 July 1956.

FM 34-130   *Intelligence Preparation of the Battlefield*. 8 July 1994.

FM 5-19   *Composite Risk Management*. 21 August 2006.

TRAINING CIRCULARS

TC 7-98-1   *Stability and Support Operations Training Support Package*. 5 June 1997.

OTHER

Handbook No. 92-3   *Fratricide Risk Assessment for Company Leadership*, Section II, Center for Army Lesson Learned, April 1992.

INTERNET WEB SITES

Some of the documents listed in these References may be downloaded from Army websites:

Air Force Publications   http://afpubs hq.af mil/.

Army Knowledge Online   https://akocomm.us.army mil/usapa/doctrine/index html.

Global Security   http://www.globalsecurity.org/military/library/report/call

NATO ISAs   http://www nato.int/docu/standard htm.

Reimer Digital Library   http://www.train.army.mil.

Index

This page intentionally left blank.

FM 3-21.12
1 July 2008

By Order of the Secretary of the Army:

GEORGE W. CASEY, JR.
General, United States Army
Chief of Staff

Official:

JOYCE E. MORROW
Administrative Assistant to the
Secretary of the Army
0817013

DISTRIBUTION: *Active Army, Army National Guard, and U.S. Army Reserve*: To be distributed in accordance with the initial distribution number (IDN) 110078 requirements for FM 3-21.12.

www.ingramcontent.com/pod-product-compliance
Lightning Source LLC
Chambersburg PA
CBHW080016280326
41934CB00015B/3370